Organizational Theory in Higher Education

The second edition of *Organizational Theory in Higher Education* is a comprehensive and accessible treatment of organizational theory and higher education administration. Noted scholar Kathleen Manning offers a fresh take on the models and lenses through which higher education can be viewed by presenting a full range of organizational theories, from traditional to current. Chapters discuss the disciplinary foundation, structure, metaphor, assumptions, characteristics, and other elements of each organizational theory and conclude with cases highlighting practical applications. Questions for discussion are provided at the end of each chapter and embedded in the cases to assist the reader in making connections to their practice. Manning's rich, interdisciplinary treatment enables readers to gain a full understanding of the perspectives that operate on a college campus and ways to adopt effective practice in the context of new and continuing tensions, contexts, and challenges.

New to this Edition:

- Revised chapters with updated material and new references that reflect current higher education issues including climate change.
- A new chapter on Institutional Theory, an expanded Feminist and Gendered chapter, and an enhanced Spirituality chapter.
- New cases throughout to address contemporary issues, and a broader range of institutional types including Historically Black and Hispanic-Serving institutions and 2-year institutions.
- Additional theoretical topics including critical race theory, queer theory, and contemplative practices.
- Updated and enhanced questions for discussion and recommended readings.

Kathleen Manning is Professor Emerita of Higher Education and Student Affairs at the University of Vermont, USA.

Core Concepts in Higher Education

Series Editors: Edward P. St. John, Marybeth Gasman and Stella Flores

Organizational Theory in Higher Education

Second Edition

Kathleen Manning

Routledge
Taylor & Francis Group

NEW YORK AND LONDON

Second edition published 2018
by Routledge
711 Third Avenue, New York, NY 10017

and by Routledge
2 Park Square, Milton Park, Abingdon, Oxon, OX14 4RN

Routledge is an imprint of the Taylor & Francis Group, an informa business

First edition published by Routledge 2013

Library of Congress Cataloging in Publication Data
Names: Manning, Kathleen, 1954– author.
Title: Organizational theory in higher education / by Kathleen Manning.
Description: Second Edition. | New York : Routledge, 2018. | Series: Core Concepts in Higher Education | "First edition published by Routledge 2013"–T.p. verso. | Includes bibliographical references and index.
Identifiers: LCCN 2017017629| ISBN 9781138668980 (Hardback) | ISBN 9781138668997 (Paperback) | ISBN 9781315618357 (ebook) | ISBN 9781315618357 (Master) | ISBN 9781317210702 (Web PDF) | ISBN 9781317210696 (ePub) | ISBN 9781317210689 (MobiPocket/Kindle)
Subjects: LCSH: Universities and colleges–Administration.
Classification: LCC LB2341 .M285 2018 | DDC 378.1/01–dc23

ISBN: 978-1-138-66898-0 (hbk)
ISBN: 978-1-138-66899-7 (pbk)
ISBN: 978-1-315-61835-7 (ebk)

Typeset in Minion
by Wearset Ltd, Boldon, Tyne and Wear

To my partner, Keith Kennedy, who has patiently supported me through two editions of the most challenging book I have ever written.

CONTENTS

LIST OF TABLES AND FIGURES

SERIES EDITOR'S INTRODUCTION

It is a great pleasure to reintroduce Kathleen Manning's *Organizational Theory in Higher Education* for the Routledge series on *Core Concepts in Higher Education*. This book not only contributes substantially to the content of higher education as a field of study, but provides case studies that have great pedagogical value in preparing anyone who works at higher education institutions. When Marybeth Gasman and I initiated this series, we wanted to encourage integration of social justice into the paradigmatic foundations of higher education scholarship. Our view was that the content typically taught did not adequately address the inequalities ushered in by globalization. Our field of higher education was rigidifying into content paradigmatic positions at a time when colleges and universities were responding to a rapid pace of change in policy, funding, student aspirations, and corporate influences.

At the outset of the *Core Concepts in Higher Education* series, we wanted to encourage a third generation of scholarship. It was time to take another step, to move beyond some of the conflicts between older paradigmatic forms and newer theory focused on critical social issues. Such movement in thought was essential to prepare a next generation of higher education scholars. These educators could then integrate an explicit emphasis on strategies for addressing inequalities within prior scholarship as well as encourage the field of higher education to advance. The authors recruited for *Core Concepts in Higher Education* have consistently demonstrated a capacity to integrate scholarship that illuminates inequality while also advancing the core content of the field. This was our priority in recruiting authors, editors, and a new series editor, Stella Flores, who has joined me and Marybeth Gasman in this endeavor.

In *Organizational Theory in Higher Education*, Manning boldly takes a step forward into the third generation of scholarship on organizations by adding institutionalism, feminism, and spirituality to the frames for examining organizational issues in higher education. In Chapter 1 of this edition, she clearly outlines how the dialectical divisions in our field continue to evolve. She also explains how the frames, coupled with discussion of case studies, can be used to encourage and support development of a new generation of practitioners who can address diverse ideas and long-standing inequalities.

Manning challenges scholars in higher education doctoral programs to take a step toward integrating their approaches to content with the pedagogies increasingly used in the education provided in masters and doctoral programs. Many of these programs used the first edition of Manning's *Organizational Theory in Higher Education* to encourage multi-frame analysis of organizational and administrative topics and issues. She also encourages all of us to step out of our own embedded ways of viewing problems in higher education by considering diverse viewpoints on issues facing college students, faculty, boards of trustee members, administrators, and other higher education stakeholders. By discussing the case studies, faculty and students in higher education and student affairs graduate programs can build the skills of listening to and considering the views of others in our field as well as the students who study within colleges and universities.

Edward P. St. John
University of Michigan

PREFACE

The major dilemma in organization theory has been between putting into the theory all the features of organizations we think are relevant and thereby making the theory unmanageable, or pruning the model down to a simple system, thereby making it unrealistic. (Cyert & March, 1959/2011, p. 140)

In 1991, Robert Birnbaum published a book outlining higher education organizational theory that became a mainstay for graduate students, administrators, faculty, and stakeholders wanting to understand "how colleges work." Birnbaum described four frames of organizational functioning and illustrated his text with examples reflective of the different types of institutions one finds in U.S. higher education. Much has changed in higher education since Birnbaum published *How Colleges Work*. You might speculate that the tensions and pressures that traditionally challenged higher education are even more prevalent today than when he first published his well-regarded text. Additionally, new challenges and theories have emerged since its publication.

In the last 20 years, there has been no shortage of pundits expressing their opinion that higher education in the United States is in crisis. The list of complaints, among others, includes unsatisfactory graduation rates, high tuition resulting in overwhelming student debt, excessive executive salaries, administrative bloat, and curricula irrelevant to global and employment needs. Despite and perhaps because of the reflection engendered through the criticisms, higher education in the United States remains a remarkable system. U.S. higher education enables scholars to generate and transmit high quality teaching, research, and service; the system drives young people to come of age and nontraditional students to craft a new life and career; colleges and universities profoundly change lives; and the system of research support enables the production of life-saving discoveries. Because of the rapid pace of change, including seismic changes occurring in countries such as China and India and regions such as the European Higher Education Area, new perspectives are warranted on the older theories about how colleges work. To be effective, as faculty, administrators, staff, and trustees, we must get out ahead of the vital, some would say disruptive, transformations occurring in higher education. While the current challenges are daunting, they are also exciting. The prospect of shaping the older organizations into newer forms holds tremendous promise for the next era of U.S. higher education. I am encouraged by the current potential within higher education institutions, a potential foreshadowed by the innovation and creativity of the earliest U.S. colleges and universities. Only with knowledge of how higher education works can we realistically explore the many options available for success.

With or without agreement about the nature of crises in higher education, colleges and universities are unique organizations. Although many borrow organizational and theoretical models from corporations, government, and other sources, those of us who work in this sector of society know that corporate, health care, and governance organizations, for example, have very different ways of operating from higher education. This book points out those differences with a focus on defining how higher education can remain relevant in today's environment.

PURPOSE OF *ORGANIZATIONAL THEORY IN HIGHER EDUCATION*

In this text, *Organizational Theory in Higher Education*, I seek to add to the higher education literature by elucidating organizational theory directly related to higher education in addition to theory from noneducational sources. As the reader studies the organizational theories in this book, several conventional theories (e.g., bureaucracy, collegial, cultural, organized anarchy, political) may appear passé. Although perhaps theoretically criticized as out-of-date, students, faculty, and administrators can easily find examples and vestiges of these approaches currently on college and university campuses. The tried-and-true frames so familiar in the past (i.e., bureaucratic, political, cultural, and collegial) are currently inadequate to the task of getting ahead of rapid and relentless changes, events that show no signs of abating. The inclusion of newer (e.g., institutional, feminist and gendered, spiritual) models provides all studying and working in higher education with a more complete and imaginative range of approaches from which to understand colleges and universities. The more contemporary theories can encourage all who are involved in higher education to be forward thinking and discover the opportunities available when a newer perspective is used to view U.S. colleges and universities.

The theories outlined in this book refer to the structures of organization as opposed to possible management or administrative approaches within higher education institutions. To imagine structure, one can visualize an image or metaphor: a pyramid, web, or circle (Morgan, 2006). There are other organizationally-related theories (e.g., academic capitalism, resource dependency, policy making, budgeting, change) that are important to organizational understanding but are less structurally oriented and, as such, are not discussed in this book. References throughout the book direct the reader to theorists who discuss additional organizational topics.

Although higher education is a global enterprise, this book focuses on the history and practices of U.S. systems of post-secondary education. While many of the models and theories can be applied to universities outside the United States, any extrapolation to a non-U.S., international setting should be approached with caution. Each country and institution has a unique organizational context and culture. Funding, admissions, governance, administrative practices, and many other factors differ from country to country. No one theory or set of theories can be applied without consideration of those unique characteristics.

ORGANIZATION OF THE THEORIES

The theories discussed in *Organizational Theory in Higher Education* are presented in alphabetical order. In this way, course instructors and higher education practitioners can choose the chapters that best suit their particular context. Because the chapters outlining the different organizational theories were written as stand-alone pieces, readers and course instructors can choose the order that best fits their purposes. Table 0.1 offers some potential orders in which the chapters could be read: alphabetical, paradigm, or significance to higher education administration. While the historical, relevance, and paradigmatic significance of the theories to higher education could certainly be debated, certain theories may be judged by the reader as being more closely related to higher education administration and leadership than others.

THEORY TO PRACTICE

The chapters discuss the disciplinary foundation, structure, metaphor, assumptions, characteristics, and other elements of each organizational theory. Each chapter concludes with a contemporary application of the theory. These contemporary discussions are completed in less depth than the theories they accompany. This is because the text was purposely written from a foundational point of view. References at the end of the chapters direct readers to more in-depth discussions of those contemporary applications.

Although the cases are matched to a specific organizational theory, each could be analyzed using more than one organizational theory. The use of only one theory per case is a heuristic, so that readers can best learn how to apply that theory to practice. Like Alfred Korzybski's saying, "A map is not the territory it represents, but if correct, it has a similar structure to the territory, which accounts for its usefulness," the organizational perspectives are not an exact depiction of life within higher education institutions. The cases are maps that can guide thinking about the specific organizational perspectives. Travel through the territory of higher education requires a complete understanding of the various organizational perspectives and comprehension of how all operate in concert

Table 0.1 Organizational Perspectives by Chronological, Paradigmatic, and Traditional Significance to Higher Education

Alphabetical Order	By Paradigm	By Significance to Traditional Higher Education Administration and Leadership
Bureaucracy	*Newtonian:*	Organized Anarchy
Collegium	Bureaucratic	Collegium
Cultural	Political	Institutional
Feminist and Gendered	Collegium	Political
Institutional	Organized Anarchy	Cultural
Organized Anarchy	Institutional	Bureaucratic
Political	*Post-Modern or Post-Industrial:*	Feminist and Gendered
Spiritual	Cultural	Spiritual
	Feminist and Gendered	
	Spiritual	

within colleges and universities. As the theories are read and understood, readers are urged to revisit previous case chapters and use different organizational perspectives to discuss the cases. Knowledge of the organizational theories can reveal the complexity of higher education organizations.

The diversity of higher education (e.g., community colleges, public, private, Historically Black Institutions, Hispanic-Serving Institutions, Asian American and Native American Pacific Islander Serving Institutions, for profit, liberal arts, specialized institutions) presents a significant challenge when attempting to write cases inclusive of the many types of institutions within the U.S. higher education system. This book, written from a broad-spectrum organizational theory perspective, is most useful when accompanied by texts that specialize in particular sectors of higher education. References to sources across the diverse sectors of U.S. higher education are included in the recommended readings for each chapter.

To lead effectively, administrators, faculty, and staff must envision solutions to organizational issues that plague college campuses. To assist the reader to make connections to their practice, questions for discussion are provided at the end of each chapter and embedded in the cases. These questions, in conjunction with the recommended readings and case studies, can assist the reader to develop an in-depth understanding of the organizational choices available.

AUDIENCES

Several audiences will find value in this text. Faculty who are seeking to understand the organizations in which they work can gain knowledge about their institutions by reading *Organizational Theory in Higher Education*. Because faculty play such a crucial role in college and university leadership and governance, the fullest understanding of organizational structure and operating factors can assist them to shape the curriculum and policy that addresses the challenges alluded to above. Graduate students who are studying higher education and related subjects must have a thorough knowledge of organizations if they are to be proficient in their field. The book was written as a concise, accessible treatment of organizational theory and higher education administration. Faculty who teach higher education organization, management, and leadership courses will find this book a foundational text to use in their courses. Both master's and doctoral students will find this a helpful introductory text. Higher education administrators and practitioners seeking to gain insight into innovative ways to approach organizations can find inspiration in this text. Through reading about the different theories, new ways of operating, making decisions, and leading can be discovered. Trustees can only effectively lead these organizations if they understand the faculty culture, historical influences, and ways of operating. State, national, and international policy makers seeking a better understanding of higher education institutions can find insights in this text.

SUGGESTED USES OF THIS BOOK IN GRADUATE LEVEL CLASSES

This book is primarily written for use in higher education administration, leadership, student affairs, and policy classes at the doctoral and masters level. The theories and cases can be used in higher education administration classes to illustrate how colleges and universities operate depending on the theoretical point of view of the administrator, faculty member, student, or other community member. For example, conflict and coalition building characteristic of the political model creates a different organizational perspective than the top-down executive decision-making and communication style of the bureaucratic perspective. An institution looks completely different again from the perspective of feminist and gendered approaches to administration and organization.

For leadership classes at the doctoral and masters level, this book provides a foundation upon which action can be understood. If leaders, whether middle managers, entry level, trustees, or executives, lack knowledge about how work is organized within the institution, it will be difficult to work cooperatively with others, impossible to jointly craft a vision, and challenging to shape a vision for the future.

Instructors of student affairs administration classes will find useful information in this book as they place that area of college and university practice into a larger context. One cannot adequately craft student-oriented policy, shape communities, or engage students without knowledge of how a university is organized.

Policy cannot be produced in a vacuum. The policies necessary, for example, to enact smooth institutional operations, fair and equitable treatment of students and employees, and adherence to local and national laws must be shaped in the context of organizational functioning. An understanding of the various organizational theories through which one can understand college and university leadership, administration, and management help define that context. This understanding allows one to shape effective policy.

While the book is intended for use in masters and doctoral classes, doctoral students require a deeper explication of the theories than is offered here. The text is meant as an introduction to various organizational theories. The desire to keep the book both affordable and accessible calls for chapters that, by necessity, do not allow the fullest treatment of the theories. The recommended readings serve as a means to supplement the chapters with additional material with which doctoral students can further delve into the intricacies of the theories. Masters students, in contrast, may be satisfied with the depth of theories offered in the book and/or could use the recommended readings for additional study.

CHANGES IN THE SECOND EDITION

This second edition of *Organizational Theory in Higher Education* includes several additions and changes.

- All chapters have been revised with updated material, new citations and references to reflect the current climate and issues in higher education.
- An entirely new chapter on Institutional Theory has been added.
- The Feminist chapter from the first edition has been renamed Feminist and Gendered, and expanded to include queer theory and more expansive concepts regarding gender.
- The New Science chapter from the first edition has been removed, although many concepts contained in that chapter are discussed in the Spirituality chapter in the present edition.
- The Conclusion has been revised and expanded with particular attention being given to how different higher education constituent groups can use the material shared in the book to understand colleges and universities.

- The theory and case chapters have been combined to enhance the connection between the practical examples and the theoretical approaches.
- The chapters have been arranged in alphabetical order by theory name to de-emphasize any hierarchical or preferential approach.
- The chapters have been written as stand-alone pieces to enable course instructors to determine their preferred order of presentation.
- Several new cases have been included to reflect current issues faced by faculty, students, administrators, trustees, and others involved in higher education.
- The cases and examples have been expanded to include additional information on Historically Black Institutions, Hispanic-Serving Institutions, community colleges, and institutions reflecting the full range of U.S. higher education.
- The questions to consider and recommended readings at the end of the theory chapters have been updated and enhanced.

As a long-term member of U.S. higher education, I am committed to the future success of these organizations. This book is an effort to achieve that goal. I hope you find it useful.

Kathleen Manning
Burlington, Vermont

1

THE CURRENT STATE OF U.S. HIGHER EDUCATION

Context over organizational forms for universities around the world … [is] not a recent development. (Pusser, 2015, p. 67)

U.S. higher education is a complex enterprise open to a range of understandings and interpretations. Complexity within this educational system is expressed in institutional type, environmental pressures, size, multiple and simultaneously occurring organizational structures, and the numerous professional identities of its members. Those working in higher education can only make sense of its complexity by understanding and using a combination of theoretical perspectives through which to understand their environment and view their practice. This book presents eight organizational theories and provides higher education administrators, faculty, staff, trustees, and students with a number of perspectives through which to understand their institution and their work within it.

U.S. HIGHER EDUCATION AS A MATURE INDUSTRY

The higher education "enterprise," in business terms, is a mature industry (Altbach, 2011; Bills, 2016; Levine, 2001). Theorists postulate that organizations progress through a life cycle: birth and early development, institutionalization, and maturity (Baden-Fuller & Stopford, 1994; Beatty & Ulrich, 1991; Doeringer, 1987; Kimberly, 1980). Mature organizations are slow to change. Their structure is concrete; some would say fossilized, with less room for nimble modifications or novel innovations. The labor force (i.e., faculty, administrators, and staff) is specialized by function with minimal flexibility within a set of self-perpetuating functions. Mature organizations are often complacent about their market niche. "Mature organizations have a choice to stay dynamic or pass into decline. Mature organizations, with their potentially fossilized structures, must actively work to remain dynamic. This entails astute environmental analysis and an adaptable belief system" (Manning, 1997, p. 6). Given the mature state of U.S. higher education organizations, a fresh look at potential organizational models can help colleges and universities rejuvenate and revitalize this important sector of U.S. education.

TRADITIONAL AND CURRENT TENSIONS WITHIN HIGHER EDUCATION

The U.S. higher education system contains several historical and current tensions (see Table 1.1). The rapidly changing and increasingly demanding contexts in which higher education currently exists exacerbate these tensions. Several of these tensions are discussed in greater depth below.

Specialization versus Integration

In terms of the curriculum, decades-long debates have raged about whether it is better to specialize in majors and minors or integrate knowledge through core curricula and general education requirements. The highly professional nature of faculty and the specialized approach of the academic department structure have limited the ability of faculty and administrators to quickly adapt to market-driven curriculum changes and student needs. Whether and how much to emphasize and the individual or the community and balance these is an argument that has long raged in higher education, particularly in residence halls, academic departments, and among members of boards of trustees. The effective mix of interdependence and independence, particularly among faculty, is an elusive goal exacerbated by the ease of communication now available through the internet and social media. Unique practices such as tenure and long-term employment

Table 1.1 Historical and Current Tensions in Higher Education

Specialization versus Integration
(particularly as expressed in the curriculum)

Sustainability versus Immediacy
(particularly as expressed with budgets)

Globalization versus Localization
(particularly as expressed in the curriculum)

Corporatization versus Liberal Arts Values
(particularly as expressed in faculty hiring patterns)

Professionalism versus Adaptability
(particularly as expressed in faculty relations)

Individualism versus Community
(particularly as expressed in student life)

Independence versus Interdependence
(particularly as expressed in academic freedom)

Structure versus Flexibility
(particularly as expressed in organizational forms)

Public versus Private Good
(particularly as expressed in public financing)

Competitive versus Collaborative
(particularly as expressed in administrative practice)

across employee groups create tension between the values of a stable structure versus the adaptability of a flexible, responsive organizational architecture.

Public versus Private Good

Whether higher education is a public or a private good is a debate that has occupied many a student and practitioner of higher education (Kezar, Chambers, & Burkhardt, 2005). The arguments in favor of the private good side of the debate resulted in a shift to loans rather than grants—an assumption that students and their families are responsible for tuition and fees—and decreases in financial support from public sources.

Competition versus Cooperation

A final tension influencing higher education is the competitive versus cooperative tendencies of all organizations. Often voiced in gender-identified language, opinions abound about whether productivity is best achieved by pitting employees in healthy competition or engaging them in cooperative approaches.

The contexts and tensions outlined here describe a higher education condition requiring significant expertise and understanding to effectively manage in today's environment. An understanding of how higher education organizations operate in circumstances of new and continuing tensions, contexts, and challenges is essential for effective leadership. This expertise extends to the varieties of organizational theories and models available for use within colleges and universities. Without an understanding of how colleges and universities work, administrators, faculty, and higher education stakeholders remain puzzled about why their institutions remain impervious to change, difficult to manage, and resistant to innovation. Without knowledge of organizational structure, faculty are hard pressed to make policy decisions regarding curriculum and other issues; trustees struggle to determine effective institutional purposes; and administrators fight to keep up with the rapid pace of change. This expansive knowledge and expertise about organizational structures is particularly important as old models of competition are replaced with newer models of collaboration.

HIGHER EDUCATION TRENDS

New computer technologies, innovative ways of communicating, borderless education, globalization, changed configurations of faculty hiring, and re-shaped pedagogies are among the developments that have profoundly altered and will continue to alter higher education.

This book presents organizational theories that can be considered against the backdrop of past, present, and future trends in U.S. higher education. Although several trends are summarized here, it is impossible to predict or foreshadow all or even most future developments. The dynamic, complex, and ever-changing nature of U.S. higher education (and global higher education in general) means that any discussion of trends will be incomplete. The recent and ongoing trends discussed in this chapter, however, bear mention accompanied with the caveat that new trends emerge continuously. These recent trends are presented with associated insights about the ways organizational theories can assist faculty, students, and administrators understand the environment in which they live and work. The multi-modal approach described below can enable all involved in higher education to gain the flexibility and creativity needed to work in complex, ever-changing higher education institutions.

Adapting to New Technologies

Perhaps no development has as much potential for change and both positive and negative disruption as computer technologies.

> Technology is reshaping pedagogy and teaching, calling into question traditional beliefs about the role of the professor. It is also spurring the development of new institutional offices and requiring innovations concerning strategy, and resource allocation. (Green, Eckel, & Barblan, 2002, p. 1)

The communication, teaching, and knowledge dissemination currently available through computer technology is unparalleled. Online journals and databases have transformed libraries. One needs only a computer and internet connection, rather than a physical presence, to access a wealth of information. Teaching delivery systems have changed teacher–student communication patterns, created new ways (e.g., chats, videos) for students to be engaged, increased methods of providing student feedback, and eliminated the time and distance limitations of the physical classroom.

Globalization and Internationalization

Higher education has always been global. Since the earliest student and scholar exchanges, higher education has welcomed international visitors, borrowed practices from distant institutions, and generated research through international collaborations. In today's environment of ubiquitous communication and virtually unlimited access to knowledge, the global reach of international higher education is greater than ever. For all its positive impact, globalization has also raised vexing issues including the overwhelming prevalence of English, the hegemony of capitalism, the dominance of developed over undeveloped and developing nations, and the diminishment of national identities and culture (Green et al., 2002, p. 1).

Dwindling Resources

The challenge of funding higher education is a national and international issue. Budget cuts, some draconian, have characterized many public institutions during the last 15 years. Nations, states, and various government structures have steadily decreased funding. Sentiment has shifted from higher education as a public good to a private one to be funded by the individual or family of the recipient. Budget cuts have been accompanied by historic tuition increases. Used to offset the revenue losses from public sources, these tuition increases have resulted in high student loan borrowing that threatens to burden future generations.

Shifts in Faculty Roles

The "graying" of the faculty is a phenomenon predicted by higher education scholars and policy makers for years. The decrease in faculty hired into tenured and tenure-track positions and increase in contingent (e.g., adjunct, part-time, multi-year contracted) faculty has accelerated significantly. Many argue that this shift will result in less support for students, exploitation of contingent faculty, and decrease the self-governance and policy-making efforts of faculty. Most at risk is academic freedom, which is protected through the tenure process.

Collaborations and Competition

Industry-related training organizations, for-profit institutions, and online options are a few of the recent developments emerging as competitors to the traditional two- and four-year higher education institutions.

To enhance their capacities universities worldwide are forming partnerships with other institutions in the same country, with institutions in other countries, and with other kinds of organizations (Green et al., 2002, p. 1).

These new configurations and collaborations promise to create innovative forms and functions in higher education. Teaching, research, and service collaborations create new forms, encourage the sharing of resources, and enhance the emerging and traditional goals of higher education. Through research consortia, teaching partnerships, articulation agreements, and university–corporate partnerships, for example, traditional forms of higher education are being re-crafted into novel possibilities.

Climate Change

Although insufficiently discussed, climate change has the potential to influence student enrollment patterns, interrupt operations due to catastrophic weather events, affect physical plant operations, and limit student and scholar mobility due to the rising costs of travel. Higher education is a major source of research on climate change with the potential to produce solutions and alternatives. The current trends of building LEED (Leadership in Energy and Environment Design) certified facilities on campus indicates a willingness to take leadership regarding this important threat.

Social Media

Once the primary purview of students, social media is now integrated into the daily professional and personal lives of faculty, staff, and administrators. Research findings take on enhanced meaning when traditional sources of knowledge dissemination are replaced with social media outlets, self-publishing, and other technology-enhanced means. Outlets for cutting edge research and ideas have increased, the time to publication has decreased, and the promise of disseminating ideas without lengthy time to publication are encouraging developments in this area. Issues concerning peer review, appropriate vetting, and trustworthiness of the knowledge shared are vexing issues raised by the use of social media and knowledge dissemination.

These and other trends yet to be identified promise to re-shape higher education in currently unimaginable ways. The organizational theories summarized in this book offer perspectives through which to view higher education institutions and the trends working upon them.

MULTI-MODAL APPROACH

The history of organizational theory is rich, lengthy, and inter-disciplinary. Many of the theories and models in this book emerged from business, sociology, political science, anthropology, and other disciplines. The approach taken is to share models and theories that can help practitioners understand the underlying structures and functions of institutions of higher education. This

> formal organizational structure reflect[s] not only technical demands and resource dependencies, but ... [is] also shaped by institutional forces, including rational myths, knowledge legitimated through the educational system and by the professions, public opinion, and law. (Powell, 2007, p. 1)

Higher education structures grow out of and are embedded in disciplinary perspectives, larger institutional structures (e.g., governments, educational systems), and societal beliefs about the "way things are done."

Dependence on only one organizational model, regardless of how powerful or explanatory, to understand higher education implies that a singular approach to theory and practice is adequate. This limited approach cannot provide the range of understanding needed to lead these complex and dynamic organizations. Models can be combined and employed to explain the various circumstances in an institution. Any one campus will certainly reflect more than one model within the institution. Readers of this book are advised to explore the models and theories with an eye for how the different choices can explain various parts of the institution.

The complexity of colleges and universities requires what Birnbaum (1991) referred to as a cybernetic approach to leadership, management, and administration. Also called multi-modal, this approach recognizes that people perceive organizations in a number of ways. The use of multiple theories to understand a college or university enables practitioners, the primary audience for this book, to most fully comprehend them. Both traditional and current theories can be used to understand organizational practices in higher education. Many practices harkening back to traditional theories such as bureaucracy remain on campus. Practices have also emerged from more current theories that account for gendered perspectives and post-modern approaches to organizational practice.

Theories do not stand alone. One theory cannot explain all the nuances and complexity of practice on a college or university campus. Instead, theories build on one another—current theorists stand on the shoulders of the theorists that went before them. Spirituality and feminist and gendered theories build on the assumptions of postmodernism.

> One of the major contributions of postmodern thought ... is to help emphasize complexity, ambiguity, continuous change, disorder, and nonlinear processes.... Previous functionalist theories emphasize the maintenance of order and the linearity of change processes, which have become the norm when thinking about organizational processes. (Kezar, 2012, p. 196)

The specific organizational context of an institution or sector of higher education requires the full range of modern and postmodern theories to understand these institutions.

Organizational theory has a long history in sociology, education, psychology, and business, among other disciplines. To better express the complexity of organizational functioning, an interdisciplinary approach underscores the organizational models discussed in this book (see Table 1.2). This approach enables readers to better understand colleges and universities as a means to support effective leadership and management. Whether called frames (Birnbaum, 1991), metaphors (Morgan, 2006), or models (Clark, 1986), the organizational theories described in this book can help administrators, faculty,

Table 1.2 Theoretical Foundations and Metaphors for Organizational Models

Organizational Perspective	Theoretical Foundation	Metaphor
Bureaucracy	modernist	machine
Collegium	sociology	circle
Cultural	anthropology	carnival and theater
Feminist and Gendered	feminist and queer theory	web
Institutional Theory	political science	concentric circles
Organized Anarchy	political philosophy	anarchy
Political	sociology	jungle
Spiritual	psychology	journey

stakeholders, and students better understand the challenges of a complex and globally connected world. Metaphors for each perspective, visually and pictorially, describe the organizational perspective as well.

As an overview of the material presented in the chapters, Table 1.3 outlines elements for each organizational theory presented. The extent of the information included in this chart merely scratches the surface of the complexity of the theories and the range that faculty and practitioners need to bring to the task of understanding colleges and universities.

Chapters discussing the theories and accompanying case study applications enable scholars and practitioners to view higher education institutions from a number of organizational perspectives. Some theories overlap with others, some conflict, some are complementary. All theories offer ways to expand the repertoire of conceptual tools available to higher education faculty, staff, administrators, students, and stakeholders. The theories offer a full range of explanatory power that takes many organizational structures and ways of operating into account.

The desire to include established, traditional theories (e.g., bureaucratic, collegial, cultural, organized anarchies, and political) and more contemporary theories (e.g., feminist and gendered, institutionalization, and spiritual) drove the choice of the eight organizational approaches included in the book. A goal was to include contemporary organizational theories often excluded from previous texts. Previous educational organizational theory texts, often written from the perspective of K–12 education, cover only four frames or theories (i.e., cultural, bureaucratic, political, and human resources). Traditional organizational theory, if used with an eye for control, order, and rationality, limits ideas about how organizations can be innovatively created and managed. This is particularly important because colleges and universities have always been "unique organizations, differing in major respects from industrial organizations, government bureaus, and business firms" (Baldridge, Curtis, Ecker, & Riley, 1974, p. 7). The interconnected and complex world in which colleges and universities exist demands more nuanced and imaginative approaches to organizing structures, functions, and processes. The older, more prescriptive theories are problematic because "the ideal-type bureaucracy does not map well onto academic organizations" (Gumport, 2012, p. 24).

The contemporary theories offered in the book can assist higher education institutions to continue to become more inclusive, entrepreneurial, and collaborative. These

Table 1.3 Summary of Organizational Models

Organizational Elements	Chapter 2 Bureaucracy	Chapter 3 Collegium	Chapter 4 Cultural	Chapter 5 Feminist and Gendered	Chapter 6 Institutional Theory	Chapter 7 Organized Anarchy	Chapter 8 Political	Chapter 9 Spiritual
Disciplinary foundation	modernity	sociology	anthropology	feminist theory	political science	political philosophy	sociology	psychology
Decision-making mode	rational decision making	participative decision making	meaning making	collaborative	choice enabled and constrained by institutions	garbage can model	compromise; conflict	cooperative and collaborative
Actions based on	technical; standard operating procedures	consensus; discussion	enactment	shared purposes	consideration of embedded institutional logics	fluid participation	conflict, loyalties, policy	intellect and gut feeling; emotions allowed
Mechanism for reality creation	"natural"; external; ideal type from nature	shared constructions	socially constructed	shared meaning	assumptions gained from wider social, cultural, and political institutions	multiple realities	defined by those in power	individual interpretation
Sources of meaning	objective rules	academic disciplines	rituals, myths, sagas, language, tradition	collaboration and relationships	institutional logics	complexity	conflict	mind, body, spirit
Power	legitimate	expert; professional	symbols, history, tradition	egalitarian	regulatory and cultural	diffused	charisma; influence	power emerges from all participants
Structure	hierarchical; pyramid	circular	varied	roughly circular; web	nested	varied	flat	varied
Metaphor	machine	circle	carnival and theater	web	concentric circles	anarchy	jungle	journey

Examples/ archetype	military; church	legal process; faculty senate; professional associations	church; sports; fraternities	corporations, colleges	pre-school, primary, elementary, secondary, and post-secondary system of education in the U.S.	colleges and universities	legislature; unions; private club	corporations, colleges
Leadership	top down; legitimate authority; leadership emanates from office	first among equals	heroes and heroines; mythical; the stuff of saga	rotating; transformational	defined by prevailing beliefs gained from overall institutional influences	constructed and symbolic	coalitions; defined by power structures and influence	rotating; transformational
Communication	top down; written predominates	protracted; oral based	explicit and implicit; oral; storytelling	power shared through open communication and other networks	flows in multiple directions	intermittent	covert	power shared through open communication and other networks
Scope of influence	institutional	faculty	institutional	global	internal and external	pockets	institutional	global
Reward structure	merit	expertise in discipline; peer review	tradition	compromise between personal and organizational goals	adherence to the assumptions and values conveyed from larger institutions	individual	connections	compromise between personal and organizational goals
Source of structure	nature	academic disciplines	culture	whole; universe	rules, laws, regulations, traditions, and assumptions	chaos	relationships; city state	whole; universe
How you perceive co-workers	worker bees	colleagues	actors and cast	fellow journeyers	associates	fellow professionals	adversaries	fellow journeyers

more inclusive theories are necessary as older economic models are supplanted with newer approaches requiring higher education degrees and increased employee skill levels. An entrepreneurial spirit is required for higher education systems that are expanding globally, embody multiple structural forms, and require a more expansive vision—one that is achievable given the recent higher education innovations. Newer ideas about collaboration in leadership, for example, will not only improve working conditions for all in higher education, but can create meaningful roles for staff, students, and those people traditionally excluded from the power structures within colleges and universities. Knowledge of these organizational theories and the complexity they depict can help all understand why higher education is so difficult to manage, a challenge to organize, and impossible to control. This book illustrates how different organizational theories can provoke more richly effective leadership and practice within higher education.

Because higher education organizations have traditionally utilized several simultaneously operating organizational theories that shape a complex range of activities, readers are strongly urged to consider the theories as gestalt, or combinations of several ways (not *a* singular way), to understand higher education. Whether as a system or a single institution, no one perspective or model will explain *all* aspects of higher education. One lens through which to view colleges and universities is not complex enough to provide the skilled leadership necessary to confront the present and future challenges that colleges and universities are encountering. Each theory is an opportunity to think differently about how colleges and universities can be organized and led. In combination, all or several theories can expose elements of higher education invisible from one theory. The theories are expressed differently across various departments and offices, and their prevalence ebbs and flows depending on the task at hand. This is only one of the many reasons why colleges and universities as organizations are complex and difficult to understand.

In addition to thinking holistically and creatively about the organizational theories, the following idioms are playful ways to consider the theories and models discussed in this text:

Bureaucratic: "A place for everyone and everyone in their place."
Collegial: "We're all equal colleagues here. Let's discuss this over coffee."
Cultural: "We have a legacy and tradition to maintain. This is not about us but about the past and the future."
Feminist and Gendered: "Let's build an organization that builds on our strengths across different identities."
Institutionalization: "We need to consider the systems and institutions that guide our work."
Organized Anarchy: "Don't try to make sense of it—just trust that it works."
Political: "I'll scratch your back if you scratch mine."
Spiritual: "If we accomplish the task but don't bring our whole selves to it, we've failed."

A discussion of the organizational theories as viewed within the higher education environment in the 21st century (see Table 1.4) can help those within and outside these institutions comprehend why they are so difficult to understand.

Table 1.4 21st-Century Challenges

- Globalization and internationalization including massification.
- Economic challenges including decreased state funding and ongoing tuition increases.
- Shift of higher education from a public to a private good.
- Increased competition and market-driven emphasis.
- Changes in management, administration, and teaching due to technological innovations.
- Increased power to administrators due to need for advanced budget and management expertise.
- Diversification of students including increased students of color, gender variant people, and women's degree attainment.
- Increased openness to students, faculty, and staff who are LGB, queer, and transgender.
- Challenges to the teaching, research, and service priorities of higher education from a public and federal government that is increasingly anti-intellectual.
- Education that is increasingly unbundled and disaggregated from faculty effort through standardized, pre-packaged curriculum.
- Tensions created by student debt load.
- Continuation of the traditional tension between vocationalism and the value of a liberal education.

Trustees, parents, and external stakeholders are frequently perplexed by characteristics of higher education organizations that are absent in other organizations such as corporations, political institutions, or other nonprofits. These characteristics include:

1. *Highly professional employees.* Although corporate models are often used to explain higher education, colleges and universities are more like hospitals, for example, than corporations. Faculty possess professional authority that places them in the role of expert, in a similar fashion to medical doctors and nurses. Administrators also possess expert knowledge and elevated professional status as evidenced by advanced degrees and highly specific job requirements.
2. *Presence of cosmopolitans.* Organizational members (e.g., faculty) often have allegiances to entities (e.g., discipline, professional associations, alma maters) outside their place of employment. These divided and potentially scattered loyalties can result in insufficient attention to circumstances and developments at the home institution.
3. *Multiple organizational structures.* Several organizational structures occur simultaneously within colleges and universities. A bureaucracy exists alongside a collegium; political dynamics can accompany feminist and gendered perspectives. Few other organizations have the complexity resulting from these simultaneously occurring structures.
4. *Conflict over the appropriate product of higher education.* Despite the urging of many state legislatures, national pundits, and critics, colleges and universities struggle to conclusively identify or measure the end product of their labors. Credits generated, retention and graduation rates, faculty–student ratios, and faculty productivity as measured by full-time equivalent measures are proxies for the true product of higher education: an educated person. Although a college degree is vigorously sought after and paid for dearly, the worth that a degree confers is difficult to definitively identify.
5. *Multiple, often-conflicting roles.* Faculty, administrators, staff, students, and external stakeholders by structure, temperament, and responsibilities play vastly different roles within higher education organizations. Sometimes at odds with one

another, the delineation of these roles is becoming more pronounced with the introduction of technology, the increasingly complex fiduciary responsibilities expected of administrators and trustees, and the raised expectations of students, parents, and other stakeholders.

The traditional tensions within higher education demand that faculty, administrators, trustees, and other stakeholders get out ahead of the current changes occurring within higher education. With the ongoing and upcoming shifts in higher education functioning, both traditional and contemporary theories should be included in the knowledge base of all who work in the sector. The traditional models can help shed light on persistent issues and odd-looking customs. The contemporary theories can be a source of innovation, collaboration, and creativity.

Questions for Discussion

- How can the organizational theories under consideration help college and university leaders get out ahead of the rapid change occurring in higher education?
- How do the different organizational theories enable or constrain innovation?
- What knowledge bases will faculty, administrators, trustees, and others involved in higher education need to develop to help these institutions thrive?
- What are the power dynamics within the different organizational theories?
- How is human agency enabled or constrained within the organizational theories?
- What aspects of an institution are best explained by a particular organizational theory? What parts are not well explained?

Recommended Readings Related to Higher Education Organizing

Bergquist, W. H., & Pawlak, K. (2008). *Engaging the six cultures of the academy* (2nd ed.). San Francisco: Jossey-Bass.

Chambers, A. C., & Burkhardt, J. C. (Eds.). (2015). *Higher education for the public good: Emerging voices from a national movement.* San Francisco: John Wiley & Sons.

Gumport, P. J. (Ed.). (2007). *Sociology of higher education: Contributions and their contexts.* Baltimore: Johns Hopkins University Press.

Hazelkorn, E. (2015). *Rankings and the reshaping of higher education: The battle for world-class excellence.* New York: Springer.

Keeling, R., & Hersh, R. (2016). *We're losing our minds: Rethinking American higher education.* New York: Springer.

Tierney, W. G., & Lanford, M. (2016). Conceptualizing innovation in higher education. In M. Paulsen (Ed.), *Higher education: Handbook of theory and research* (pp. 1–40). New York: Springer.

2

BUREAUCRACY

Virtually all colleges and universities have been organized at least partly along bureaucratic lines, so it is important to understand their advantages and disadvantages. (Bess & Dee, 2008, p. 203)

INTRODUCTION

Organizations, from a bureaucratic perspective, are "rationally ordered instruments for the achievement of stated goals" (Selznick, 1948/2016, p. 116). Bureaucratic principles are so inculcated into modern living that they are often considered inherent parts of daily life. Bureaucracy is an undeniable and enduring perspective through which to view organizational functions in higher education. In reality, bureaucracy is just one of many ways to organize collective human behavior. Though many decry the red tape and glacial pace of bureaucracies, it is difficult to imagine administrative operations without this form. While this book describes a number of ways to think about organizational structure, aspects of bureaucracy either shape a number of those theories or exist as the norm against which other forms are compared. Despite the ubiquitous nature of bureaucracy in institutions of higher education, the presence of this dominant organizational form was not always the case.

Early universities, if one can call those early forms by that term, were not bureaucracies. Operating with an informal paternalistic style, scholars set up shop in a cafe or public establishment and attracted paying students. Scholars were deemed as such because they owned the book; the technology of the time that made learning possible. These early scholars were not associated with an institution but were self-employed, independent scholars. While non-institution-affiliated scholars exist in today's higher education system, they are the exception rather than the rule. In modern day colleges and universities, rank, title, and employment with an organization are formalized. Many take these organizational elements for granted, but each is based on bureaucratic principles as defined by early theorists such as Max Weber and Henri Fayol. Using bureaucratic principles of standardization and specification, learning is classified into majors, degrees, and certificates. Students, like professors, find their place in higher education through their association with a formal educational institution. Through this connection they earn credits and, ultimately, a degree.

MODERNIST ASSUMPTIONS AS A FOUNDATION FOR THE BUREAUCRATIC PERSPECTIVE

Max Weber, the father of bureaucracy, made this organizational form decidedly modern by emphasizing precision and efficiency (Merton, 1957/2011): "Weber's ideas were based on his presumption of the importance of rationality, impersonality, and objectivity in decision making and in the application of rules" (Bess & Dee, 2008, p. 204). Borrowing from the Enlightenment, Weber built the modernist assumptions of logic and progress into the theory of bureaucracy. These underlying principles endure in today's bureaucratic forms (see Table 2.1).

Weber built rationality into every principle and characteristic of bureaucracy (Merton, 1957/2011). This rationality is particularly expressed in the goal orientation that underlies all organizational activities. True to the modernist perspective, people in bureaucratic organizations assume that progressive movement toward goals is essential. This movement is achieved by the competent action of the people who fill the ranks of institutional staff and management. Progress is also reflected in principles regarding growth that underscore modern organizations. Bigger is better in bureaucracies as, in the case of higher education institutions, student bodies grow in size, majors are added, new ways of teaching are developed, and economies of scale are applied.

Today, those who work in bureaucracies, use services within these organizations, or consume products produced through bureaucratic procedures often have a negative view of this organizational form. The cumbersome, time-consuming processes common in bureaucracies (i.e., "red tape") are the source of frequent complaints. Despite its current problems, bureaucracy was a revolutionary and forward-thinking concept when Weber first theorized its principles.

Prior to the bureaucratic innovation, paternalism was the predominant style of organization. Early organizations relied on leadership approaches emphasizing authoritarianism and arbitrary treatment of employees. The Great Man Theory (i.e., leaders are born, not made) (Lipman-Blumen, 2014), outdated by today's egalitarian standards, was firmly rooted in the early paternalistic higher education organizations. These early and in some

Table 2.1 Strengths and Weaknesses of the Modernist Theoretical Foundation for Higher Education

Strengths	Weaknesses
Objectivity introduced increased fairness and objectivity into organizations.	Constant progress may not be sustainable given declining fossil fuel resources.
Rationality encouraged logic into organizations, which spurred consistency and increased efficiency.	Progress is a Western civilization concept not transferable across all cultures.
Progress opened to door to a plethora of modernist inventions and successes: modern medicine, the industrial revolution, heightened quality of life, and universal education, among others.	Objectivity can diminish individual initiative and accomplishment.
	Rationality may crowd out passion that sparks innovation.

cases current paternalistic organizations lack consistent policies and procedures. The organizational leader operated as the "head of the family" with unlimited power and arbitrary, at times capricious, rule. Bureaucracy was invented to revolutionize the excesses, favoritism, nepotism, and lack of procedures of paternal organizations. Credentials replaced favoritism; standard operating procedures traded for opinion; and objectivity supplanted subjectivity.

Modernist assumptions as related to higher education institutions include the following:

- Efficiency regarding budget, organization of staff, and use of institutional resources is an organizing principle.
- Progress and growth as indicated in increased institutional size, addition of academic programs, and provision of services are institutional priorities.
- Accountability, particularly to government agencies, is an essential aspect of organizational life.
- Organizational issues, conflicts, and inefficiencies can be resolved through restructuring and re-engineering.

METAPHOR

Quintessential bureaucratic organizations include the military, Catholic Church, and McDonald's. Each conjures the image of a well-oiled machine (Morgan, 2006). In McDonald's, every action—from the way customers are greeted to the salt on the fries—is routinized. Consistency is assured through standard operating procedures. A McDonald's franchise whether in Paris, France, or Bloomington, Indiana produces its trademark product with minor variations. This worldwide standardization is possible because individual staff choice is eliminated. Any McDonald's staff member, trained in the procedures, can substitute for another staff member. Each employee is a cog in the wheel of the machine created from a central corporate location and, as such, is expendable (Ferguson, 1985). Standardization as illustrated on an organizational chart dictates "'A place for everything and everything in its place'" and "'A place for everyone and everyone in his [*sic*] place'" (Fayol, 1916/2016, p. 62).

STRUCTURE

Bureaucratic theory holds that organizations should follow an ideal, natural, or perfect order (Fayol, 1916/2016; Ferguson, 1985), one in which human action follows the hierarchy of nature. Following this natural, ideal order, bureaucracies adopt a hierarchical, pyramid shaped structure. Mimicking the forms found in nature, early proponents of bureaucracies used authority and responsibility as a way to vertically organize organizations. Bureaucracies are "natural" in their organization from simple to complex, lower to higher, and smaller to greater. They are complex because employees with more complicated jobs are positioned near the top of the organization. They are higher in the ways that responsibility increases as one goes up the hierarchy. They are greater in the ways that power is concentrated at the top of the hierarchy. Despite advice by early bureaucratic theorists (Fayol, 1916/2016) about the need for flexibility and artful application of principles, bureaucratic organizations tend to "fossilize." Their ways of operating and standard operating procedures become an impediment, a sea of red tape that frustrates everyone associated with these organizations. Although many are tempted, bureaucratic theorists advise against changing the structure to accommodate or make allowances for individual personalities. To do so interferes with the rational order and can result in a Byzantine organization that lacks logic, rationality, and objectivity.

MAJOR CONCEPTS, CHARACTERISTICS, AND TERMS

In her feminist critique of bureaucracy, Ferguson (1985, p. 7) outlined the major characteristics of this organizational form as originated by Weber:

> A complex rational division of labor, with fixed duties and jurisdictions; stable, rule-governed authority channels and universally applied performance guidelines; a horizontal division of graded authority, or hierarchy, entailing supervision from above; a complex system of written record-keeping, based on scientific procedures that standardize communications and increase control; objective recruitment based on impersonal standards of expertise; predictable, standardized management procedures following general rules; and a tendency to require total loyalty from its members toward the way of life the organization requires.

Although the list of bureaucratic characteristics described by Ferguson and others is extensive, for the purposes of this introductory text, only the basic characteristics are discussed in this chapter (see Table 2.2). Bureaucratic concepts that may be of interest but which are not discussed here are outlined in Table 2.3. Additional readings on bureaucracies are located at the end of the chapter.

Appointment of Staff

The move away from the nepotism and patronage systems of pre-bureaucratic, paternalistic organizations introduced meritocratic organizational practices. In a meritocracy, one gains a position because one has the necessary qualifications (Weber, 1946/2016).

Table 2.2   Basic Characteristics of Bureaucracies

Concept	Description
Structure	Hierarchy.
Appointment of Staff	Obtain their office through expertise and credentials.
Authority	Concentrated at the top of the hierarchy.
Communication	Formal vertically and informal laterally.
Decision Making	Rational and top down.
Ways of Operating	Standard operating procedures.
Labor Organization	Division of work by specialization.
Span of Control	Number and range of direct reports.
Stability of Personnel	Constancy of staff that enables organizational effectiveness and efficiency.
Centralization/Decentralization	Location and focus of power and/or control of organizational processes.

Table 2.3 Additional Bureaucratic Concepts

Concept	Description
Unity of Direction	One head, one plan. Unity and coordination of action among the employees in a given area is a goal of bureaucracies.
Unity of Command	One employee, one supervisor.
Remuneration of Personnel	Employees should receive a salary based on the cost of living, availability of personnel, business conditions, and economics.
Individual Interest Subordinated to the General Interest	The interest or interests of one employee or group should not take precedence over the interests and concerns of the organization.
Scalar Chain	Line of authority ranges from the ultimate authority (e.g., university president) to the lowest ranks (e.g., non-classified staff members).

Source: Fayol, 1916/2016; Gulick, 1937/2016.

Objective credentials and qualifications are used to judge whether the candidate is suitable for hiring, theoretically regardless of personal connections or family background. People are hired as employees, not unique individuals, and paid to fill an office. The bureaucratic principle of appointment to a role was and is best exemplified in assembly lines and fast-food companies such as McDonald's.

Being hired into an office is one of the major ways that employees are viewed as cogs in the mechanistic wheel of bureaucracies. When an office becomes vacant, another "part" (i.e., employee) can theoretically and easily fill the vacancy. If the structure is well constructed, employees are interchangeable. Organizational success is not based on personal qualities but on a set of time and performance based criteria. Rational action is thus built into human organizations (Selznick, 1948/2016). By removing the personal and emphasizing the functional, organizational success is independent of the person, but rather, depends on the way the organization or bureaucracy is organized to withstand ups and downs in staffing. This objective, impersonal process assures the continuation of the organization, regardless of those who occupy it.

Weber theorized that a bureaucratic position should be held for life, as a vocation, not a "job." Vocational-style employment is a bureaucratic principle widely applied in higher education institutions where lifelong employment as guaranteed by tenure for faculty is widely accepted. These characteristics of employment apply equally to administrators and staff who occupy their positions, or ones similar to them, for their professional lifetime.

The meritocratic principles of appointment imply that the "best" person, based on objectively determined criteria, is hired to fulfill an identified role. Although this principle of merit exists theoretically, it is rarely enacted in practice. Critical race theorists (Delgado & Stefancic, 2012; Ladson-Billings, 1998, 2013) and feminist theorists (Dobbin, Schrage, & Kalev, 2015; Ferguson, 1985; Mullins, 2014) have debunked the assumptions of objectivity and merit. In reality, favoritism, propinquity (i.e., hiring someone because he or she shares similar characteristics to one's own), and gender, racial, sexual orientation, and other biases exist within all organizations. While the value of subjectivity versus objectivity can be debated, the solely merit-based philosophy fails in practice.

Authority

The efficient and effective operation of an organization depends on authority; the authority to plan, organize, staff, direct, coordinate, report, and budget (Gulick, 1937/2016). In bureaucracies, managers and executives, referred to as line officers, possess the formal authority to execute these responsibilities. In the traditional bureaucratic tradition, "[a]uthority is the right to give orders and the power to exact obedience" (Fayol, 1916/2016, p. 54). Also called bureaucratic authority, formal authority is attached to the office or position held by the employee (Morgan, 2006). Bureaucratic or formal authority is vastly different from charismatic, political, expert, or reference power. "Distinction must be made between a manager's official authority deriving from office and personal authority, compounded of intelligence, experience, moral worth, ability to lead, past services, etc." (Fayol, 1916/2016, p. 54). Higher education organizations, as seen from the bureaucratic perspective, contain considerable authority in the executive offices of the president and provost. Authority emanates from the position or office, but real power comes from those being supervised, directed, or governed. Despite the "ideal" authority embedded in bureaucratic positions, authority cannot be exercised unless subordinates agree to be led and influenced.

> To the extent that authority is translated into power through the assent of those falling under the pattern of command, the authority structure is also a power structure ... authority becomes effective only to the extent that it is legitimized from below. (Morgan, 2006, p. 168)

Authority and its related concept, power, must be earned. Organized in order of the authority imbedded in organizational roles, positions are hierarchically organized from lowest to highest order of importance. In classic bureaucracies, the number of positions decreases and authority increases as one moves up the hierarchy (see Figure 2.1).

Authority, power, and responsibility are interrelated concepts in organizations. One can have responsibility with the required authority but lack the power to execute the role. A college president, for example, can possess the responsibility of the office without the accompanying personal power to effectively execute the duties of the position. Responsibility and the exercise of authority to achieve goals are more difficult as one proceeds up the chain of command due to increasingly complex work, larger numbers of workers, and tasks for which the results are more elusive (Fayol, 1916/2016). Authority without responsibility to exercise it is wasted; responsibility without authority is unproductive.

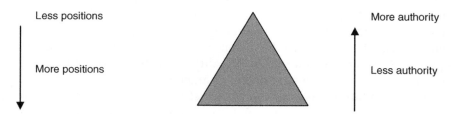

Figure 2.1 Relationship between Positions and Power

Authority and power have long been sources of tension on college campuses. The presence of academic freedom and tenure, student activism, and administrative professional power create a complicated mix of circumstances regarding how authority and power are exercised. In professional and educational environments such as higher education, skilled management and successful leadership depend on the delegation of responsibility within the organization. Traditional bureaucratic theory defines authority and power in ways that do not adequately express the dynamics of colleges and universities.

The prevalence of bureaucracies persuades many organizational members that the existing authority configuration is the only choice available. But, powerful counterstories about a wider variety of organizational forms challenge traditional notions of authority by illustrating collaborative, generative, and more equitable approaches (Bordas, 2012; Ferguson, 1985, 1994; Helgesen, 2006; Lipmen-Blumen, 1992, 1998, 2002, 2014). Authority, according to these countertheorists, is possessed and exercised by all in the organization.

Communication

Communication patterns in bureaucracies are determined by the vertical and horizontal direction of its flow (Guetzkow, 1965). The vertical form includes top-down communication; for example, supervisor directives to subordinates, executive missives to the entire institution, and activities involving multiple levels of the organization. This formal communication type represents a major task of administrators as they oversee subordinates, plan and execute goals, and direct organizational purposes.

Communication patterns, in keeping with the objective, rational nature of bureaucracies, are formal and prescribed. Rules governing bureaucratic communication, each of which is dictated by the role, status, and power held by the speaker, include the following:

1. Subordinates respect the chain of command by only communicating directly with their bosses. It is unacceptable and precarious to skip levels (e.g., talk to your boss's boss).
2. Requests must be made "in writing."
3. Incidents, procedures, and consequential actions (e.g., firing) must be documented through a paper trail.
4. Meetings include protocols about who is allowed to speak (and who can speak out of turn), the length of time one can speak, and tolerance for side conversations.

These communication patterns are predominantly one-way with limited opportunity for dialogue, feedback, or dissent. "In order to do business with bureaucrats, one must engage in conversation with them; this requires that one learn their language, play their game, and come onto their turf" (Ferguson, 1985, p. 15). Communication in bureaucracies becomes real in the form of written documents, through commands given by those in authority, and within prescribed and formal channels. In reality, communication also flows horizontally through rumor mills and a variety of informal means (Roethlisberger, 1941; Simon, 1957; Taylor, 1947; Weber, 1947). Horizontal communication is less formal and more "independent of the formal structural size of the organization as a whole" (Guetzkow, 1965, p. 541). This form takes place primarily across similar bureaucratic levels (e.g., between secretaries, among faculty). The strength of the horizontal communication is measured by the initiative it engenders within the staff (Fayol, 1916/2016). The success of this method depends on the network of personal contacts held by the administrator. Horizontal communication can be powerful with both effective and ineffective outcomes. It can enhance and facilitate communication within the organization. It can also undercut superiors, cause confusion, and perpetuate rumors.

Communication within organizations has changed dramatically with the advent of electronic mail, the internet, social media, cellular phones, and other instantaneous and ubiquitous means of communication. Technology has enabled more widespread access to information accompanied by the means to communicate across bureaucratic levels. Etiquette within bureaucracies continues to dictate older patterns established by the classic organizational theorists, but new forms have radically changed how information is controlled and communication achieved.

Communication is intricately connected to authority, specifically, the authority of the office that has the legitimacy to control the frequency and nature of communication. Administrators at higher levels within the hierarchy have wider and more formal means of communication (Guetzkow, 1965). These administrators possess a wide range of organizational resources (e.g., calling meetings, writing memos, utilizing distribution lists) through which to disseminate their messages. For example, organization-wide e-mail distribution lists are tightly controlled through the president's office, human resources, or public relations. Also, only a few in a college or university (e.g., president, provost, faculty senate president) could effectively call a community-wide meeting that administrators, students, faculty, or staff would attend.

Decision Making

In keeping with the assumptions of authority, power, and control within bureaucracies, the leader or leaders in a bureaucracy are charged with making rational choices. Theoretically, bureaucratic decision making, called the rational model of decision making, proceeds through seven steps: (a) identify the problem or opportunity, (b) gather information, (c) analyze the situation, (d) develop options, (e) evaluate the alternatives, (f) select an alternative, and (g) act on the decision (Simon, 1955, 1979). "From the gut" or subjective decisions, although commonplace, are discouraged by a bureaucratic mind-set. The belief in the efficacy of the rational model can be so strong that administrators often "retrospectively" construct these steps for a decision that was in reality achieved differently, even subjectively, haphazardly, or through "drift."

Simon (1956) recognized that the rational model of decision making was more myth than fact. He suggested that decisions are more often made through a process of satisficing. Rather than an exhaustive process that explores options, most bureaucrats find a solution that is "good enough," one that satisfies sufficient parameters of the decision situation. This solution is adopted and perhaps adapted. In this way, time—a valuable commodity within organizations—is not wasted on identifying solutions that will never be enacted.

Standard Operating Procedures

Bureaucratic organizations have accepted standards for the ways they are to function. "The management of the office follows general rules, which are more or less stable, more or less exhaustive, and which can be learned" (Weber, 1946/2016, p. 79). In organizations such as hospital emergency rooms and the military, where variation can have dire consequences, these standard operating procedures (SOPs) strictly dictate behavior and action. SOPs are represented in higher education organizations through, for example, staff and faculty manuals and union collective bargaining agreements. Hiring and firing procedures, timelines for tenure and promotion, and schedules for budgets are often strictly and legally maintained through SOPs.

Organization of Personnel

People make sense of an organization's structure, lines of authority, and reporting configuration by examining the organizational chart. These charts represent the ideals of specialization and division of labor (Fayol, 1916/2016; Gulick, 1937/2016). From this familiar image, a job applicant, new employee, or seasoned organizational member can determine the areas of responsibility for personnel within the organization. In fact, one could drill down through various division and department organizational charts to see the roles and responsibilities of nearly everyone within the college or university.

In bureaucracies, tasks and responsibilities are systematically divided into offices and among people. With efficiency as the goal, organizational personnel work to avoid repetition, map out clear lines of communication and effort, and delineate responsibility: "The object of division of work is to produce more and better work with the same effort" (Fayol, 1916/2016, p. 53). Efficiency is achieved because this approach allows management to (a) take advantage of employees' different skills and aptitudes, (b) eliminate lost time when people are assigned only the tasks for which they are trained, and (c) better utilize lower skilled workers (Gulick, 1937/2016).

An important function of the division of labor and specialization is the separation of thinking as performed by management versus doing as performed by staff. This division of labor becomes the justification for salary, power, and status differences within the organization. The separation of thinking and doing is evident in the division of labor and specialization among faculty, administrators, and staff in higher education organizations. In higher education institutions, lower level staff positions are primarily filled by women (Acker, 2009).

The organization of faculty and their academic work also represents specialization and division of labor. Disciplines (e.g., English) are divided into specializations (e.g., African American literature) and subdisciplines that are represented in the departments that comprise the academic structure of a college or university. The myriad departments and programs representing disciplinary specialization is more complex today than when the University of Vermont established academic departments in 1826, the University of Wisconsin in 1836, and the University of Michigan in 1841.

Span of Control

The bureaucratic concept of span of control refers to the number of departments, staff, and areas of responsibility coordinated by an administrator who is a specialist hired for her or his expertise in those areas. Most people can adequately direct only a few people (Gulick, 1937/2016). The manager's knowledge constrains and that person's time and energy limits the span of control. The supervisor's limitations on knowledge are more significant today than when Gulick wrote about span of control. The wide range of technologies and specialities required to manage a modern college or university are substantial. Higher education executives often manage broad spans of control. It is not unusual, in fact it is commonplace, for a director to supervise employees who are proficient in areas unfamiliar to the supervisor. Provosts, in particular, can be responsible for academic affairs (through coordination of a number of deans or directors), institutional finances, teaching and learning initiatives, student affairs, diversity initiatives, and any number of areas. Although close supervision is not an expectation at that level, according to bureaucratic theory, the wide span of control can threaten effective and strategic management of a college or university.

Space and physical facilities are additional complicating elements regarding span of control (Gulick, 1937/2016). Coordination, even with a broad span of control, is more effective when supervised personnel are located nearby. The introduction of branch and satellite campuses, including international campuses, significantly impacts span of control, coordination, and effective management. Technologies such as e-mail and video-aided telecommunications augmented with regular local and international travel are now standard expectations of many higher education administrators.

Stability of Personnel

Stability and constancy within bureaucracies occur through consistency of personnel. Unless hired on a temporary basis, most administrators and staff are employed with the expectation that long-term employment is possible and desirable. Retirement and medical benefits, vacation accrual, and the promise of advancement are elements that shape the expectation that stability is expected and rewarded. This stability allows the employee to become familiar with the organization and the work of the unit, gain experience useful to the organization, and build loyalty to and connection with the institution.

Centralization/Decentralization

The choice whether to centralize authority in one or several offices or to decentralize and share authority across a wider range of offices is a difficult one for any organization. In higher education, with its multiple goals and purposes, the centralization–decentralization dilemma is particularly acute. The professional and disciplinary expertise of deans and faculty exacerbate the centralization–decentralization tensions in academic bureaucracies. Centralization enhances standardization, control, and consistency. Decentralization can allow multiple purposes to exist within the organization because oversight is less vigilant. Leadership across a wider range of offices and units is possible because responsibility is diffuse, located away from the center of the organization. An advantage of decentralization is that "local" management can make up for leadership deficiencies at the executive (e.g., president and provost) level. But, too much decentralization can be detrimental to organizations. Goals become too disparate, results are wasted from duplication of effort, and power struggles erupt throughout the organization.

> Unless the sentiment of general interest be constantly revived by higher authority, it becomes blurred and weakened and each section tends to regard itself as its own aim and end and forgets that it is only a cog in a big machine, all of whose parts must work in concert. It becomes isolated, cloistered, aware only of the line of authority. (Fayol, 1916/2016, p. 62)

The size and nature of higher education institutions, except for the smallest of colleges, drive these organizations to a more decentralized form. It is a rare dean or department chair who takes orders in the way envisioned by the original bureaucracy theorists.

STRENGTHS AND WEAKNESSES OF THE BUREAUCRATIC MODEL

The bureaucratic model is perhaps one of the most highly criticized organizational approaches (Briskin, 1996; Ferguson, 1985; Fleischman, 2009). As with all organizational perspectives, this perspective contains strengths and weaknesses (see Table 2.4).

NEXT STEPS: BRINGING THE BUREAUCRATIC PERSPECTIVE INTO CURRENT USE

Although elements of bureaucracies exist in every college and university, the form is a difficult fit in organizations with democratic-style governance systems (e.g., faculty senates), collegial mechanisms, disciplinary priorities, and faculty professionalism. Furthermore, the time-honored practice of student activism works against the ideal-type mechanisms advanced by Weber and others.

> The presumptions of an ideal-type Weberian bureaucracy do not hold. Top-down directives fail without faculty buy-in, or at least extensive consultation processes. Academic change is slow, and it is not sustained without faculty ownership. (Gumport, 2012, p. 24)

An organizational theory based on ideas about networks and systems has taken hold over the last 20 years with the potential to bring this organizational form into more current use.

Karen Stephenson is a leading theorist on heterarchy and social networks within organizations. With a background in anthropology, chemistry, and art, Stephenson uses the term heterarchy to describe the ways that networks of hierarchies can be combined to produce extremely complex organizational forms. Heterarchy "is an organizational form somewhere between hierarchy and network that provides horizontal links permitting different elements of an organization to cooperate" (Stephenson, 2010, p. 2).

Table 2.4 Strengths and Weaknesses of the Bureaucratic Model

Strengths	Weaknesses
Provides a familiar way for people to view organizations.	Discourages innovation through the imposition of order and rationality.
Seeks to build order and rationality by imposing a structure from external sources.	Assumes an ideal type of organization, eliminating other possible forms.
Can provide measurable units for accountability and planning purposes.	Cannot account for the less tangible, hard to measure products of organizational systems.
Eliminates duplication of effort through reductionism and specialization.	Can be biased against women, gender minorities, people of color, and others who do not reflect the "standard" way of being in bureaucracies.
Seeks to minimize patronage, favoritism, and nepotism through standardization and objectivity.	Breeds alienation among employees who may feel infantilized and misused in a system that does not recognize their full potential.
Works well in settings where routinization of task is needed to produce a standard outcome or product.	Cannot quickly adapt to the changing environments typical of higher education institutions.

Heterarchical structures can be imagined as a double helix in which hierarchy and networks influence and benefit each other to create more effective organizational structures (Kleiner, 2002). In higher education, these heterarchies could be different divisions, academic departments, and schools/colleges in the same institution or a group of institutions within a system or consortium.

Stephenson's work recognizes the existence of hierarchies, including the long-standing characteristics built into bureaucracies, but extends those principles to examine organizations as disparate as corporations and terrorist groups. Hierarchies emphasize, perhaps to excess, the vertical connections within an organization; heterarchy emphasizes the vertical *and* horizontal connections (Hedlund, 1986). Networks are critical components of heterarchies. With relationships at the center of the perspective, networks enable connections to form and change to occur. Both hierarchy and network characteristics exist in heterarchical configurations.

While some might welcome the demise of pure hierarchies, heterarchies include this all too familiar structure while also incorporating the interrelationships and connections of networks. Heterarchy theorists do not propose to replace hierarchy but to understand that this widely accepted structural form tells only part of the organizational story.

> Hierarchy is an important aspect of an organization's structural integrity. It is, in fact, half of the knowledge equation. But hierarchy's power cannot be confused with that of the equally real and relevant social networks that account for so much organizational knowledge. In the final analysis, hierarchy and networks should be yoked together to ensure balance and accountability. (Stephenson, 2005, p. 263)

Stephenson's image of heterarchy contrasts sharply with the image of hierarchies in which people on different layers, particularly as depicted on an organizational chart, can be blind to the full impact of the rich array of connections between and among the layers. When leaders and other organizational members are unaware of these connections, they fail to understand that managing institutions is difficult, often impossible.

> Any network can unravel a hierarchy and any hierarchy can crush a network. Hierarchy without network is austere; network without hierarchy is anarchy. Together they form a natural tension in the dance of discovery. (Stephenson, 2001, p. 5)

Without a structure such as hierarchy, it is difficult to imagine how networks form and endure. Without networks built on trust to humanize hierarchy's form, organizational purposes could not be achieved. Heterarchies depend on networks, connections, and, most importantly, trust for their organizational form and effectiveness. "Networks are built from trust and trust is invisible and ubiquitous" (Stephenson, 2004, p. 2). Stephenson (2005) warns of the dire consequences that can ensue when trust-based networks are ignored.

Heterarchy as an organizational form is a helpful concept to explain college and university structures. Higher education institutions have a side-by-side structure of hierarchy and collegium (see Chapter 3). The collegium acts as a powerful disciplinary, social, and collegial network while the hierarchy provides a structure upon which to manage administrative tasks. Individual colleges and universities are their own heterarchical structures that cooperatively network in a loose state and federal structure with formal and informal networks. Individual colleges and universities are further connected through faculty disciplinary associations, professional associations, and consortia. The goals of each structure combine to form a regional, federal, and global system that offers higher learning, enacts social change, enables class mobility, and realizes social justice. Any one college or university alone could not achieve these societal goals. They can only be realized through the cooperation and networked efforts of the entire higher education system.

CONCLUSIONS

Bureaucratically organized institutions are more effective in stable, unchanging environments than in volatile, constantly changing ones. Unfortunately, the former do not exist in higher education. Despite this fundamental conflict, effective work in higher education institutions warrants an understanding of bureaucracy and how this type of organization operates. Even the most skeptical of critics concerning this organizational form will find elements of it everywhere, even in the most loosely organized college or university. But proponents of bureaucracies might take heed of an observation by Stephenson (2010) concerning the efficacy of this form. She claims that bureaucracies "demand constant tending and feeding to be sustained; awe arises because they are mercurial, magically summoning power from unknowable depths to kill an innovation or destroy a career with aplomb" (Stephenson, 2010, p. 1). If higher education is to achieve its current purposes and rise up to meet future challenges, the energy expended to maintain the bureaucratic form may be better invested in other places.

Questions for Discussion

- To what extent are the bureaucracies you have experienced been effective at being rational organizations with progressive movement toward goals?
- Some bureaucracies have stringent rules of communication as mentioned in this chapter. In what contexts (institutional and departmental) would these types of rules help an organization to function better? In what contexts might such rules impede functioning?
- Are the ideas and techniques of traditional bureaucratic theory relevant to contemporary higher education?
- How can higher education leaders use the concepts of heterarchy to effect change within their institution?
- How do bureaucratic principles enable higher education effectiveness? How do they constrain effectiveness?
- In what ways and why do bureaucratic ways of organizing persist in contemporary higher education institutions?
- How do bureaucratic ways of organizing enhance higher education leaders' ability to transform society? Constrain their ability?

Recommended Readings in the Bureaucracy and Heterarchy Perspectives:

Cohen, A. M., & Brawer, F. B. (2003). *The American community college*. San Francisco: John Wiley & Sons.

du Gay, P. (2005). *The values of bureaucracy*. Oxford: Oxford University Press.

Evans, C., & Holmes, L. (Eds.). (2016). *Re-Tayloring management: Scientific management a century on*. New York: Routledge.

Fumasoli, T., & Stensaker, B. (2013). Organizational studies in higher education: A reflection on historical themes and prospective trends. *Higher Education Policy, 26*(4), 479–496.

Nevarez, C., Wood, J. L., & Penrose, R. (2013). *Leadership theory and the community college: Applying theory to practice*. Sterling, VA: Stylus Publishing.

Olsen, J. P. (2005). Maybe it is time to rediscover bureaucracy. *Journal of Public Administration Research and Theory, 16*, 1–24.

Peters, M. A. (2013). Managerialism and the neoliberal university: Prospects for new forms of "open management" in higher education. *Contemporary Readings in Law and Social Justice, 5*(1), 11–26.

Powell, W. W. (1990). Neither market nor hierarchy: Network forms of organization. *Research in Organizational Behavior, 12*, 295–336.

Stephenson, K. (2006). Trusted connections. *World Business, 6*, 56–59.

Stephenson, K. (2007). The community network solution. *Strategy + Business, 49*, 32–37.

Stephenson, K. (2009). Neither hierarchy nor network: An argument for heterarchy. *People and Strategy, 32*(1), 4–7.

Stephenson, K. (2011). From Tiananmen to Tahrir: Knowing one's place in the 21st century. *Organizational Dynamics, 40*, 281–291.

CASE: EXECUTIVE LEADERSHIP AND THE CORPORATIZATION OF HIGHER EDUCATION

The corporatization of higher education has been a topic of significant interest in recent years. Higher education has been pushed toward corporate-inspired ways of operating by the rise in tuition, decreased levels of public funding, the increased emergence of higher education as a private good, and demands for accountability, among other trends (Andrews, 2006). The common use of the term chief executive officer (CEO), as applied to higher education presidents, points to the current practice of applying corporate ideas to higher education. The corporatization of higher education, as argued by Aronowitz (2000), Bok (2003), Giroux (2002), and Levine (2000), among others, is a deleterious development in higher education, one that is shifting the very foundation and values of these long-standing institutions.

For opponents of higher education corporatization, business practices such as branding, cost savings through decreased employee benefits, and the use of nonacademic amenities to recruit students are viewed as negative higher education management trends. Andrews (2006) provided a checklist against which faculty, the focus of that author's attention, can compare their institution (see Table 2.5). Answering affirmatively

Table 2.5   A Corporatization Checklist

- Is your college or university hiring low-paid, non-tenured contingent faculty to replace departing tenured and tenure-track faculty?
- Has your institution decreased need-based financial aid? Has there been a corresponding increase in merit-based scholarships?
- Are high corporate-level salaries (especially when compared with faculty salaries) being paid to administrators?
- Is there an increasing reliance on search firms—expensive and inadequate substitutes for an appropriately constituted, well directed, and faculty-dominated search committee?
- Are faculty members' teaching and service contributions being devalued while pressure to obtain external funding for research is increasing?
- Have health and retirement benefits for faculty decreased in an environment in which the costs of health care and retirement are rising rapidly?
- Have courses and curricular programs formerly regarded as essential to a college education been eliminated? Are for-profit courses being established without regard to their long-term educational value?
- Is there an increasing emphasis on intercollegiate athletics as a selling point for admissions and fund raising? Is this trend complemented by increased spending on teams that is not matched by increased spending on teaching, research, or financial aid?

to these questions can provide information about the extent to which an institution is adopting corporate practices.

Income generation through auxiliary services, online and distance learning, and fee-for-service programs has become a required means to keep institutions solvent. Outsourcing as a way to economize and develop new services, including residence halls, is common. Multimillion dollar and complex financial models require additional staff to undertake cost–benefit analyses, responsibility centered budgeting, and other financial processes borrowed from the corporate world. College and university presidents, responsible to a wide array of intra- and extra-institutional stakeholders, must juggle the medieval academic structure of the collegium and the corporate structure of a modern bureaucracy. The rapid rate of change that exists on today's college and university campus is congruent with a corporate approach to management but incongruent with traditional models of higher education organization.

Questions to Consider
- What are several internal and external pressures on today's higher education that are driving corporatization?
- What long-standing values and traditions of higher education must change when an institution adopts a corporate approach?
- What value is attained when colleges and universities are operated "like a business"?
- What is gained with a corporate approach to higher education management?

Change Through a Presidential Search

Bergquist and Phillips (as cited in Bergquist & Pawlak, 2008) suggested structure, process, and attitude as three organizational development domains related to change within higher education institutions. Organizational change, a frequently sought goal, can be affected by influencing these three domains. Changes in organizational charts, reward systems, and institutional policies and procedures result in structural changes. When communication configurations, decision-making approaches, conflict management methods, or management styles change, process adaptation follows. Attitude, the third domain of organizational development, entails "how people feel about working" in the structures and processes of the organization (Bergquist & Pawlak, 2008, p. 82). All three domains work together: attitude is affected by structure and process, while process is influenced by attitude and structure.

A search for a new president, or CEO in corporate parlance, is a particularly salient opportunity for change. A new president can bring change in all three domains of process, structure, and attitude. Particularly during the honeymoon period of a president's new administration, changes are possible that are difficult if not impossible to institute in later stages of the presidency. Existing senior administrators often tender their resignations; new administrators are hired. Departments and divisions shift into new configurations. Programs are eliminated. New communication, management, and decision-making styles are brought into institutional practice.

Questions to Consider
- What structural changes might a new president make to solidify a base of support for new initiatives?

- What process changes might be necessary to garner support for a new vision for an institution?
- How does loyalty among staff members impact the success of a new president?
- How does objectivity and distance by presidents inform the principles of bureaucracies?

Boards of trustees, regents, or visitors, as they are sometimes called, have four primary purposes on college campuses: to hire and fire the president, review programs for introduction or termination, exercise fiduciary responsibility for the institution by reviewing the budget, and assure the mission and direction of the institution (Chait, Holland, & Taylor, 1996; Kezar, 2006; Tierney, 2004). The bureaucratic principle of unity of command (Morgan, 2006), stating that each person should receive orders from one source, is most evident during presidential searches. With the chair of the Board of Trustees as the titular or actual chair of the search committee, the reporting line between the president and Board becomes abundantly clear. With all deference to stakeholders notwithstanding, the president's definitive "boss" is the Board of Trustees. While members of the Board of Trustees normally use closed executive sessions to issue presidential evaluations and directives, presidential searches are regularly conducted using the democratic processes of representation, open forums, and abundant feedback.

THE CASE

This case discusses bureaucratic principles involved in a presidential search. Particularly illustrated are the concepts of line and staff, division of labor, stability of personnel, responsibility as endowed in the office, and scalar chain.

Institutional Context

Prize University (a pseudonym) is a private, doctoral highest research activity institution as designated by the Carnegie Classification (Carnegie Foundation, 2015). The institution with its 11,000 students is located in a state of approximately 25 million people. Prize University has high admissions standards, attracts extremely qualified faculty, and boasts a high rate of research funding. After nine years of uninterrupted presidential leadership, Prize University is searching for a new chief executive. Citing health concerns, the former president resigned a year ahead of schedule; the vice president for administration and finance stepped in as interim president.

Characters

Mr. Frank Harrison: Mr. Harrison, a retired CEO of a local Fortune 500 firm, has served as the chair of the Board of Regents of Prize University for five years. A veteran of university politics, Mr. Harrison feels that the president of this institution with its $3 billion budget needs to have an executive leader with business experience. As a member of the board for seven years prior to becoming chair (12 years in total), he has been consistently puzzled by the University faculty's insistence that the president be an academic. In Harrison's mind, the provost could manage the academics. The president needed to be a CEO, someone familiar with the intricacies of financial planning, personnel management, and leadership. Leaders from the corporate world or government sector could manage the substantial budget. Harrison believes the job was unsuited for someone with a career spent in academia.

In addition to serving as board chair, Harrison is leading the presidential search committee, a position he takes seriously. While past search committee chairs allowed the president's executive assistant staff to manage the committee, he is extremely involved in the process. While some administrators and faculty have complained that he is micromanaging, he feels that he is exercising his legal and fiduciary responsibility as board chair.

Interim President John Creamer: Creamer has served as a vice president of the institution for 25 years. Prior to the presidency, he filled a variety of roles including associate vice president for finance, director of human resources, and, most recently, senior vice president for administration and finance. An alumnus of the institution, Creamer has spent his adult life at Prize University. He is extremely loyal to the institution and enjoys his role as interim president. He served under the most recent president, Dr. William Hunter, a strong academic leader who had minimal understanding of the intricacies of the budget. Dr. Hunter had made it clear from the start that he would delegate the financial matters to Creamer. As such, the vice president had a free hand with how money was allocated throughout the institution. This approach resulted in a disconnection between the academic, research, and administrative functions of the institution. When he assumed the interim president position, Creamer promised not to apply for the job. On the urging of numerous administrators within the institution and government officials outside the university, however, he is regretting that decision. His plan is to talk to Chair Harrison and see if he could become a candidate, even at this late stage of the search.

Dr. Gary Kegan: A veteran of three presidents, Kegan is the executive assistant to the president. A veteran of university administration, Dr. Kegan has been on the committee or staffed three presidential searches. In addition to his experience with these essential university search functions, he has also staffed a number of provost and vice-presidential searches. He is familiar with Mr. Harrison's desire to be an active search committee chair and welcomes his involvement, but in his experience, trustee chairs are usually figureheads. They are chair in name but leave it to the staff to manage the committee's proceedings. This search promised to be very different. Kegan is looking forward to the change.

Dr. Mary Glazer: Glazer is a relatively new faculty member at the university. She was recruited from her old institution because of the substantial research dollars she brought with her. Her work in molecular biology is cutting edge and has left her with little time for university service. When she was invited by interim president John Creamer to be on the committee, she reluctantly agreed. She knew that Creamer was using her international reputation as a way to recruit top candidates. Despite her misgivings about serving on the committee, she agreed because she feared that the corporatization of the university was eroding the research mission. While she understands that research dollars are viewed as a substantial revenue source for the university, Glazer has a purist view of the research enterprise. Her academic career has been dedicated to the pursuit of new knowledge. She feels strongly that the next president needs to be an academic who fully understands the research mission of an institution like Prize.

Questions to Consider

- How are the roles of different staff and faculty informed by the bureaucratic model?
- What are the roles of line and staff employees in this case?
- What standard operating procedures exist to guide the presidential search committee proceedings?

Authority and Power

Dr. Kegan is a traditionalist regarding presidential leadership. A student of bureaucracy and advocate of its use, Kegan believes in separating the person from the office. As a first-hand observer of several Prize University presidents, Kegan has witnessed good results when an administrator's personal and public personas are unconnected, as much as that is possible. His first president, Steven Curtis, a man of considerable talent, had gotten himself into trouble when he let his personal beliefs interfere with professional business. An unenlightened administrator regarding diversity, Curtis based his hiring on the racial and gender identities with which he was comfortable. The consistent practice of hiring White men was met by challenges from students and faculty and became a primary reason for Curtis's early retirement.

Like Kegan, Board Chair Harrison also adheres to bureaucratic principles. He believes that legitimate power is the most effective way to achieve change within an institution. Harrison has struggled with faculty claims about expert power and believes that true power comes from the authority endowed in a position or office. University presidents, like corporate CEOs, were at the pinnacle of power and, therefore, most able to effect organizational change. As Board chair, Harrison takes his authority role regarding the president seriously. He and the other Board of Trustee members are the boss. They have been invested in the success of the institution and use the means at their disposal to exercise power and communicate their vision. Budget approval and vision, mission, and strategic plan authorization are their major means to keep the institution on track. They delegate the day-to-day operation and other responsibilities to the president and the staff and then hold them responsible for assuring that their identified course of action was followed.

In conversations during the presidential search committee retreat, it became clear that Harrison and Kegan were like-minded concerning presidential leadership. Both felt that leadership and management acumen needed to take precedence over academic credentials. At the urging of the Board, substantial progress on financial reform had been achieved under Interim President Creamer's leadership. This was accomplished without the need to explain financial management details to the president. They had had years of financially inexperienced presidents who lacked the necessary knowledge and background for fiscal management. On-the-job training and nationally sponsored professional development had helped but did not alleviate the need for trustee intervention when the president did not have all the skills necessary to lead a multibillion dollar operation.

Questions to Consider

- What conflicts can you envision between the academic-related qualities of the president and the bureaucratic responsibilities and expectations of that executive position?

- What qualities and skills gained from a president's experience as an academic and scholar enhance that person's ability to undertake the presidential role?
- What do you envision as the skills necessary for a president over the next 20 years in higher education? How can those skills be taught to today's academic leaders?

Traditional Views of the Office of the President

The search committee was deep into conversation during their off-campus retreat. The group was evenly split between people who believed that traditional bureaucratic principles were the best means of leadership and those who believed that a more academically oriented, collegial approach was necessary. The collegial group, led informally by Dr. Glazer, felt the institution would benefit from a president who was socially and personally more accessible to administrators and faculty. Glazer felt strongly that Interim President Creamer lacked knowledge of the importance of knowledge generation and research as central to the university's mission. From her perspective, he understood how research dollars through indirect costs flowed into the institution, but lacked an understanding of how basic research, even the most arcane, advanced knowledge in today's society.

Board Chair Harrison led the bureaucratically inclined group that felt it was necessary for the CEO to exercise authority and strong management. This approach involved a decisive leadership style, distance from employees to convey authority, and logistical use of the presidential accoutrements to convey power and leadership. Harrison knew that vision flows from the president's office, often in consultation with others, but ultimately directly from the CEO.

Questions to Consider

- How do power and privilege intersect in bureaucracies? How are both expressed through the presidential role?
- What is the relationship between the trappings of the president's office and presidential authority?
- How are the symbols of the president's office viewed from a bureaucratic perspective?
- How does presidential authority from a bureaucratic perspective create the opportunity for change? How can this authority create barriers to change?

Presidential Qualifications

Administrative and staff hiring in bureaucracies, including higher education institutions, is based on qualifications and criteria. Whether a presidential search is managed externally through an executive search firm or internally via committee, qualifications are determined as a first step in the recruitment process. Often symbolized in the job description, the qualifications only tell part of the story about the qualities sought in a president.

At their retreat, the presidential search committee at Prize University determined a list of requirements for the position. A posting for a presidential search at the University of Utah had summarized the herculean qualities desired of a president. The search committee agreed that the presidency of Prize University demanded similar heroic attributes:

> Ideal candidates must have broad administrative and management experience, a proven record of administrative and scholarly achievement in higher education, experience and success in fundraising, and leadership qualities essential for the administration of a large, culturally diverse, and complex academic and research institution. (The Chronicle of Higher Education, 2011)

This paragraph exemplifies the tension existing for today's college and university presidents: they must have spent significant time honing their academic credentials and scholarship while simultaneously gaining the requisite management skills to oversee a multimillion or multibillion dollar institution. Few other contemporary organizations require such a wide array of qualities for its CEO. Using presidential job descriptions from competing institutions, materials from past searches, and information from the higher education literature, the following qualifications were included in the job description.

1. *Highly* experienced as an academic of high (e.g., full professor) rank with impeccable teaching and scholarly experience;
2. Proficiency in fund raising;
3. Understanding of strategic planning, problem solving, financial management, and executive administration processes;
4. Possession of a vision with the capability to communicate this to the university community;
5. Prior experience managing a multimillion or multibillion dollar institution;
6. Knowledge of how to work with internal and external stakeholders including elected city officials, students, alumni/ae, parents, and local businesspeople; and
7. A change-oriented approach matched with an understanding of institutional administrative practices.

Questions to Consider

- If you were to write a job description for the presidential search at this institution, what qualifications would you include?
- How can strong academic credentials be balanced with the need for executive management skills?
- In what ways can structure and administrative personnel be used to balance the skills needed by a university president?
- What are the necessary skills for the next generation of presidents?

Interviews, Open Forums, and Community Input

The presidential search committee spent weeks reviewing applications, informally checking references, and determining the pool of candidates for in-person interviews. After interviewing 10 candidates in airport conversations (i.e., a process whereby the search committee travels to a central location and interviews multiple candidates in short meetings), the on-campus interview pool was whittled down to four candidates. Because the search was entering the public phase, candidate materials (e.g., vitas) were posted on a presidential search website. The committee knew that conflicting opinions being played out on the committee would be amplified through campus community input.

Dr. Glazer was looking forward to the open forums. Through numerous conversations with faculty and staff on campus, she knew that people wanted a change from the traditional bureaucratic approach to presidential leadership. Her colleagues were interested in a president who was less bureaucratic and more collaborative. She believed you could be an effective administrator while also being open, participative, and exercising first among equals leadership. While several committee members agreed with her, others, most notably Board Chair Harrison, believed that top-down, decisive, and commanding leadership was needed at this point in the institution's history. In his mind, leaders who portrayed vision from the top, who set the tone, were strong and decisive, had served the institution well in the past. Glazer believed that these traditionalists could be swayed if campus community members shared their alternative point of view about leadership and administration. She encouraged many to attend the open forums and express views about a more up-to-date way to lead, one that was collaborative, participative, and empowering.

The existence of two different approaches to presidential leadership, bureaucratic and collaborative, was well represented on the search committee and among the candidates, who were split evenly into two groups by leadership style: two candidates exemplified "command and control" leadership and two exhibited a collaborative approach.

Questions to Consider
- What campus practices dictate the inclusion of community input in presidential appointments?
- In what ways does campus-wide inclusion reflect (or not reflect) a bureaucratic approach to administration?
- Which style of leadership and administration most resonates with your approach to higher education management and organization?

Four presidential candidates visited the university for on-campus interviews. Much to the disappointment of search committee members, the open forums for each candidate were sparsely attended. Although committee members had encouraged involvement from the community, people voiced the opinion that the ultimate decision on who was hired was determined by the trustees. They felt that their opinion would not be heeded in the open forums or follow-up evaluation. With the burden of too much work to be completed, they told Glazer, "What's the point? The trustees are going to appoint whomever they want. It's a waste of time for us to attend the meetings and provide input."

Questions to Consider
- In what ways do bureaucracies disempower the voice of those lower on the hierarchy?
- What communication patterns exist in bureaucracies that encourage the flow of communication between hierarchical layers?
- How do power, position, and privilege overlap in bureaucratic structures?

The search committee met for their final meeting to determine an unranked list of candidates with narrative about each individual's strengths and weaknesses. This list was presented to, and a final decision made by, the Board of Trustees. The committee's role was to give recommendations, not select the candidate. In this way, the lines of authority between the president and the Board of Trustees were clear. The search committee was advisory; the ultimate decision rested with the Board.

The committee, as reflected in previous deliberations and discussions, was split in their opinions about the best candidate or candidates. Many felt strongly that the candidate with a strong research record and recent experience as a provost at an institution similar to Prize University was the most likely choice. This coalition of committee members, led by Dr. Glazer, lobbied hard for this candidate to be discussed in a manner that highlighted obvious strengths as an academic and researcher. Board Chair Harrison and his contingent had other plans for the list. His choice for president was also clear: the candidate who was a sitting president at an institution similar in size and scope, but not reputation, to Prize University. In this way, Prize would benefit from the administrative and managerial expertise of a seasoned professional and the candidate would be attracted to the academic excellence of Prize. Although the deliberations were lively, even heated, Harrison knew his perspective would prevail. It was his responsibility to carry the unranked candidate narratives to the Board. In a closed-door session, he would give his perspective on the strengths and weaknesses of each candidate and his opinion on what was best for the institution. His choice for the next CEO would need to tackle the issues facing Prize: a complex budget situation, a marketing plan that portrayed the institution effectively, and an imperative to contain costs through salary savings and outsourcing. Harrison knew that his choice would command a high salary and an attractive contract, including a severance package at the end of the tenure, but the outcome would be worth the price.

The Board of Trustees met to determine the outcome of the presidential search with Harrison's candidate as the obvious choice. They felt that the process had maintained the integrity of the search process by creating opportunities for input and a democratically-oriented search committee. They were confident in their choice.

Questions to Consider

- Using a bureaucratic perspective, how might you influence the search as a member of the search committee?
- What are the strengths and weaknesses of the bureaucratic leadership perspective?
- What are the strengths and weaknesses of a collaborative, participative approach to leadership and administration?
- To what extent is your present (or recent past) institution characterized by the items in Table 2.5? Do these items help or hinder institutional effectiveness at achieving its primary mission?

CONCLUSIONS

Depending on the perspective of the viewer, a presidential search committee can be viewed as a fait accompli, the inevitable outcome of bureaucratic principles laid down in earlier decades. Or, the appointment of a new president can be an opportunity to transform leadership styles, institutional trajectory, and organizational practices. As with all perspectives, each has its positive and negative aspects. There is stability and constancy in bureaucratic procedures that offer continuity over time. In bureaucracies, the lines of authority and power are very clear. Each entity, from the boards of trustees to the lowest staff member on the hierarchy, has a job description and operating procedures that, at maximum, dictate or, at minimum, shape the rules of operation. Presidential searches are opportunities to observe the written and unwritten rules of an organization at work. Assumptions become more evident, reporting lines are revealed, and power becomes visible. This case sought to illustrate some of the tensions within bureaucracies when a new executive is chosen. In the current world of higher education, a significant tension exists between the desire of the Board of Trustees to hire an experienced executive and the faculty (and others) who wish to hire an academic or researcher. This tension, played out for decades, promises to continue into the future.

3

COLLEGIUM

The "Idea of a University" was a village with its priests. The "Idea of a Modern University" was a town—a one-industry town—with its intellectual oligarchy. "The Idea of a Multiuniversity" is a city of infinite variety. (Kerr, 2001, p. 31)

INTRODUCTION

Nowhere is the simultaneous existence of several organizational models within a single institution more apparent than at the intersection of faculty and administration. Faculty adhere predominantly to a collegial model while administrators typically operate as a bureaucracy with aspects of the political and organized anarchy models often obvious. This chapter discusses the collegial model, the original model for higher education organizations. Although collegial behavior may exist among administrators such as student affairs professionals, the collegium is most often associated with the faculty.

The collegium traces its origins to medieval universities such as Bologna in Italy, Oxford in England, and Paris in France. The faculty tradition started in early universities where teaching guilds or student nations were organized in 12th-century Europe (Rosser, 2003).

> The guilds or nations were voluntary associations of scholars and students who shared a common ethnic or regional identity and a common vernacular language. In the Southern European tradition of Bologna, Italy, universities were formed as students' *collegia* (Haskins, 1984). The student collegia were associations of foreign apprentice-scholars or guilds of students who wanted instruction…. In … the Northern European tradition of Paris, France, guilds of faculty members came together and formed a university or institution. Renowned faculty members from specialized disciplines began to attract large numbers of students. (Rosser, 2003, p. 4)

Over time, multiple organizational models have evolved and now occur simultaneously within the same college or university. Although several combinations are possible, the most common is the collegium and bureaucracy (see Table 3.1). This unique feature of

Table 3.1 Coexisting Bureaucratic and Collegial Aspects of Higher Education

Organizational Element	Collegium	Bureaucracy
Structure	Fluid	Rigid and stable
Authority	Expert, decentralized, emanates from the academic discipline and expertise	Legitimate, centralized, emanates from the position
Goals	Ambiguous, changing, and contested	Unified
Relationships	Autonomous	Interrelated
Purpose	Teaching, research, and service	Achieve organizational goals and maintain standards of performance
Institutional Purposes	Primary	Secondary
Context	Aligned or seek alignment with national and international disciplinary communities	Aligned or seek alignment with local communities
Coupling with Other Departments	Independent	Loose and interdependent
Change	Change adverse	Use change as a way to achieve institutional goals
Long Range	Tenured	Nontenured
Measures of Effectiveness	Measurable product for teaching, research, and service difficult to achieve	Demand measurable product

Source: Adapted from Alpert, 1985 and Birnbaum, 1991.

higher education institutions accounts for the complexity of organizational structures in colleges and universities and the multiple ways of operating within the same institution. Bureaucracies and collegiums have vastly different practices, goals, and priorities. Major differences include approaches to autonomy, connections outside the institution, and different approaches to accountability. Although often at odds, the uneasy coexistence of bureaucratic and collegial structures enables faculty to conduct teaching and research without time-consuming administrative responsibilities. It also enables administrators to build organizations based on excellence and distinctive goals.

Several characteristics of current academic life that evolved from the medieval guild structure and—although frequently challenged and adapted to meet current needs— persist today include peer review, faculty control of the curriculum, and academic freedom. The longevity of the collegial structure of higher education institutions means that colleges and universities have one of the longest lasting organizational structures in the world.

SOCIOLOGY AS A FOUNDATION FOR THE COLLEGIAL MODEL

Sociology provides a useful lens through which to view faculty guilds and their evolved structure, the collegium (Childers, 1981). In sociology, the group, society, and community are the units of analysis and interest. This group emphasis is expressed in the collegium through peer review, professorial authority, self-governance, and the community of scholars. In a wider sense, societal institutions (e.g., U.S. society) and communal goals (e.g., equality) are central to the mission and purposes of higher education institutions.

Sociology can be used to build understanding of higher education environments by considering the following:

- Social movements have historically been closely linked to higher education through activism, access initiatives, and social change.
- Human rights movements have a profound impact on the mission and purposes of higher education.
- Analysis of higher education from a sociological perspective speaks to social mobility, human rights, equity, and justice.
- Higher education is closely related to socialization, societal transformation, class mobility, social change, and collective advancement. (Clark, 2007; Meyer, Ramirez, Frank, & Schofer, 2007)

As with any theoretical foundation, there are strengths and weaknesses to this foundational perspective (see Table 3.2).

METAPHOR

Whether describing chairs drawn together in a circle during class discussion, the shape of a table for contract negotiations, or the configuration of an organizational structure with "first among equals" leadership, the circle conveys collegiality, cooperation, and equality. The metaphor of a circle most aptly describes the spirit of collaboration at the heart of the collegial model. In addition to conveying equality and collegiality, the circle metaphor further expresses the structural configuration of collegiums. The structure is nonhierarchical and depicts peer rather than authority relationships as the valued means of interaction and association. This flat structure exists in marked contrast to the power and role differentiation of the bureaucratic hierarchy in which administrators work.

STRUCTURE

With the elements of the collegium (e.g., leadership, information flow, power) arranged in a flat structure lacking the differentiated authority of hierarchy, this model may confound those unfamiliar with it. Collegium members lack close supervision; they are

Table 3.2 Strengths and Weaknesses of the Sociological Theoretical Perspective for Higher Education

Strengths	Weaknesses
Conveys insights about community building.	If ideas about human agency are neglected, some sociological concepts may appear deterministic.
Builds understanding about socialization mechanisms in human groups and organizations.	Does not provide an adequate analysis of leadership in organizations.
Provides explanations for individual and communal behavior.	Can advance over-generalized explanations for human behavior.
Assumes that humans are social beings shaped by social interaction.	Can over-emphasize the importance of group and under-emphasize individual characteristics.

autonomous and independent; and they function in a structure that has expert power, which is variable and independent, to a large extent, from position. The dependence on expert power and absence of positional authority can be particularly disconcerting to trustees and administrators who lack experience as faculty. With department and program first-among-equal leaders who have variable and diffuse power and authority, one may be hard pressed to determine who is in charge.

MAJOR CONCEPTS, CHARACTERISTICS, AND PRINCIPLES

Like other organizational models, collegiums have unique characteristics including faculty rank and expert power; circular communication patterns; leadership as first among equals; faculty socialization; and academic freedom, tenure, peer review, and self-governance.

Faculty Culture

In literature that would become a classic in the higher education field, Burton Clark (1963, 1980) described the values, attitudes, and behavior of American higher education faculty members as a culture. Referring primarily to full-time, tenure-track faculty at four-year institutions, Clark viewed faculty culture as a formidable force that significantly shapes higher education. The strength of faculty culture is shaped by, among other characteristics, institutional size, type (e.g., public, private; single sex, coed), and academic discipline.

Due to dissimilar underlying assumptions, faculty culture can complement and clash with administrative culture. Whereas administrators (even those who began their academic careers as faculty) value efficiency, decisiveness, and expedience, faculty prefer thorough explication of a topic, consideration of long-term implications, and adherence to tradition.

Faculty culture has changed significantly since the 1960s and 1980s when Clark produced his formative works. Since that time tenure, academic freedom, and other mainstays of faculty culture have eroded as the ranks of tenure faculty have decreased (Haviland, Alleman, & Allen, 2015). The diversity of institutions including community colleges, Hispanic-Serving Institutions, Historically Black Colleges and Universities, and Asian American/Pacific Islander Serving Institutions preclude the uniform, homogeneous, and dated approach to faculty culture. Although only outlined here, the reader is urged to consider the ways that a diversity of faculty at different types of institutions shape faculty culture. Like faculty culture, "institutional culture is arguably pluralistic, fragmented, and even ambiguous" (Levin, Haberler, Walker, & Jackson-Boothby, 2014, p. 57).

Disciplinary Orientation

Although collegium structures are flat, a hierarchy of disciplines is built into faculty culture. "Certain fields have been defined historically as areas of pure, disinterested study (the liberal arts), while other fields are defined as areas of application of the ideas generated in the 'basic disciplines'" (Clark, 1963, p. 42). Academic majors represent the approximate ranking of this order. Some disciplines (e.g., physics, philosophy) are viewed as theoretically "pure," while others (e.g., education, nursing, business administration) are "applied." A vestige of past prejudice remains against so-called women's disciplines, and disciplines that do not reflect dominant, traditional academic culture.

Queer, ethnic and racial, and gender studies are frequently marginalized to the status of minors or under-resourced departments. These distinctions remain in attitudes toward the liberal arts versus professional disciplines: "The distinction between the pure and the applied often bitterly divides a faculty" (Clark, 1963, p. 42).

The hierarchy of disciplines dates back to the original seven liberal arts, divided into a *trivium* of grammar, logic, and rhetoric and a *quadrivium* of arithmetic, geometry, astronomy, and music (Brubacher, 1990, p. 78). These original, highly respected academic subjects have evolved into different configurations, but the principle of greater and lesser valued disciplines remains. This early rank ordering of disciplines remains evident in salary differences among faculty, the earning power of different majors, and the value of scientific and theoretical developments.

Loyalty to the College: Cosmopolitans and Locals

Academic specialization and loyalty to one's discipline are other key characteristics of faculty culture (Clark, 1963). Working from earlier ideas about latent roles in organizations outlined by sociologist Alvin Gouldner (1957, 1958), Clark discussed two types of faculty, cosmopolitans and locals, as a way to describe the discipline versus institutional loyalty of faculty.

Faculty who are cosmopolitans shape their professional identity in the context of their national or international disciplinary communities. Clark (1963, p. 41) described cosmopolitans as

> low on loyalty to the college, highly committed to specialized skills, and oriented to an outer reference group. What counts for the Cosmopolitan is the work and opinion of a professional or disciplinary peers, who ordinarily are in other places; when the better professional opportunity appears ... [the cosmopolitan] is gone ... an itinerant expert.

They are more loyal to their discipline (e.g., biology, political science) than to the institution that employs them. According to Clark's conception, cosmopolitans often lack the time or interest to be involved in campus administrative and political activities. These faculty focus their professional energies outside the institution through national and international allegiances and activities, particularly research.

A configuration that applies mainly to research universities and is eschewed in community colleges and other teaching-oriented institutions, cosmopolitans are often researchers, frequently well known and lauded in national and international settings but perhaps unknown on their home campuses. Their teaching duties are often minimal because they are "bought out" of classes through research grants. Their interest lies in research and scholarship more than in teaching and service. Energies regarding service are directed toward their disciplinary professional organizations.

Faculty who are less involved in their discipline's professional communities, more involved on campus, and focused internally were coined locals by Clark. Locals are first and foremost loyal to their institution. They are "low on commitment to specialized skills, and [use] a group within the college as a point of reference" (Clark, 1963, p. 41). They serve on institutional committees, are involved in administrative matters, and keep their focus on students and institutional politics. Their closest colleagues are on the immediate campus. Locals put more emphasis on teaching and service than research (Clark, 1963).

Institutional type is the most significant determinant of whether a faculty member is a local or cosmopolitan. Large research universities are less inclined to hire locals; community colleges are less interested in the activities of a cosmopolitan. In addition to institutional type as a determinant of institutional versus disciplinary involvement, the characteristics of faculty can be viewed along a continuum. Regardless of whether they see themselves more as locals or cosmopolitans, faculty are fiercely loyal to their academic disciplines. The focus of their life's work, expertise, and professional identity are intimately tied to the discipline to which they committed at a young age. This tight connection to their discipline creates one of the most difficult aspects of higher education administration and organizational management. Tenure and disciplinary allegiance tie faculty to an academic department or program. They neither want nor are qualified to teach subjects in a different area. A history professor would be hard pressed to teach English. An engineering professor can rarely teach philosophy. This close identification with their discipline results in an inflexible structure in which faculty may be permanently assigned (i.e., tenured) to departments though they may teach insufficient numbers of students to meet course enrollment targets. Academic administrators are left with the task of balancing institutional resources, faculty time, expertise, and effort, within an inflexible structure (Saltzman, 2008).

Today, faculty members are not as easily separated into locals and cosmopolitans as when Clark coined the terms (Martin, Manning, & Ramaley, 2001). Rhoades, Kiyama, McCormick, and Quiroz (2008) call professionals with a mix of local and cosmopolitan characteristics "intermediates." These authors refashioned the local–cosmopolitan dichotomy in different terms. Locals, in their estimation, did not simply mean connection to the institution but was expanded to include the local community. They questioned the "assumptions embedded in the dominant model of being a professional, with an eye … to conceptualizing and enacting the professor role in relation to serving local communities" (Rhoades et al., 2008, p. 212). In fact, these authors re-shaped the local–cosmopolitan discussion to point out that many women and people of color who are faculty use the term local as a means "to recalibrate the overriding emphasis on cosmopolitan aspects of academic work, in ways that link to social change and justice" (Rhoades et al., 2008, p. 216).

The advent of the internet and electronic communication and expanded platforms has significantly changed the local–cosmopolitan dynamic. Given the global reach afforded by technology, the on-campus pressures to generate research dollars, and the relationship between campus decision making and academic life, few, if any faculty, are true locals. The information explosion and immediate, easy access to knowledge are pushing academic majors and disciplines to change rapidly. All faculty members, whether cosmopolitan or local, must remain up-to-date regarding their disciplines through engagement with national and international communities of colleagues. The internationalization and globalization of higher education mean that even faculty inclined to stay close to home have contact with students, faculty, and administrators in other institutions and countries. E-mail and technologies such as social media blur the local–cosmopolitan continuum; all can now adopt the habits of a cosmopolitan. Similarly, those inclined to be cosmopolitans, particularly at senior faculty ranks, are taking on the concerns of locals. Financial pressures, changes regarding tenure, threats to academic freedom, and the encroachment of academic capitalism (e.g., corporate-style practices) require resilient faculty involvement in campus decision making, strategic planning, and policy setting (Rhoades & Slaughter, 2004; Tierney, 2006). Senior faculty, who have traditionally been rewarded for their research productivity, are increasingly involved in local campus governance and politics as a means to articulate the importance of the faculty role and values of academic culture.

Faculty Rank and Expert Power

There are many titles for the various faculty positions (e.g., adjunct, clinical, research), but there are only three possible ranks: assistant, associate, and full professor. (The emeritus/emerita rank is assigned only upon retirement.) Faculty responsibilities (i.e., teaching, research, and service) within these ranks are virtually indistinguishable. The work of professors is similar across the ranks as they conduct research, teach, and serve on, for example, institutional committees and assume professional association roles. This flat hierarchy contrasts sharply with bureaucratic structures in which those at higher levels (e.g., vice presidents) rarely interact with lower level administrators (e.g., residence directors). In the absence of a role and power structure based on position within a hierarchy, prestige and expert power among faculty is based on disciplinary expertise. For example, junior faculty colleagues (e.g., assistant professors) with robust reputations and active research dollar generation may wield more power than senior faculty (e.g., associate or full professors) with weak or nonexistent professional and research reputations.

Because power in collegiums depends on expert and professional knowledge, the organizational characteristics of this model can be difficult to ascertain or predict. As expertise and professional knowledge are valued, faculty exercise their power in several ways. They have been adamant about control of the curriculum (Bowen & Tobin, 2015), a position that has eroded recently with budget cuts and decreased tenured and tenure-track faculty. They believe that decision making in curricular and faculty review and promotion matters rests on a tradition of expert authority—authority that only faculty possess. Expert power among faculty is the source of their authority to challenge executives (e.g., presidents) with votes of no confidence, an action that has no legislative force but can impact presidential reputations and influence.

While power and authority are contextual for all organizational models, this is particularly the case for collegiums. A faculty member's power in a particular circumstance may fail to carry over to a different setting.

> Although administrators and trustees at many colleges and universities have welcomed faculty participation in many areas of decision-making ... there has been no widespread institutionalization of faculty authority outside the basic areas of faculty appointments/advancements and responsibility for maintaining academic standards. (Bowen & Tobin, 2015, p. 144)

Faculty who feel their power is secure may find their efforts thwarted in a situation where their expertise is neither wanted nor respected. This variable power dynamic creates an ever-changing situation for administrators and faculty. It is extremely difficult to predict or shape the outcome of a committee's deliberation, a faculty senate vote, or a policy review due to the dynamic and complex power structure within higher education institutions. This power dynamic is at the heart of observations by organizational theorists who stress that the political model provides significant explanatory power for higher education organizations (Baldridge, Curtis, Ecker, & Riley, 1978).

Consensus Decision Making

Like power and authority structures, communication patterns in collegiums are flat and variable. Communication proceeds in a circular manner as topics are dissected and analyzed to a greater extent than in organizational models such as bureaucracies which have efficiency as a core operating assumption. A seemingly inconsequential topic can gain substantial symbolic momentum during a senate meeting as faculty use their discipline-honed skills of analysis and critique. Informal communication plays an important role as personal contacts, long-standing collegial relationships, and history affect communication patterns.

Nowhere is the circular and protracted pattern of communication in collegiums more evident than during decision making. In the past, faculty decision making involved "participation, consensus, professional expertise and competency" (Childers, 1981, p. 26). Decisions predominantly occur through democratic (e.g., majority vote) processes. These time-consuming practices, often frustrating for those who are not faculty, entail lengthy and protracted discussion that may or may not result in an outcome. Communication can flow in various directions without a discernible central focus or stopping point. The purpose of the thorough discussion is for each individual to share an interpretation of the issue with the goal of swaying others to a particular way of thinking. This process often results in interesting combinations and collaborations for a more informed, relevant decision. At other times, it results in the metaphorical horse created by a committee—a camel. In most circumstances, a loose consensus results (Clark, 1963). The extended and circular communication style of collegiums is further complicated by the fluid participation of faculty (Cohen & March, 1986). Meeting attendance is neither mandatory nor, for many, central to their work at the institution. This means that the faculty present for a final vote may be different from those attending preliminary meetings and discussions. Fundamental questions may be rehashed as new participants are updated. While many, particularly administrators, may find the decision-making process in collegiums tortuous, Birnbaum (1991) argued that this method is effective over time. The time-consuming nature of decision making by faculty can prevent overly ambitious (and potentially transient) presidents and provosts from making decisions that have short-term positive effects but disastrous long-term consequences.

The value placed on consensus is a stark point of contrast between collegiums and other organizational models. Top-down style is abjured in collegiums. Presidents are well advised to consult with faculty or their elected representatives in faculty governance on major decisions. This is particularly important regarding curriculum decisions. Faculty believe that sound decision making requires the exercise of their professional knowledge, their knowledge of institutional traditions, and their opinions about what is best for the institution.

Leadership as First Among Equals

Each organizational model summarized in this book has a particular style of leadership that is used and valued in that approach. In collegiums, leadership as first among equals is the preferred style. "The basic idea of the collegial leader is less to command than to listen, less to lead than to gather expert judgments, less to manage than to facilitate, less to order than to persuade and negotiate" (Baldridge et al., 1978, p. 45). Leaders who take a first among equals role gain respect through listening, building consensus, and creating compromise. While their power comes from the professional expertise they wield in the academic arena, their success as a leader is based on proficient knowledge of faculty culture and processes. Emanating from the values embodied in collegiality, leaders in collegiums know they are performing a service to their professional community. Leadership selection (from department chairs to faculty senate presidents) is generally accomplished through faculty vote or designation. Though it does happen in some types of institutions and in certain circumstances, administrative selection is to be avoided for faculty appointments. In fact, the designee's colleagues may view with suspicion leaders who have been appointed by executive administrators.

Academic Freedom and Tenure

Academic freedom has a long history in the U.S. and in international higher education. In its *1940 Statement of Principles on Academic Freedom and Tenure*, the definitive statement on academic freedom, the American Association of University Professors (AAUP) asserted:

1. Teachers are entitled to full freedom in research and in the publication of the results, subject to the adequate performance of their other academic duties; but research for pecuniary return should be based upon an understanding with the authorities of the institution.
2. Teachers are entitled to freedom in the classroom in discussing their subject, but they should be careful not to introduce into their teaching controversial matter which has no relation to their subject. (American Association of University Professors, 1940/1990, p. 3)

Academic freedom, and its sister concept, tenure, are often misunderstood. Students, parents, administrators, and, unfortunately, some faculty, believe that the practice of academic freedom means "anything goes" in teaching or research.

> Critics charge that the professoriate is abusing the classroom in four particular ways: (1) instructors "indoctrinate" rather than educate; (2) instructors fail fairly to present conflicting views on contentious subjects, thereby depriving students of educationally essential "diversity" or "balance"; (3) instructors are intolerant of students' religious, political, or socioeconomic views, thereby creating a hostile atmosphere inimical to learning; and (4) instructors persistently interject material, especially of a political or ideological character, irrelevant to the subject of instruction. (Finkin, Post, Nelson, & Benjamin, 2007, p. 54)

In fact, as stated above, academic freedom relates to professional expertise within one's discipline. The principle does not give the faculty member latitude to introduce any topic, particularly one that is untested or patently false, into the learning environment. By protecting academic freedom, though imperfectly, tenure in the form of employment for life creates a "protected space" for intellectual pursuits in teaching and research (Kolodny, 2008). The AAUP has extensive information and procedures for ways to safeguard academic freedom, including precautions regarding faculty who misuse this principle (AAUP, 2008; Finkin, et al., 2007; Saltzman, 2008).

Academic freedom is a tradition originally established in German research universities. Tenure track professors, graduate teaching assistants, contingent and adjunct professors, with degrees of application, possess academic freedom or *Lehrfreiheit*, the "right of the university professor to freedom of inquiry and to freedom of teaching, the right to study and to report on his [*sic*] findings in an atmosphere of consent" (Rudolph, 1990, p. 412). Students also possess academic freedom or *Lerhrfreiheit*, the

> absence of administrative coercion which freed the ... student to roam from university to university, to take what course he [*sic*] chose, live where he [*sic*] would, and to be free from all those restrictions ... hostile to an atmosphere of dedicated study and research. (Rudolph, 1990, p. 412)

Academic freedom as expressed through these two concepts is essential to higher education's community of scholars and marketplace of ideas (Goodman, 1962).

In 1957, the U.S. Supreme Court reinforced the right to academic freedom as expressed by the AAUP. They supported the idea that academic freedom, as an aspect of higher education, was essential to a healthy society.

> The essentiality of freedom in the community of American universities is almost self-evident.... To impose any straitjacket upon the intellectual leaders in our colleges and universities would imperil the future of our nation.... Teachers and students must always remain free to inquire, to study and to evaluate, to gain new maturity and understanding; otherwise, our civilization will stagnate and die. (*Sweeney* v. *New Hampshire*, 1957: 250 as cited in Tierney, 1998, p. 41)

Often mischaracterized as only job security, tenure is, in actuality, intimately connected to academic freedom. Tenure, which guarantees faculty employment for life within certain conditions, shields faculty from reprisal so they can research and teach without restriction (AAUP, 2008; DeGeorge, 2003; Tierney, 1998). In essence, it guarantees the right to due process (Saltzman, 2008). One cannot understand academic freedom without comprehending tenure, its sister concept. Both tenure and academic freedom, embattled features of academic life, are central features of faculty culture and collegiums.

> If a faculty member lacks the freedom to teach unpopular or controversial subjects out of fear of losing her or his position, then the free exchange of ideas is compromised. Faculty members without tenure will hardly risk pursuing cutting edge or potentially controversial research and publication (if they even have time for research), and they will avoid raising controversial or contentious subjects with their students. Tenure was designed, in large part, to protect academic freedom in research and teaching. (Kolodny, 2008, p. 5)

The protection tenure affords academic freedom has not always existed in higher education. One can easily identify examples of faculty who were fired or threatened with sanctions and reprisals for a variety of perceived transgressions: disagreeing with administrators, teaching unpopular or controversial subjects, conducting research at odds with the values of the institution, or tangling with trustees. Higher education history is peppered with cases of faculty members being fired due to an unpopular stance on institutional, national, or international matters (Ehrenberg, 2012).

The AAUP, establishing tenure as a means to assure academic freedom, published the *Statement of Principles of Academic Freedom and Tenure* in 1940 (AAUP, 1990), a document that remains the pivotal statement on these matters. Seen on a continuum from being an immutable aspect of faculty life to being a relic of a bygone era, tenure generates strong feelings among many people associated with higher education. "Legislators do not understand its necessity. Public critics attack tenure for its ability to populate the academy with 'radicals'" (Tierney, 1998, p. 38). The litany of complaints (see Table 3.3) against this long-standing and well-established system is extensive.

From an organizational point of view, tenure is an expensive practice that limits management options within higher education institutions. The practice reduces budget flexibility and organizational responsiveness; it "rigidifies" positions (Tierney, 1998) by limiting the ability of deans, department chairs, and other administrators to change programs, initiate experimental programs, and move faculty across departments. When a faculty member receives tenure, the decision, unless the faculty member chooses to leave the institution, is an institutional commitment for the length of the faculty member's career. Every tenure decision is a multimillion dollar commitment. This is particularly relevant in light of the 1994 ruling eliminating a mandatory retirement age for faculty. Boards of trustees, state legislatures, parents, students, and other higher education stakeholders determinedly test the continuation of this practice.

Dismissal of a Tenured Faculty Member

Most people within and outside of higher education believe that a tenured faculty member cannot be dismissed. In fact, a joint AAUP and American Association of Colleges statement in the 1973 Commission on Academic Tenure outlines the reasons why a tenured faculty member can be released due to "adequate cause." The reasons must include:

> (a) demonstrated incompetence or dishonesty in teaching or research, (b) substantial and manifest neglect of duty, and (c) personal conduct which substantially impairs the individual's fulfillment of his institutional responsibilities. (AAC & AAUP as cited in Saltzman, 2008, p. 59)

Tenure can be revoked due to financial exigency, moral turpitude, or incompetence. Any of these three actions has major consequences for the individual and the institution.

Table 3.3 Complaints and Criticisms of Tenure

- Separates faculty from the mechanisms of the labor market.
- Tenured faculty do not work hard.
- Lack of accountability among tenured faculty.
- Enables "deadwood" (i.e., unproductive faculty) to retain their positions.
- Allows research to take precedence over teaching.
- Can lead to an abuse of faculty power, including unethical conduct toward students.
- Limits structural flexibility regarding reassignment of faculty lines out of departments with low enrollment majors.
- Prevents the hiring of new faculty in departments that are "tenured in."

An institution, through action of the board of trustees, must formally declare financial exigency, the institutional equivalent of bankruptcy. The declaration of financial exigency is a last resort for many institutions teetering on the brink of closure. It is an uncommon step that results in serious institutional consequences (e.g., drop in enrollment, loss of faculty and staff).

Moral turpitude is defined as the

> kind of behavior which goes beyond simply warranting discharge and is so utterly blameworthy as to make it inappropriate to require the offering of a year's teaching or pay. The standard is not that the moral sensibilities of persons in the particular community have been affronted. The standard is behavior that would evoke condemnation by the academic community generally. (American Association of University Professors, 1940/1990, p. 7)

Over the years, the limits of moral turpitude have been stretched. This criterion for the revocation of tenure is an extremely difficult test to meet.

Many assume that the incompetence criterion for revoking tenure entails ineffective classroom teaching, advising, and research. Lack of skill in the classroom is a difficult measure to endorse, particularly if it is to result in the radical action of revoking tenure. Today, incompetence has taken on a different hue with mental illness or other maladies being the test for revoking tenure. Teaching ineffectiveness is generally not grounds for removal. An example of a policy regarding this reason for revoking tenure is available from Michigan State University:

> Faculty members may be found to be incompetent if … their performance is judged to be substantially below their relevant unit's(s') standards and criteria for acceptable faculty performance…. Dismissal of faculty members for incompetence is an extreme remedy, and other avenues, including the disciplinary procedures … should be carefully considered as possible alternatives to correct unacceptable performance. Colleagues in departments and schools play a primary role in determining if individuals are competent to serve as faculty members…. Units (and especially the department chair) have primary responsibility to identify those rare cases where faculty members belonging to their unit are no longer competent to perform their duties at an acceptable level. (Michigan State University, 2010, p. 43)

Tenured faculty can be dismissed if their department or program is eliminated, although the AAUP recommends that every effort be made to relocate faculty members to another suitable department or program. Dismissing a tenured professor need not be the only recourse for a higher education institution regarding an underperforming faculty member. The AAUP has several possible sanctions that it recommends including a reprimand (e.g., a letter in the employee's personnel file), suspension without pay, demotion, or revocation of the faculty member's tenure.

A significant challenge to tenure and the traditional responsibilities as filled by full-time, tenured or tenure-track professors is the shift toward hiring part-time and adjunct faculty (Haviland et al., 2015; Kezar, Lester, & Anderson, 2006; Yakoboski, 2016). Often called contingent faculty made up of full-time nontenure track or part-time instructors, this group of faculty has significantly increased in number. In 1975, part-time faculty composed 30.2% of total faculty ranks. In 2016, this group of faculty composed 70% of the faculty across all institutional types. Between 1975 and 2007, full-time tenured and tenure-track faculty decreased in inverse proportion to contingent faculty: 1975, 56.8% and 2007, 31.2% (AAUP, 2007). The percentage of tenure versus contingent faculty differs by type of higher education institution. Examples of the percentage of tenure across institutional types between the academic years 1993–1994 and 2013–2014 are summarized in Table 3.4.

When fewer faculty members on any campus enjoy the protections of tenure, academic freedom is imperiled (Kolodny, 2008). Contingent faculty ranks are increasing due to cost control efforts, desire to have flexibility to fill gaps in course coverage, and demand for a more diverse set of roles (Yakoboski, 2016). "Managers have greater discretion related to academic programs at the institutional periphery taught by temporary faculty or core faculty on overload" (Toma, 2012, p. 147).

In addition to the threat to academic freedom, the prevalence of continent faculty creates a situation where fewer faculty are available to fulfill institutional service requirements (e.g., committee work; governance; reappointment, tenure, and promotion review). Adjunct faculty members are contracted to teach, not advise or meet with students outside the classroom. Adjunct faculty, who have been described as the "indentured servants" of academia (Duncan, 1999), are paid considerably less than tenured and tenure-track faculty, carry heavier teaching loads, and have lower job satisfaction than tenured professors (Yakoboski, 2016). The limited faculty time available to students diminishes mentoring and advisement. For example,

> Part-time faculty are not unqualified, but they are exploited. Most part-time faculty earn very low "per course" salaries and few, if any, benefits. The nature of their employment (many have a full-time job off campus) often does not enable them to advise students adequately, conduct research or contribute to the academic direction of the institution. (National Education Association, n.d.)

These faculty often lack health insurance, are ineligible for retirement contributions, and do not receive other benefits available to tenure and tenure-track faculty. The decreased hiring of tenured and tenure-track faculty and increased reliance on part-time faculty members places full-time and tenured faculty, adjuncts, and students all at a disadvantage.

While the day-to-day autonomy of faculty may lead some to think that these employees are rarely evaluated or supervised, a closer look at the reappointment, promotion, and

Table 3.4   Percentage of Faculty with Tenure by Institutional Type (%)

Type of Institution	1993–1994	2013–2014
All Institutions	56.2	48.3
Public 4-year	56.3	47.3
Public 2-year	69.9	67.2
Non-profit 4-year	49.5	43.8
Non-profit 2-year	47.9	31.5
For-profit All	33.8	19.8

Source: NCES, 2015, Table 316.80.

tenure processes belies this impression. The rigorous review, reappointment, and tenure processes (e.g., six years' probation at most four-year institutions, three years at community colleges that grant tenure) are intended to assure peers and academic administrators that the lifelong tenure commitment is warranted. The evaluation period is admittedly "front loaded" at the beginning of a faculty member's career. In fact, many probationary faculty do not proceed to the tenure review. Instead, they change careers, are hired at a different faculty rank (e.g., from assistant professor on tenure track to nontenure track lecturer or adjunct), take administrative or research positions, or leave higher education completely.

External review of tenure and promotion dossiers, editorial board appraisal of manuscripts, conference paper evaluation, and expert assessment of grant proposals are part and parcel of faculty life. Whether performed on campus as part of curricular change processes or off campus through journal review processes, peer review permeates faculty culture. This aspect of academic life is based on assumptions about disciplinary expertise, including the belief that faculty can only be effectively evaluated by the same or similar discipline peers. Anyone outside this collegial circle (including administrators, students, and trustees) is considered un- or less qualified to pass judgment on the work performed in the context of the discipline. The outsider is unfamiliar with the knowledge bases, theoretical models, disciplinary practices, and ethical considerations of the discipline. In addition to peer review, expert authority and knowledge underscores another aspect of faculty culture—self-governance.

Self-Governance

Collegiums afford faculty the opportunity to determine policy, review programs, and provide input on institutional matters. These essential institutional activities occur in the context of faculty governance organizations (e.g., faculty senates). Through a variety of possible structural configurations (e.g., town meeting format, representative approach), faculty deliberate and make decisions on curricular affairs, long-range planning, and budget considerations, among other institutional matters (Austin & Jones, 2015; Hendrickson, Lane, Harris, & Dorman, 2013).

Whether advisory or determinative (Eckel, 2000), faculty use governance structures to cooperate with the administration and other institutional governance organizations (e.g., student government associations, staff councils). This system of shared governance is "composed of structures and processes, through which faculty, administrators, and other campus constituents make collective institutional decisions" (Eckel, 2000, p. 16). Tradition and desire for participative decision making dictate that faculty be consulted on major decisions undertaken by the administration (Birnbaum, 1992). In addition to the shared decision and policy making that occurs via faculty governance groups, these senates and related organizations enable faculty to exert jurisdiction over the curriculum. Faculty use peer review through the governance system to (a) approve, in the case of new majors; (b) review, in the case of program evaluation; and (c) discontinue, in the case of obsolete academic programs. A variety of administrative and policy decisions may come before a faculty governance group, but it is the curricular deliberations that garner the most attention. Faculty hold fast to their duty to control the curriculum; a responsibility represented in the often-heard expression, "the faculty own the curriculum."

STRENGTHS AND WEAKNESSES OF COLLEGIUMS

The collegial model contains strengths and weaknesses (see Table 3.5) that add to the complexity and intricacies of higher education institutions.

NEXT STEPS: BRINGING THE THEORY INTO CURRENT USE

The image of colleges and universities invoked in the media is often bucolic, a pastoral environment where faculty contemplate the life of the mind, write impressive tomes, and discourse with students and colleagues. All who work in today's higher education environment know that those images of campus life are very different from the reality. This section offers academic capitalism, as discussed by Rhoades and Slaughter (2004), Schrecker (2010), and Cantwell and Kauppinen (2014) and the advocacy culture as posited by Bergquist and Pawlak (2008) as updated approaches to the collegial model.

ACADEMIC CAPITALISM

Academic capitalism, the antithesis of the collegial model, is the inclusion of corporate practices into higher education. Outsourcing, encouraging institutionally-based revenue-generating corporate start-ups, corporate style executive compensation, recruitment of international students for revenue purposes, and erosion of tenure and academic freedom are among the trends changing U.S. higher education from a collegially-based educational system to a market and commercially-based one (Rhoades & Slaughter, 2004; Schrecker, 2010; Slaughter & Leslie, 1997).

Slaughter and Rhoades (2004, p. 107) define academic capitalism as

> an alternative system of rewards in which discovery is valued because of its commercial properties and economic rewards, broad scientific questions are couched

Table 3.5 Strengths and Weaknesses of Collegiums

Strengths	Weaknesses
Provides a structure that enables faculty autonomy while creating disciplinary communities.	The emphasis on academic excellence and disciplinary accolades can breed competition among like-discipline peers.
Facilitates participative decision making at an institution-wide level.	May divide cosmopolitans who emphasize research and national and international discipline activities and locals who emphasize institution-based and service activities.
Creates a range of options for faculty involvement in institutional planning, decision making, and policy making.	Can lead to disengagement of some faculty in institutional affairs.
Allows for an array of academic excellence, both locally at the institution level and globally at the discipline level.	The value placed on extensive discussion and protracted decision making can conflict with bureaucratic expediency and today's pace of organizational activity.
The formidable community within collegiums provides history about the institution's identity, values, and standards.	Strong collegiums are resistant to influence from the external environment and from collegium members who differ from the dominant norms. This circumstance can lead to missed cues and outmoded ideas of practice.

so that they are relevant to commercial possibilities (biotechnology, telecommunications, computer science), knowledge is regarded as a commodity rather than a free good, and universities have the organization capacity (and are permitted by law) to license, invest, and profit from these commodities.

Academic capitalism is justified by administrators as a way to cut costs, generate revenues in times of decreasing state and other allocations, and manage tuition increases. Many faculty, particularly through activism led by the AAUP, see this trend as an erosion of the principles upon which higher education was founded, particularly education as a public good and higher education as a site for the development of critical and democratic citizens (Bok, 2003; Giroux, 2014; Guinier, 2015). The critique offered by academic capitalism is an important development closely related to the values and assumptions long held in the collegium model. The diminished values resulting from this trend include many principles of the collegial model: shared governance, faculty control of the curriculum, the role of knowledge generation, academic freedom, and consensus-style decision making.

Academic capitalism is objectionable because it erodes the belief that higher education and education in general is a public good. As higher education institutions accept neoliberal emphases on commercialization, capitalism, and markets, arguments for higher education as a private good, one that should be paid for solely by individuals, are strengthened.

> Corporate models for operating colleges and universities value short-term profits over long-term investment in education, and they regard students not only as products but also as customers. Professors are commodities to be exploited and traded, and academic administrators are managers whose decisions make shared governance and due process inefficient and unnecessary. (Andrews, 2006, p. 1)

Given the high cost of higher education and historical struggles to include members from under-represented groups, the corporate practices of academic capitalism represent a significant threat to academic integrity and access to higher education (Pasque, 2007).

Academic capitalism practices include corporate-style salaries of presidents; the adoption of corporate language and mentalities; outsourcing, oftentimes to companies that lack sustainability, fair labor, livable wages, and social justice practices; expansion of higher education into income generating auxiliary services (e.g., shopping centers) with weak links to the educational mission; and high visibility athletics as an admissions recruitment tool. As these practices are embraced, universities adopt the goals of capitalism (e.g., profits) rather than those of education (e.g., holistic growth, intellectual engagement). But the most significant threat regarding academic capitalism has been the shift in philosophy regarding decreasing public funding of colleges and universities.

Recent changes in faculty hiring practices strengthen academic capitalism and weaken higher education values. The lack of protection for adjunct, contingent, and nontenured faculty through long held principles of academic freedom, faculty autonomy, and tenure erodes traditional collegial approaches. While contingent faculty colleagues bring significant expertise to higher education, the provision of short-term contracts in exchange for their services and inadequate pay for their labor reinforces academic capitalism.

In addition to the corporate revenue-generating practices and industry-style approaches, a significant threat to traditional collegial values concerns intellectual property rights. Academic capitalism in the new economy is not just a matter of institutions seeking to commercialize and capitalize on the intellectual products of individual faculty; it also involves bringing new actors (less autonomous adjunct faculty and professional staff) into the process by which instruction is developed and delivered (Rhoades & Slaughter, 2004). The curriculum, long the purview of the faculty, is increasingly "managed" by professionals outside the faculty. Whether through distance and online learning approaches, centers for teaching and learning staffed by nonfaculty professionals, or syllabi developed for piecemeal delivery, faculty work is increasingly homogenized and standardized. Intellectual products are being packaged with the goal of creating marketable, revenue-generating products. Through this process, the intellectual property rights and professional standing of faculty are eroding.

If one contrasts the values of the collegium with those of academic capitalism, a clash of cultures is obvious. The collegium values the life of the mind; academic capitalism values the generation of capital. Where the collegium emphasizes the acquisition of social and cultural capital, academic capitalism stresses the acquisition of wealth. Academia has a long history of skilled, intelligent people rejecting the goals of capitalism for altruistic goals and a different way of life. Academic capitalism thwarts those goals.

ADVOCACY CULTURE

Advocacy culture, as conceived by Bergquist and Pawlak (2008), is a significant means of combatting academic capitalism. This type of higher education culture is one of the six proposed by Bergquist and Pawlak as ways to understand the unique environments of colleges and universities. The other five cultures are collegial, managerial, developmental, virtual, and tangible. Bergquist and Pawlak (2008, p. 111) define advocacy culture as

> A culture that finds meaning primarily in the establishment of equitable and egalitarian policies and procedures for the distribution of resources and benefits in the institution; that values confrontation and fair bargaining among constituencies, primarily management and faculty or staff, who have vested interests that are inherently in opposition; that holds assumptions about the ultimate role of power and the frequent need for outside mediation in a viable academic institution; and that conceives of the institution's enterprise as either the undesirable promulgation of existing (often repressive) social attitudes and structures or the establishment of new and more liberating social attitudes and structures.

Advocacy culture is best represented in faculty and staff unions. In advocacy culture, the traditional union issues of salary and personnel matters are accompanied by concerns about curriculum, teaching–learning, tenure, and part-time faculty issues, among others (Bergquist & Pawlak, 2008). Although the 1980 Supreme Court decision in *National Labor Relations Board* v. *Yeshiva University* (444 U.S. 672) dampened union organizing efforts at private universities, with or without unions, faculty employ the traditions of advocacy culture to advocate for causes and resist managerial attempts at increased control of the curriculum and other faculty matters. Faculty unions, academic senates, and academic freedom provide room for advocacy and engagement. Proponents of advocacy culture seek equitable and egalitarian policies and procedures as a goal of advocacy actions. They use collective bargaining as a means to obtain and retain employee considerations, sometimes in opposition to administrative interests. Power struggles typify relations between faculty and administrators with appeals to outside mediation (e.g., labor relations boards) when necessary. Institutional change is a goal of negotiations and other actions, often through committees or involvement in strategic and institutional planning.

Although associated with faculty unions and collective bargaining, advocacy culture has a longer history than union formation. Academic freedom, the defense of the free exchange of ideas, and the presence of communities of scholars has long endowed faculty with the propensity to advocate. Collective action through student organizations and faculty advocacy is a major means to combat the changes which threaten the long-standing values of higher education. Collaboration with students is a strategy to achieve mutual goals, and faculty frequently march with student activists or support their causes.

CONCLUSIONS

The collegial model provides a culturally and tradition-rich approach to higher education organizations. New faculty, students, administrators, and stakeholders cannot understand colleges and universities without being familiar with the values and practices of the collegial model. Faculty self-governance, peer review, control of the curriculum, academic freedom and tenure are aspects of the collegial model that are contested terrain in higher education. The introduction of academic capitalism has decreased faculty voice and influence. As multimillion dollar higher education operations grow in complexity and orientation to the student market, the areas where faculty can realistically exert influence decrease.

Questions for Discussion

- To what extent is academic freedom on campus imperiled by the declining numbers of full-time, tenured, and tenure-track faculty?
- How might traditional ideas about academic freedom be incorporated into the current trend toward contingent faculty?
- How does the faculty role change with the blurring of the local–cosmopolitan continuum?
- What changes in faculty governance need to occur to keep pace with the current challenges within higher education?

Recommended Readings for the Collegial Model

Altbach, P. G., Berdahl, R. O., & Gumport, P. J. (Eds.). (2011). *American higher education in the twenty-first century* (3rd ed.). Baltimore: Johns Hopkins University Press.

American Association of University Professors. (1970). *Statement of principles on academic freedom and tenure with 1970 interpretive comments.* Washington, DC: Author.

American Association of University Professors. (1999a). *Post-tenure review: An AAUP response.* Washington, DC: Author.

American Association of University Professors. (1999b). *Recommended institutional regulations on academic freedom and tenure.* Washington, DC: Author. (Original work published 1957).

Armacher, R. C., & Meiners, R. E. (2004). *Faculty towers: Tenure and the structure of higher education.* Oakland, CA: The Independent Institute.

Bowen, W. G., & Tobin, E. M. (2015). *Locus of authority: The evolution of faculty roles in the governance of higher education.* Princeton, NJ: Princeton University Press.

Brown, M. C., Lane, J. E., & Zamani-Gallaher, E. M. (2010). *Organization and governance in higher education* (6th ed.). Boston: Pearson Custom.

Chait, R. (Ed.). (2002). *The questions of tenure.* Cambridge, MA: Harvard University Press.

Clark, B. R. (2008). *On higher education: Selected writings, 1956–2006.* Baltimore: Johns Hopkins University Press.

Hendrickson, R. M., Lane, J. E., Harris, J. T., & Dorman, R. H. (2013). *Academic leadership and governance of higher education: A guide for trustees, leaders, and aspiring leaders of two- and four-year institutions.* Sterling, VA: Stylus.

Lechuga, V. M. (2016). *The changing landscape of the academic profession: Faculty culture at for-profit colleges and universities.* New York: Routledge.

Macfarlane, B. (2013). *Intellectual leadership in higher education: Renewing the role of the university professor.* New York: Routledge.

Palfreyman, D., & Tapper, T. (2013). *Oxford and the decline of the collegiate tradition.* New York: Routledge.

Rhoades, G. (2007). The study of the academic profession. In P. J. Gumport (Ed.), *Sociology of higher education: Contributions and their contexts* (pp. 113–146). Baltimore: Johns Hopkins University Press.

Tight, M. (2014). Collegiality and managerialism: A false dichotomy? Evidence from the higher education literature. *Tertiary Education and Management, 20*(4), 294–306.

Van Note Chism, N., Baldwin, R. G., & Chang, D. A. (Eds.). (2010). *Faculty and faculty issues in universities and colleges* (3rd ed.). Boston: Pearson Custom.

CASE: COLLEGIALITY AND DISCIPLINARY LOYALTY IN REAPPOINTMENT, PROMOTION, AND TENURE

Collegiality, peer review, and faculty socialization underscore the processes by which reappointment, promotion, and tenure are awarded in higher education. During these fundamental processes of higher education, aspects of faculty culture are readily apparent. The reappointment, promotion, and tenure processes are often times of anxiety for junior faculty. This section discusses the collegium and its characteristics through a case of reappointment, promotion, and tenure in a regional university formerly focused on teacher training.

Each university has a standard set of reappointment, promotion, and tenure criteria, determined through the faculty governance system. These criteria tend to be broadly defined with individual colleges and schools (e.g., education, engineering) providing specific standards, timelines, and processes. The means through which tenure is awarded varies from institution to institution, and the details can be found in an institution's faculty collective bargaining agreements for unionized faculty and institutional faculty documents (e.g., handbooks) for nonunionized faculty. Some higher education institutions downplay research in the name of a teaching mission; others accept scholarship in addition to original data-driven research; service may be more important at certain stages of a faculty member's career. Generalizations about reappointment, tenure, and promotion are hard to make but one aspect remains similar across institution type: tenure is a vital issue for most faculty. Peer review, a noteworthy aspect of faculty culture, is part and parcel of the tenure process.

When a faculty member is hired "on tenure track" that person is considered "probationary for tenure" (American Association of University Professors, 1968). In the instance provided in the case presented in this section, tenure-track faculty members have five years (see Figure 3.1) to prepare their tenure and promotion dossier. These faculty usually carry the title of "assistant professor," which changes to "associate professor" if tenure is accompanied by a promotion in rank. The traditional ranks in a college or university are assistant

| 1st year | 2nd year | 3rd year | 4th year | 5th year | Sabbatical or Job Search |

| 2-year contract upon hire | reappointment 2-year contract | reappointment 2-year contract; tenure review in 5th year |

Figure 3.1 Tenure Probationary Period Example

professor (can be tenured or nontenured), associate professor (usually tenured), and full professor. There are a wide variety of additional faculty titles (e.g., research assistant, associate, or full professor; clinical professor; adjunct professor; lecturer; assistant professor without tenure) but, for the purposes of this discussion, the three traditional ranks for tenure-track professors will be examined.

Timelines and Preparation for Reappointment, Promotion, and Tenure

During the probationary period, a junior faculty member will experience reviews for "reappointment." In the example illustrated in Figure 3.1, a faculty member will be hired in year 1 and have 12 to 15 months to submit refereed journal articles, apply for grants, establish a service record, and prepare a dossier for reappointment. In the example outlined in Figure 3.1, the reappointment dossier, a curtailed version of the tenure profile, is submitted in the second year of service. Reappointment papers are reviewed at the department and college/school with the standard of review being "promise" of future achievements in teaching, research, and scholarship. A positive review for reappointment results in several multiple year contract renewals, feedback about the progress being made, and, for the candidate, experience with the review process. Questions asked at both the department and college/school dean level include:

- Has the candidate established a research agenda?
- What progress has the candidate made toward publication?
- What is the quality of the publications?
- Is teaching of sufficient quality?
- What advice can be given to support the faculty member's progress toward tenure?

The probationary faculty member in the case presented here "goes up for tenure" in the fifth year after multiple year contracts and two reappointments. The reappointment, promotion, and tenure reviews follow similar procedures with an external review by faculty within the candidate's field and several review layers added for tenure decisions. The nature of the assessment shifts between reappointment and tenure. For the tenure review, committee members and deans no longer use the standard of "future promise" in their assessment. Rather, the tenure candidate must present evidence of achievement and quality in teaching, research, and service.

Peer Review

As part of academic life, faculty members are subjected to various kinds of peer review. Manuscripts for publication are submitted to journals that use peer review to decide whether the piece warrants publication. Research grant applications, conference program proposals, and papers for presentation go through a similar peer review process. Colleagues, particularly department chairs, are invited into tenure-track professors' classrooms to assess the quality of teaching and to provide feedback to junior professors. When going up for reappointment, promotion, or tenure (see the example in Figure 3.2), peers assess the dossier of the tenure candidate and offer their professional judgment on the worthiness of the faculty member's teaching, research, and service.

In addition to the internal peer review processes, an external peer review process is typically added for tenure (and promotion to full professor). Several outside tenured reviewers, often with full professor rank depending on the candidate's institutional type, are solicited to read samples of the tenure or promotion candidate's work and render a judgment. Faculty members are selected who are "at arm's length" to the candidate. Former professors, members of the candidate's dissertation committee, personal friends, and research colleagues, among others, are not eligible to serve as external reviewers.

Research and scholarship are the only basis for the external review. The external review is deemed effective if the reviewer is familiar with the candidate's work because the research and scholarship has had an impact on the field. Journal articles and other publications are reviewed to judge their quality. External reviewers do not assess teaching and service, promotion, and tenure activities internal to the institution. The resulting letters from external reviewers are "redacted" (i.e., any identifying information is removed) and placed in the candidate's tenure dossier. Redaction occurs so the review

Department Review
Papers are reviewed by department members and votes tendered.

Department Chair Review
The Department Chair writes a commentary summarizing the department faculty members' feedback and votes, which is included in the dossier.

College/School Review Committee
A representative committee of tenured faculty from across the college/school reviews the papers and advises the Dean.

Dean Review
The Dean writes a commentary, which is included in the candidate's papers. The vote from the College/School Review Committee is recorded.

Reappointment reviews stop here

University-Wide Review Committee
A representative committee from various institutional schools and colleges reviews the papers and makes a recommendation to the Provost.

Provost Review
The Provost (or a designee) reviews all tenure papers and makes a determination about the receipt of tenure based on the feedback from the previous levels of review.

Figure 3.2 Hierarchy of Tenure Review (example, for illustration purposes only)

can be "blind," though not double blind. Reviewers know the identity of the tenure or promotion candidate but the candidate does not know the identity of the external reviewers.

Some institutions invite the faculty tenure or promotion candidate to suggest a list of names from which the department chair draws external reviewers. Other institutions depend on the department chair's knowledge of the discipline to identify external reviewers. In both cases of tenure and promotion, the department chair manages the external review process. Its success depends on the administrative acumen of the department chair, familiarity with the candidate's discipline, and even-handedness regarding the process.

The Reappointment and Tenure Review Process

The reappointment and tenure review proceeds through a hierarchical process during which the faculty member's papers proceed up a ladder of committees and academic administrators. The number of steps in the process is determined by the size of the institution, its academic and administrative structures, and the specific review processes at the college or university.

The First Level of Review: The Department

The first level of review is by the faculty member's department colleagues. Faculty in the department read the reappointment or tenure papers and render a decision, which is reported to the department chair. Questions posed at this level include:

- Does the candidate have a well-defined and cohesive research agenda?
- Is the candidate's work cutting edge or in keeping with the expectations of the discipline?
- Was the quality of the journals in which the candidate's work is published in keeping with the expectations of the college/school and institution?
- Do the student teaching evaluations reflect the quality of teaching expected in the department and college/school?
- Is the faculty member involved in service at the department, college/school, or university levels?
- What is the involvement of the candidate in national or international service work within the respective discipline?

The department chair summarizes the vote of the department and writes an evaluation based on department faculty members' feedback and assessment of the candidate's progress.

To many candidates, this stage of the process is the most important—although sometimes fraught with difficulty and political pitfalls. Because peer review is central to the reappointment, tenure, and promotion process, those colleagues most familiar with the faculty member's work and discipline are, it is argued, the most qualified to make the assessment. But, political battles, professional jealousy, and research and generational differences are among the issues that can emerge at this stage in the process. Probationary or junior faculty are advised to get to know senior faculty who will be voting on their reappointment, promotion, and tenure. Through the five to six years of probation, junior faculty are advised to tread lightly, avoid strong opinions, and play a political game with the end result of a positive tenure decision by colleagues.

In addition to possible difficult relations among colleagues, the department chair and faculty candidate relationship can be problematic. The department chair is simultaneously the candidate's mentor and assessor. This person has the task of both encouraging the candidate's career and success through the reappointment and tenure processes while balancing the goal of maintaining institutional quality within the department, college or school, and institution. If relations are strained between the chair and probationary faculty member, this balance can be a difficult one to achieve. Questions asked during the department chair review might include:

- Has the candidate met the tenure requirements as conveyed in institutional policies?
- Has the faculty candidate made a significant contribution to the academic program, institution, and discipline?
- Do the external review assessments indicate that the candidate's research and scholarship are in keeping with the ideals of the discipline?
- As indicated by the external reviewers, is the candidate's research known within his or her discipline?

The Second Level of Review: The College Faculty Evaluation Committee

A college/school committee follows the department's evaluation. The committee is composed of tenured faculty who represent different departments within the college or school. Questions asked at this level are similar to those posed at the department level. At each step of the process, the candidate's record is assessed against the criteria set by the institution and the individual college/school. Budget considerations, personality conflicts, and differences in disciplinary perspectives are not to be considered in reappointment, promotion, and tenure decisions. Instead, the candidate's record and quality of work produced is the deciding factor.

Often advisory to the dean, these committees represent some of the best aspects of peer review. Large numbers of dossiers are often reviewed, depending on that year's number of candidates. Positive and negative decisions have serious, long-term consequences. Committee members know that theirs is a once-in-a-lifetime multimillion dollar decision and they take their work seriously. Once a faculty member is tenured, they are, unless they change institutions, colleagues for life. Candidates denied tenure may see their academic careers conclude with a negative review.

The Third Level of Review: Dean's Review

Following the college/school committee review, the dean of the college or school makes an assessment. Similarly deemed one of the most important reviews, the dean is familiar with the faculty member's work and academic field. The endorsement or lack of the same at this level has a ripple effect felt throughout the remaining steps in the process. If the review is for reappointment, in some review instances, the hierarchical process often concludes here and does not advance to the institution-wide committee for deliberation and decision.

Questions asked at this stage might include:

- Is the candidate's record meritorious enough to warrant tenure?

- If there are weaknesses in the record, can those be justified in the dean's letter that accompanies the dossier through the remaining steps of the process?
- Does the candidate match the quality of faculty sought in the dean's vision of the college or school?
- Did the candidate receive sufficient support at the department and college or school committee levels to warrant a positive review?
- Does the candidate's record indicate a trajectory toward continuing success?

The Fourth Level of Review: Institutional Committee Review

In the case of a tenure or full professor promotion decision, the dean's review is followed by an assessment by an institution-wide committee, usually of the faculty senate or other governing group. This committee contains representatives from the colleges and schools within the institution. Notably at this point in the process, colleagues less familiar with the candidate's discipline deliberate on the papers. While assessments of quality certainly occur at the institution-wide level, prior reviews at the department and dean's level are crucial to the work at this stage. Without those prior reviews, faculty from disciplines other than the candidate's would be at a loss to judge the quality of a discipline unfamiliar to them. Questions asked at the institutional level may include:

- Does the quality of the candidate's research meet institutional expectations?
- How did the candidate's departmental colleagues assess the dossier? Did they deem it as appropriate within their respective disciplines?
- How does the candidate's quality of work compare with others within the college/ school and the institution as a whole?

At the conclusion of the institution-wide committee's deliberation, a vote of the committee is taken and the decision is forwarded to the chief academic officer (i.e., provost).

The Fifth Level of Review: Provost Review

The provost or a designee accomplishes the final step in the review process. A daunting task, this is as important a step in the process as all the others. The provost sets the tone for academic excellence in an institution. Contrary to popular belief, the provost review is rarely a rubber stamp but a genuine review of the candidate's papers and the procedures followed to date. Although provosts often delegate the thorough reading of the papers to an associate provost or similarly ranked administrator, the ultimate decision about whether or not to award tenure or promotion rests with the provost. The results of the provost's decision are forwarded to the board of trustees (and sometimes the president). Although reversals of decisions can occur at these levels, they are rare and point to political disputes or feelings of no confidence on the part of those reversing the decision.

Summary

The reappointment, promotion, and tenure processes can be a watershed experience in an academic's career. These are moments when one can take stock of a career path; when progress can be assessed and midcourse corrections made. Extensive feedback about the candidate's work is an opportunity to acutely understand the impact (or lack of impact) the faculty member is making on a field. Although annual evaluations and subsequent promotions take place, tenure may be the most substantial level of review experienced in a lifetime as an academic.

While the institution is making a commitment to the faculty member, that person is making a long-term, in many cases, lifelong commitment to the college or university. Faculty are certainly free to change jobs and institutions; however, having tenure often means that the majority of a faculty member's career takes place at one institution. Faculty members with tenure are often reluctant to move to a different institution without a guarantee that their tenured status will continue. One may be inclined to move to an institution with a better reputation and standard of quality, but tenure at these institutions is not always guaranteed. Senior faculty with academic successes and the rigors of the reappointment, promotion, and tenure processes behind them are often loath to move to an untenured position. While some faculty have given up the privileges of tenure in lieu of alternative arrangements (e.g., short or long range contracts, a position in an institution without the option of tenure), most remain at the institution in which their tenure was granted. As such, tenure can be a "golden handcuff."

THE CASE

Institutional Context

Baker University is a public, regional institution established in 1954. Founded as a teacher's college, the university has evolved over the years to fulfill a broad mission. Located 150 miles from the state's flagship institution, Baker has always existed in its shadow. Students denied admission at the flagship but who desire an in-state public education tend to enroll at Baker. The faculty at Baker University fall into the category of "graying." With its aging faculty, Baker has a reputation for a traditional approach to the curriculum. Cutting edge ideas and new theories are for the flagship institution, not Baker. The faculty acknowledge that scholarship and research are important but many received tenure before the institutional values shifted away from teaching and toward research. Few have made the shift with the institution, and instead devote their energies to their students rather than to an agenda with research and scholarship at the center.

The executive leadership at Baker has ambitious plans for the institution and readily awaits the retirement of many traditional faculty. They anticipate that the arrival of new faculty will bring novel ideas, theories, and connections to national and international academic colleagues. To achieve this institutional transformation, the provost has pushed his deans to recruit cutting edge scholars, particularly faculty of color and women. Research dollars have been designated to help this effort. While the executive level is committed to institutional transformation from a regional to a world-class institution, financial difficulties continually derail the process. Admissions requirements have been adjusted downward to fill incoming classes of first year students. An ambitious building project including an addition to the library has been put on hold. Programs and services have been cut. It is widely believed that staff layoffs in the upcoming year are the only solution to the looming fiscal crisis.

Characters

Dr. Darlene McPhail: Dr. McPhail is a junior faculty member (i.e., assistant professor) in the educational foundations department of the College of Education. Having received her PhD a year prior to being hired at Baker University, Dr. McPhail specializes in critical race theory. Because her scholarship is at the cutting edge of theoretical developments in her field, Dr. McPhail was highly sought after as a candidate for assistant professor positions. She is an up-and-coming African American scholar with several publications in refereed journals prior to her appointment at Baker University. Dr. McPhail believes that scholars should go outside the confines of traditional academic publications. As such, she is extremely active on social media. She is a frequent blogger, offers comments on news media, maintains a current and highly active website, and engages with colleagues on Twitter and other social media. She sees her involvement on social media as an important aspect of her scholarship.

While she feels she has had substantial support from the department chair and dean since her arrival, Dr. McPhail works in a department that is heavily "tenured in." The colleague closest in age to Dr. McPhail is 20 years her senior and most were tenured 30 years ago. She is the only faculty member with her theoretical expertise, which is a new area for the college. She is also the only faculty member who engages in social media as an aspect of her scholarship.

Dean John Sachs: Dr. Sachs has been the Dean of the College of Education for three years. He committed to work at Baker University because he believed in the president's mandate to bring the College of Education into line with contemporary theoretical developments in education. Despite his initial enthusiasm and determination to makeover the College, his three years have been fraught with controversy. Because this is Sachs's first position as dean, senior faculty view him as lacking the political acumen to navigate the university environment. His former roles as assistant dean and associate provost provided him with extensive experience in building academic programs and improving the curriculum but minimal experience with faculty development, particularly mentoring faculty through the reappointment, promotion, and tenure processes.

Dr. Robin Willis: Dr. Willis has served as a department chair for 20 years. As an experienced chair, he has seen no less than 10 junior faculty through the tenure process and three colleagues to full professor promotions. No junior faculty member under his mentorship has failed to achieve tenure. His record is so strong that he gives presentations at AAUP conferences on tenure, academic freedom, and mentoring junior faculty.

Dr. Marge Martin: Dr. Martin is the chairwoman of the Faculty Evaluation Committee at the College of Education. A full professor with nearly 30 years' experience at Baker, Dr. Martin is a well-known researcher and scholar in her field. She is an avid supporter of new faculty and believes that senior faculty should do everything in their power to help junior faculty succeed through the reappointment, promotion, and tenure process. Dr. Martin possesses a substantial amount of political capital within the College of Education and the University.

Questions to Consider

- What are the considerations for junior faculty as they determine their research agenda?
- What aspects of the collegial model might appeal to a new faculty member? Not appeal?
- How does social media complement or clash with the collegial model?

Background for the Case

The case of tenure-track professor, Dr. Darlene McPhail, is typical in the way that it proceeds in a hierarchical manner, contains potential pitfalls, encompasses conflicting values regarding disciplinary values, and engages several types of peer review.

Professor McPhail's Perspective

Darlene McPhail had aspired to be a university faculty member since high school. At that time, she toyed with the idea of becoming a high school teacher but it was during college that she fell in love with theory and research. She knew that she would someday become a university professor who was well known and respected in her field. An ethnic studies major in college, Dr. McPhail developed a love of critical race theory, an interest that continued throughout her master's and doctoral degree programs in educational foundations. Her doctoral advisor, a leading scholar in the critical race theory area, involved Dr. McPhail in a number of research projects. As a result, Dr. McPhail arrived at Baker University with two published articles and a third in review. For each of these articles, she was the fourth author, following three tenured faculty members.

Questions to Consider

- What values in the collegial model drive the traditional order of the authors in academic publications?
- How does the traditional hierarchy of disciplines reflect on Dr. McPhail's choice of research agenda?
- What characteristics of faculty culture are evident in this case?

Year 1

Dr. McPhail eagerly anticipated starting her tenure-track position at Baker University. She was the only junior faculty member in her department, the only person of color, the only person who taught critical race theory, and the only person who used social media as an outlet for her scholarship. Of the 13 faculty members in her department, only one was familiar with the subject matter, and his knowledge was rudimentary. Dr. McPhail's first year as a professor was hectic. With four new course preparations (as a new professor, she was given one course release), she struggled to get classes prepared and assignments read. She was unable to make any further progress on her research agenda focusing on critical race theory but was confident that the summer would be productive.

Year 2—First Reappointment

As she prepared her papers for reappointment, Dr. McPhail was advised to follow the format for tenure dossiers. She closely documented her progress in the areas of teaching, research, and service and felt good about her first two years. She administered and compiled her teaching evaluations, made progress on two journal articles during the summer, and kept good records about her service. Most importantly, she continued her research with her dissertation advisor but not to the degree she would have liked. The distance and adjustment in the advisor/advisee relationship dictated changed circumstances.

Although Dr. McPhail did not meet her goal of three published articles in her first two years as an assistant professor, she did publish one and the second manuscript was in draft form. Her first article was well received and honored as "Research Article of the Year" by the major professional association in her field. Her real accomplishments, she felt, were in the area of social media. She had 2,000 followers on her blog and 2,300 followers on Twitter. Her scholarly life was lively with frequent social media collaborations with nationally-based colleagues. Dr. McPhail knew her scholarship was making an impact through her entries on her blog that discussed critical race theory and its analysis of current public education events. Dr. McPhail's teaching, as evidenced in student evaluations, was excellent. They appreciated her up-to-date engagement techniques and challenging theoretical material. Students reported that her classes were life changing and regularly commented how nice it was to have someone of her caliber at the institution.

For service, Dr. McPhail only served on one committee, in the interests of time. Her dissertation advisor had warned her that service was neither rewarded nor the best use of her time as she pursued tenure. Her committee involvement, therefore, consisted of the Faculty Senate Nominations Committee. This group met once a semester and involved minimal time commitment and negligible political risk. She was pleased to have found a committee that allowed her the time for her research, teaching, and social media responsibilities.

Questions to Consider

- Who decides whether a faculty member is reappointed?
- How do the reappointment and tenure processes differ?
- How can colleague familiarity with the subject matter assist a candidate for reappointment or tenure? How can familiarity disadvantage the candidate?

Department Chair Willis's Perspective

Chairman Willis was worried. Using his knowledge as a seasoned department chair, he had advised the dean against hiring Darlene McPhail. Because Baker is a regional university in the midst of a budget crisis, the department could not afford to hire a professor with such concentrated expertise and focused research agenda. The department, he had argued, needed generalists, people who could teach across a wide range of areas. Behind closed doors with the Dean, Willis argued that although McPhail's papers were well-written and contained evidence of teaching excellence, she was not fitting in well with her fellow colleagues, did not take her service commitments seriously, and only taught courses within a narrow range of expertise. Her publication record showed some strength but she made the mistake of counting her two pre-hire publications as progress. She had not heeded his instructions, issued during their meeting to discuss the dossier preparation, that only articles since her appointment as an assistant professor could be listed on the dossier. In addition to these concerns, Willis was particularly alarmed by the inclusion of social media activity as scholarship. Because blogs, news comments, and other social media activity could not be peer reviewed, Willis did not see how this activity could be considered scholarship. He had warned McPhail to curb her social media activity, advice that had obviously been ignored.

Department members were split on their vote for reappointment. Chairman Willis's department was a traditional educational foundations department, which covered required classes in history of education, psychological perspectives on education, and philosophy of education. They were cautious and did not allow just anyone to teach the educational foundation classes because the faculty member needed a rich background in liberal arts to meet the needs of the department. Dr. McPhail lacked this background and, instead, brought strength in an area, critical race theory, that was not valued by the department. In the reappointment vote, half the department felt that Dr. McPhail was making sufficient progress toward tenure and half did not.

Questions to Consider

- In what ways can social media activity be considered in reappointment, promotion, and tenure?
- What characteristics of faculty culture and the collegial model might you use to assess social media as scholarship?
- As a dean, how might you resolve the rift between McPhail and Willis?

Chairwoman Marge Martin's Perspective

Dr. Martin was angry. She believed that Darlene McPhail had more than met the requirements for reappointment. No matter how hard she argued in the Faculty Evaluation Committee meeting, the faculty with traditional views about the primacy of quantitative research, the importance of a broad liberal arts background, limited awareness of contemporary theories, and disdain or disinclination for social media activity argued that Dr. McPhail had not made sufficient progress toward tenure. They pointed to the mixed department vote as support for their point of view. While they saw value in her teaching, this area was not a top priority for the eventual tenure vote; research was the lynchpin. She needed to conduct research; in their minds, what was needed was hard, quantitative analysis of pressing issues in education. While they believed that equity and justice were important, Dr. McPhail's theoretical explorations of critical race theory were not, in their minds, going to change the condition of children, youth, and families in the school systems. Dr. Martin argued that the journal article published in Dr. McPhail's first year as a professor had won accolades and awards for its theoretical depth and connection to the field. Those arguments were not persuasive.

Questions to Consider

- How is teaching, research, and service assessed in reappointment, tenure, and promotion decisions?
- How did the faculty culture values of peer review, collegiality, and loyalty to one's discipline influence this case?
- What is the role of the department chair in mentoring a junior faculty member through the reappointment, promotion, and tenure processes?
- What political and professional conflicts could potentially arise between the department chair and the faculty candidate?

Year 4—Second Reappointment

Given her preparation for the faculty role through her doctoral degree, Dr. McPhail was shocked by the results of her first reappointment. Having prevailed in her first reappointment vote by a slim margin, she was determined to present herself in the best possible light for her second reappointment. She had published two articles with a third in press. This brought her total number of refereed journal articles to five; two published prior to her faculty appointment and three published in her first four years as a professor. She knew that many of her department colleagues had not published any articles in the last 10 years so she felt that her progress was above average for the department.

Dr. McPhail was not as confident as she would have liked to be about her research agenda. She had failed to obtain any of the eight grants she had applied for. She continued to write about critical race theory despite the urgings of her department chair to broaden her research agenda. Because she received such positive responses from her professional colleagues outside the college, she was reluctant to take his advice. She was also reluctant to take his advice about her social media activity. Dr. McPhail believed strongly that she reached more people through her public communications on social media than she could through journal articles. Journal articles, in her mind, were read by very few. Her blog posts, news comments, and critical theory analysis of current events on social media reached and affected thousands of people.

Dr. McPhail's teaching remained strong and she had a strong following of students who signed up for all her classes, which reached maximum enrollment each semester. McPhail felt that her skilled teaching was a double-edged sword. As a former teacher's college, Baker University placed a high priority on teaching excellence. But the time and effort that she put into her teaching kept her from pursuing her research agenda to the degree required for excellence in that area. On the advice of her department chair, Dr. McPhail increased her service. She accepted an invitation from the president's office to join the President's Commission on Lesbian, Gay, Bisexual, and Transgender Issues. Her term on the Senate Nomination Committee had expired so she became involved in the College of Education's Diversity Committee. Despite this increased service, she followed her plan, based on the advice of her doctoral advisor and mentor, to avoid extending herself with too much service. This was particularly the case because, as the only African American professor in the College of Education, she carried a heavy load of formal and informal advisees, particularly students of color.

Questions to Consider

- Is Dr. McPhail a "local" or "cosmopolitan" according to Clark's definition?
- What are some of the unique circumstances regarding service and advising for faculty of color?
- What are some of the challenges of balancing teaching, research, and service? How does this balance change across the lifetime of a faculty member's career?
- How can faculty balance the traditional demands of research and scholarship with the more current possibilities of social media influence?

Dean Sachs's Perspective

Dean Sachs knew of the political battle in the Educational Foundations Department, but trusted that they could work it out. He had his own battles to fight and had little time to resolve disciplinary differences within the departments. The university had passed down a rescission of $1 million to the colleges and schools. This translated into a $250,000 cut for his college. In each of the three years of his tenure as dean, he had seen six figure cuts. They were cut to the bone and Sachs could not imagine finding another quarter of a million dollars. Willis and McPhail were going to have to find their own way out of their mess.

Chair Willis's Perspective

Willis was through advocating for Darlene McPhail's success. Despite strong evidence of his success in mentoring junior faculty, she refused to take his advice. She had not broadened her research agenda beyond the critical race theory work, she insisted on joining college and university committees that were, in his mind, tangential to the department's and college's work at the university, and she continued her excessive involvement in social media. He would wait and see what the results of the second reappointment were but he was already thinking through the discussion during which he discouraged Dr. McPhail from pursuing tenure.

Questions to Consider

- What generational and theoretical differences between Willis and McPhail have led to differences in priorities and perspectives?
- What balance must Willis strike between the success of the junior professor and what he sees as the good of the department?
- How does the context of the university influence the emphasis placed on teaching, research, and service?
- If you were Darlene McPhail, what decisions might you make about research, teaching, and service?

Year 5—Tenure Review

Summer had been very difficult for Darlene McPhail. Shortly before the end of last spring semester, her department chair had a very formal conversation with her. He advised her not to go up for tenure in her fifth year. He presented the evidence of the split department and college Faculty Evaluation Committee votes as an indication that her tenure bid would not be successful. She consulted with Dr. Martin who no longer chaired the College of Education Faculty Evaluation Committee but had been a strong advocate for Dr. McPhail's success behind the scenes. Dr. Martin encouraged her to go up despite the chair's advice but warned her that it would be a tough fight.

Questions to Consider

- If Dr. McPhail were to switch from tenure track to nontenure track, what are some ramifications?
- How might the situation change if the Faculty Affairs Committee of the Faculty Senate included social media activity as a criterion for reappointment, promotion, and tenure? What do you see as parameters of this criterion?
- What long-term consequences exist for taking legal action, filing a grievance, or pursuing other routes?

Option 1: Cut Her Losses

Despite Marge Martin's encouragement, Darlene McPhail chose not to go up for tenure. She knew the statistics for women of color and tenure and chose not to fight a battle she did not believe she could win. Instead, she depended on her strong reputation as an up-and-coming scholar in her field and the firm support of her doctoral advisor to pursue other opportunities. After a few months of job-hunting, she was successful at finding an assistant professor, tenure-track position at a large research university. Her new institution specifically set out to recruit a critical race theorist and assured her that she would not face the disciplinary issues she experienced at Baker University. She left at the end of her fifth year at Baker to pursue her new position.

Option 2: File a Grievance

Dr. McPhail never felt comfortable with Willis as chair. He seemed to have his own agenda about what her research should entail and how she should pursue her professional goals. Instead of working closely with Willis, she took advantage of the Faculty Mentoring Program that existed at her university to get independent advice on the reappointment, tenure, and promotion process. Her mentor was a member of the College of Arts and Sciences who was very involved in the faculty union. After numerous conversations with her university mentor and a lawyer, Dr. McPhail filed a grievance. Since grievances can only be based on procedural irregularities, she was struggling to find a rationale for her case.

Option 3: Pursue Tenure without the Support of the Department Chair

Dr. McPhail was confident about her record of teaching, research, and service. She believed that she was on the right track as identified by the president and provost of Baker University. Although the department vote might be split or negative, Dr. McPhail felt, after conversations with colleagues outside the College of Education, that she would prevail at the university levels of the review. She went into the tenure process with 10 juried journal articles and three book chapters. Most were coauthored but several were single authored. She had set down roots in the Baker community and was willing to take a chance on tenure. Dr. McPhail believed in the process and the new mission of the institution.

Questions to Consider

- What are the roles and responsibilities of the dean in the tenure process? of the department chair?
- How might department dynamics play a part in reappointment, promotion, and tenure?
- How does the racial identity of a faculty candidate influence the reappointment, promotion, and tenure decisions?
- How do budget considerations influence reappointment, tenure, and promotion decisions?

DISCUSSION

Reappointment and tenure may be one of the richest opportunities for the nuances of collegiality, disciplinary loyalty, and faculty culture to be expressed. While most reappointment, promotion, and tenure processes proceed without the difficulties and priority conflicts illustrated in this case, it is not unusual for political and personal clashes to be played out among faculty. The AAUP has a collection of guidelines on tenure, self-governance, and collegiality that can inform faculty and administrators on helpful ways to shape reappointment, promotion, and tenure procedures. Solid procedures assuring fairness and equitability can help assure that reappointment, promotion, and tenure processes are not overly defined by those challenges.

4

CULTURAL

Institutions do not always behave in ways they purport to or perhaps even want to, developing "rationalizing myths." These ... narratives ... are reassuring to those inside and outside the organization, while also connecting with institutional purposes. (Toma, 2012, p. 150)

INTRODUCTION

Culture is a ubiquitous word on college campuses, with references to this elusive concept readily available. A culture of evidence, an entitlement culture, African American student culture, and faculty culture are phrases used in the higher education vernacular. Such expressions attempt to define the character of an institution or perhaps the character to which the institution aspires. These depictions of institutional character and ways of operating convey the idea of "organizations as meaning systems" (Parker, 2000, p. 13); that is, meaning systems crafted by the people within them. This chapter uses the rich offerings from anthropology as a foundation from which to discuss culture as a way of viewing higher education organizations. This perspective can help make meaning of the rituals and ceremonies, architecture, sagas, language, and other cultural features that exist within colleges and universities.

Anthropologists began their studies of culture within business and corporate organizations during the 1930s and 1940s. With the dwindling of interest in the human relations school, most famously highlighted in the Hawthorne experiments (Mayo, 1946; Roethlisberger, 1941), anthropologists paid less attention to human relations (Hamada, 1989). Increased interest in organizational culture arose when Japan emerged as an economic power, particularly in the 1980s (see, for example, Deal & Kennedy, 1982; Frost, Moore, Louis, Lundberg, & Martin, 1985; Ouchi, 1982; Peters, Waterman, & Jones, 1982; Smircich, 1983). That phenomenon, combined with the globalization of business and disillusionment with hard, quantifiable management, spurred managers and theorists to search for models of organizational functioning that better explained the less tangible aspects of institutional life: "The 'hard S's' of strategy, structure and systems needed to be supplemented by the 'soft S's' of style, skills and staff" (Parker, 2000, p. 21). Practitioners and organizational theorists felt that the hard science approach crushed creativity and was inappropriate and ineffective in modern organizations. Using a cultural lens, organizational members sought to understand the ways that different perspectives impact day-to-day and long-range operations.

George Kuh and associates ushered the organizational culture perspective into higher education in the 1980s and 1990s (Kuh, 1993; Kuh, Schuh, Whitt, & Associates, 1991; Kuh & Whitt, 1988; Manning, 2000). This chapter primarily relies on the literature written from anthropological and higher education perspectives to shed light on organizations from a cultural perspective. Using this approach, faculty, administrators, students, and other stakeholders in higher education can achieve a richer, more complex understanding of organizations. This nuanced and multifaceted approach is particularly useful during decision making, program development, and planning.

Organizational theorists in higher education have claimed that the organizational culture perspective no longer has relevance in the sector, that theorists have moved on to perspectives with a more scientific basis (Tierney, 2012). While newer theories provide additional insights regarding institutional functioning, the older, established theories continue to afford awareness and understanding. Organizations are built in the past and continue into the future. Vestiges of past models continue in the everyday practices of an organization. Higher education in particular has, for example, remains of the medieval structures and practices of the collegium and bureaucracy. The principles outlined in the organizational culture literature can help higher education practitioners understand the symbolism embodied in academic regalia and the meaning conveyed in a graduation ceremony. In this way, the ideas outlined in this theory continue.

ANTHROPOLOGY AS A FOUNDATION FOR THE CULTURAL PERSPECTIVE

Organizational culture theory can take two different approaches. The corporate culture approach advantages upper level administrators, assumes culture can be "managed," and holds executive leaders responsible for the substantial messages and meanings about culture. The second perspective, an anthropological framework, embraces an egalitarian approach and offers a deeper understanding of organizational life. In the anthropological perspective, all organizational members play a role in shaping culture and in the construction of meaning from individual and collective experiences. In this chapter, the anthropological perspective is highlighted in the assumptions and discussion; concepts informed by the corporate culture literature that are congruent with the anthropological perspective are shared in the characteristics section of the chapter.

Several underlying assumptions define the anthropological perspective:

- A cultural group, over time, forms a unique culture made visible in its rituals, language(s), architecture, stories, and other tangible and intangible outcomes of cultural action (Kuh & Whitt, 1988).
- Organizations encompass unique cultures that can be understood and interpreted through ethnographic techniques such as interviewing, participant observation, and document analysis (Museus, 2007; Whitt, 1993).

- Organizations, like cultures, are rehearsals, performances, and enactments (Turner & Bruner, 1986). The "mis-steps," gaffes, and faux pas are folded into the culture, history, and collective memory of the group.
- Dynamism and change characterize culture as exemplified by the saying, "you can never step into the same river twice."

The strengths and weaknesses of the anthropological perspective are summarized in Table 4.1. Clifford Geertz, a well-known interpretive anthropologist, provides a useful definition of culture, which can be used to understand higher education organizations:

> [Culture] denotes an historically transmitted pattern of meanings embodied in symbols, a system of inherited conceptions expressed in symbolic forms ... [to] communicate, perpetuate, and develop ... knowledge about and attitudes toward life. (Geertz, 1973, p. 89)

In the time since Geertz penned this definition of culture, feminist and postmodern anthropologists, among others, have expanded ideas about culture to include the concepts of dynamism, power, and gender.

Departing from the modernist approach of bureaucracies, from a cultural perspective organizations are not "natural phenomena" inherently determined by forces outside the organization. Organizations from a cultural view form through the actions of people who live and work within them. "Organizational culture is a process which is locally produced by people, but ... it can also be usefully talked about as a thing with particular effects on people ... it is both a verb and a noun" (Parker, 2000, p. 83). As a verb, culture is a medium through which people dynamically and continuously take action, create meaning, and achieve purposes. As a noun, culture builds congruence, gathers people as a community, creates clarity, builds consensus, and endows meaning.

To understand college and university organizational cultures, one must learn to read and interpret the ways of operating, languages, and cultural elements within the setting. As institutions built on medieval structures (even new higher education institutions have vestiges of the earliest universities), these organizations are unquestionably culture bearing. Of all the modern organizations, higher education institutions fiercely maintain their underlying values through ceremonies, rituals, and traditions such as graduations, convocations, and a myriad of other traditions that shape and build culture (Manning, 2000).

Table 4.1 Strengths and Weaknesses of the Anthropological Theoretical Perspective for Higher Education

Strengths	Weaknesses
Explains how people make meaning within the day-to-day of organizational life.	May seem extraneous to the missions and priorities of higher education in the 21st century.
Illuminates connections among communities, cultures, and organizational lives.	Provides limited explanatory value about economic priorities within higher education.
Clarifies how people become connected to organizations, including colleges and universities, in meaningful and long-lasting ways.	May situate higher education and its traditions in the past rather than the future.
Describes the importance and central role of ritual, tradition, and other cultural artifacts.	Can appear out of step with current issues in higher education (e.g., affordability, globalization, loss of public trust).

The literature on corporate organizational culture contrasts strong and weak cultures (Schein, 2010). In a higher education context, women's colleges, Historically Black Institutions, and Ivy League institutions with their historical traditions are often cited as "strong" cultures. Community colleges, commuter-based campuses, and more recently established institutions supposedly have "weak" cultures. The anthropological perspective adopted in this chapter avoids these distinctions. All institutions have cultures with their strengths and weaknesses. A culture is effective only to the degree that its practices fit the institution in which it is embodied. The traditions of a Historically Black College or University would lack historical context and be out of place at a predominantly White institution. The traditions of a Seven Sisters college (Manning, 2000) are vastly different from the culture of a community college (Shaw, Valadez, & Rhoads, 1999). While not purporting that all, even destructive, cultures are equal (i.e., cultural relativism), any college or university has effective and ineffective features crafted into its unique institutional culture.

METAPHOR

Carnival and theater are two metaphors that portray the cultural perspective on organizations. Because both images imply performance, the dynamism and ever-changing nature of organizations are captured in these images. Carnivals and theaters have actors and audiences, performers and observers. All involved in the performance exercise vital roles in culture building. With so many players, actors, and constituents composing, arranging, and living within organizations,

> sense-making is often contested, as organizational members defend alternative understandings of identity against the organization's attempt to reduce them to one-dimensional role players. Everyday life becomes a drama, a stage managed presentation with the continual danger of confusion lying beneath the surface. (Parker, 2000, p. 50)

The uncertain, idiosyncratic, and ambiguous nature of human action is reflected in organizations. Complexity and ambiguity are as normal in organizations as they are in human living and, in the case of higher education institutions, are long-standing features. Rather than something to be fixed, complexity, multiple meanings, and paradoxical messages create opportunities for interpretation, clarification, and learning, urging critical thinking and deep reflection.

STRUCTURE

From an anthropological perspective, "an organization is a set of meanings that people act out, talk out, and back up with their own armamentarium of forces—psychological, moral and physical" (Greenfield, 1986, p. 154). Organizations as cultures are not isolated entities but institutions situated in a context that includes history, past players, and traditions that serve as the fodder for and backdrop to any culture building experience. From a cultural perspective, organizations do not reflect one given structure such as hierarchy. Culture is reflected across a variety of organizational forms: circles, webs, pyramids.

MAJOR CONCEPTS, CHARACTERISTICS, AND PRINCIPLES

Organizations as cultures are marked by several characteristics, concepts, and principles. The following are briefly described below: values and assumptions; subcultures; history, tradition, and context; language; organizational saga; symbols; and architecture.

Values and Assumptions

Every organization has a set of values and assumptions that are embedded in mission statements, founding documents, and other historical artifacts. Although contested, these values and assumptions are debated in practices that can lead to clarification and change or disagreement and impasse. Values and assumptions pinpoint guidelines for everyday behavior, provide a common focus, and identify heroines and heroes. Due to the contestation and rich context of discussion and debate, a homogeneous culture is impossible in colleges and universities. The presence of a highly professional staff (e.g., faculty and administrators), lofty societal expectations, and various constituent groups (e.g., students, alumni/ae, legislators, parents) guarantees the presence of multiple and potentially conflicting values and assumptions. The veracity of these assumptions changes depending on the vantage point used to view the organization. Whether formally built into the organization's structure through reward systems or informally through member-to-member communication, new affiliates quickly become familiar with the underlying assumptions and values. If not, these new organizational members voluntarily or involuntarily leave the institution or stay and continually struggle to find their place within it.

Values and assumptions are particularly important to higher education institutions because they are represented in the root metaphor and integrating symbols of an organization—"built into a college in tradition and legend, in administrative arrangements, in emphases of the curriculum" (Clark & Trow, 1966, p. 37). Whether consciously understood or not, metaphors and symbols communicate

> the ways groups evolve and characterize themselves. Cultural messages are communicated via institutional actors but also through the material culture of buildings, office layout, language, and other artifacts. (Schein, 2010, pp. 16–17)

Root metaphors that reflect the institution's values and assumptions can include, for example, social justice, leadership, and environmental stewardship. Social justice messages are conveyed in institutional policies and practices that determine space allocation, verbal messages during ceremony, holidays celebrated, and funds allocated.

The staying power of cultural artifacts and their importance to organizational members is evident in debates about institutional mascots, particularly enacted during athletic events. These mascots frequently embody outdated, oppressive, and disrespectful images (e.g., Confederate symbols or Native American stereotypes) (Bollinger, 2016; Hofmann, 2005; Stegman & Phillips, 2014). Likenesses of the mascot can literally be built into material culture (e.g., athletic stadiums and campus buildings). Arguments that these symbols simply have historical, not present-day, meaning are disingenuous to those who recognize that the oftentimes offensive values communicated through these symbols are perpetuated through daily enactment. Through protests, many mascots have been changed but many remain untouched.

Manning (2000) discussed values and assumptions from an anthropological context in her discussion of higher education rituals and traditions. Values and assumptions, espoused and enacted during traditions, ceremonies and rituals are communicated through the messages and interpreted as meanings during those events. Messages are multivocal (i.e., people experience cultural events differently); meanings are individually and socially constructed. The complexity of higher education organizations can, in part, be attributed to the multiple messages and meanings that abound within these institutions.

The multivocal and multiple expressions of values, assumptions, messages, and meanings lend strength to higher education organizations, which have always existed in turbulent environments. The presence of numerous values enables organizational members to express multiple beliefs and quickly move to a latent or less emphasized set when the circumstance allows or requires. The presence of both traditional assumptions and values and cutting-edge assumptions and values creates an adaptable foundation upon which the institution can operate.

The multiple and potentially conflicting values and assumptions support the idea that organizations are not unitary phenomena. Broad consensus across constituencies entails the idea that people and ideas conflict in organizations (Parker, 2000). Colleges and universities are sites of contestation, and multiple meanings. Though frustrating to many, others who value diverse perspectives revel in the fact that many institutional definitions and goals can exist simultaneously (Cohen & March, 1986). Birnbaum (1991) went so far as to attribute the success of higher education to the presence of multiple goals and stated that this characteristic enables colleges and universities to be highly productive organizations. For a university medical college, pure research on cancer may be the primary purpose of their work; in education, creating healthy, active learning environments for children and youth may be a goal; for student affairs professionals, creating programs, policies, and services that facilitate student engagement and success may be of utmost importance. No one goal need take precedence; all can exist simultaneously.

Subcultures

The anthropological cultural perspective on organizations eschews rigid and deterministic hierarchical arrangements of human perspectives and behavior (Parker, 2000). Rather than subcultures with the "sub" prefix implying a diminished value, a less hierarchical approach promotes the idea that there are many equally valid cultures within any organization. This perspective addresses a basic problem with the concept of subculture that "we immediately need to specify what kind of culture the subculture is subordinate to" (Parker, 2000, p. 84). A vivid example of this issue can be seen when students of color are said to occupy a "sub-culture" within the organization. This point of view positions them as "outsiders" or visitors, a group never fully welcomed or part of the organization. When respectfully viewed as members of one of many cultures within an institution, the primacy of their points of view, ways of being, and right to membership become transparent. Rather than a hierarchy of subcultures where one is superior to a subordinate other, cultures within an organization are nested, embedded, and overlapped.

People do not belong to a single subculture; their cultural identity is shaped by their gender, ethnicity, social class, sexual orientation, and age, among many other aspects of identity.... A single subcultural category is unlikely to capture the richness and diversity of organizational life in a college or university. (Bess & Dee, 2008, p. 387)

A complexity of cultures existing simultaneously in the same organization is an image that better fits institutions of higher education. Faculty, student, staff, and administrative cultures weave together and exist separately, all at the same time. Each of these is not monolithic; each has a culture in its own right. Although these cultures share some assumptions and values, their beliefs also diverge. Efficiency, autonomy, innovation, and experimentation are examples of values that may define a distinct culture or are shared across cultures.

History, Tradition, and Context

Colleges and universities possess delightfully varied cultural forms that evolve over time and remain dynamic through human actions. Through habit, repetition, and socially constructed organizational forms (e.g., decentralized and centralized structures, religious and secular affiliations), a cultural context takes shape.

Since culture is created through human action, organizations are rich places for meaning and culture building: "Clothes, spaces, symbols, games, roles and rituals are seen to be deployed and arranged in complex constellations" (Parker, 2000, p. 50). These constellations form a unique perspective on an organization reflected in its history, mission, and stories. It is literally built into the architecture and physical features of the institution.

While humans create culture in the moment, they also re-create the culture enacted in the past and foretell the culture of the future.

A college is not simply an aggregation of students, teachers, and administrators. Although the character of a college is greatly influenced by the nature of its staff and students, it also has qualities and characteristics which are to some extent independent of the people who fill its halls and offices at any given moment. (Clark & Trow, 1966, p. 18)

Architecture, language, ceremonies, stories—the physical, mental, and symbolic elements of organizational life—become the raw material for culture building. For the culture to have long-term, significant meaning for the organization's members, the organizational elements and actions should be grounded in its values and assumptions. This culture building process could be shaped by intervention and the influence of members of the organization and even some external to the college or university (e.g., legislators, board of trustee members) (Parker, 2000). Precise management and purposeful manipulation is impossible. From an anthropological perspective, human action is simply not that malleable or predictable. Unexpected consequences abound.

Language

Language within an organization is more than simply a means to communicate. It is a fundamental and highly symbolic aspect of culture. Language represents and recreates habits of thinking, mental models, and organizational paradigms (Schein, 2010). Taught to newcomers through socialization processes, the jargon of a field, terms employed within a group, and expressions unique to a college or university distinguish membership and cultural belonging.

> Language, in its most general sense, is central, since an organization's culture is manifested in and through its local languages. Slang, jargon, acronym and technicality hence become exemplifiers of cultural processes because they are ... illustrative of the kinds of communities that organizational members inhabit. (Parker, 2000, p. 70)

In addition to signals about membership and belonging, language has the capacity to shape reality. The use of first names for executives, the custom of addressing people as "doctor" or "professor" during meetings, and evocation of traditional phrases during graduation and campus ceremonies convey and shape the power of administrators, faculty, and students. Although allowances are made for students and others unfamiliar with established practice, breaches of protocol are discouraged (e.g., student protests during trustees' meetings, excessively emotional expressions during meetings). "Language is power. It literally makes reality appear and disappear. Those who control language control thought, and thereby themselves and others" (Greenfield, 1986, p. 154).

Organizational Saga

Language is powerfully used by storytellers to convey organizational culture (Kuh et al., 1991). Values and assumptions are communicated to those new to the organization through these myths and sagas (Bess & Dee, 2008). Clark defined saga within higher education contexts as "a collective understanding of current institutional character that refers to a historical struggle and is embellished emotionally and loaded with meaning" (1986, p. 82). These cultural artifacts serve many purposes including (a) establishing normative behavior, (b) creating standards for excellence, (c) honoring founders, and (d) communicating core values (Birnbaum, 1991). Saga reveal the values about which organizational members feel deeply. They identify the behaviors that are acceptable as well as adding to the organization's future (Bess & Dee, 2008).

Saga tells the tales of the organization's heroes and heroines. For example, there are stories told of Mount Holyoke College's founder, Mary Lyon, and her efforts to collect small amounts of money from local farmwomen. These accounts shape community ideas about fortitude and persistence in hard times. The values of egalitarianism, equality, and openness are relayed through the saga of Notre Dame University students, who late at night upon seeing the office light of former President Hesburgh, climbed the fire escape to speak to the famous university president. Through telling and retellings, sagas become explanations and shape expectations of the "way things are done here." The people whose activities are repeated in sagas need not be institutional leaders in a positional leader sense. Dining service workers often exemplify powerful institutional values regarding student-centeredness and an ethic of care (Kuh, Kinzie, Schuh, Whitt, & Associates, 2005/2010). Sagas can erupt at any location within the organization and carry their messages throughout the institution.

Symbols

Every action contains meaning within it that refers to or symbolizes something else. Everything is symbolic (Parker, 2000) and all actions are symbolic acts. The complex nature of symbols is particularly evident in higher education organizations, which encompass multiple cultures in the same institutional space. Academic regalia at a university ceremony could symbolize curricular excellence to faculty members, the achievement of a career goal to students, or elitism to a local community member. A statue of the founder on the campus green could represent pride for one group and oppressive values of sexism, racism, or homophobia to another. Diplomas represent an obligation to family for a traditionally-aged undergraduate and the fulfillment of a lifelong dream to an adult learner. Used effectively, symbols can set expectations and provide messages that shape meaning. When a college president uses a convocation address to convey who "we" are, expectations for community building are shaped. A significantly different message is conveyed when an interim president moves into the president's quarters. One is about communal action; the other about establishing power and presence. As with all cultural forms, symbols have the potential to express mixed messages. Symbols that are meant to include can inadvertently exclude. Action meant to set expectations for excellence can chafe against student expectations of adult freedom and independence.

Architecture

The architecture of a campus immediately communicates the values, aspirations, and character of an institution (Bergquist & Pawlak, 2008; Kuh & Whitt, 1988; Kuh et al., 1991). These qualities may be explicitly expressed in mission statements and include beliefs about academic excellence, leadership, and access. Less explicit ideals are also conveyed through the built culture of a college campus. The physical space of colleges and universities, when placed, for example, on top of a city hill or sequestered behind forbidding walls conveys exclusion, elitism, and separation. The physical height of bell towers, steeples, and administration buildings communicates the desire to pursue lofty ideas (Bergquist & Pawlak, 2008). Campuses that choose less conventional approaches to their physical space (e.g., classes in a local high school) are communicating an equally valuable approach (e.g., access) to higher education and academic achievement. Physical space can enable and constrain an institution's values. Civic engagement may be contradicted by a college campus built at a distance from local communities. In contrast, global citizenship may be tangibly conveyed through art and architecture.

The direction that buildings face, placement of parking, and the position of academic buildings in relation to other structures tangibly convey institutional values and intentions. Residential campuses often focus inward, community college and commuter-based campuses project outward (Bergquist & Pawlak, 2008). A quick tour of a campus provides students with an impression about what is important to a campus, how they will be treated, and what kind of community they can expect.

> Where buildings are placed, what they look like, and how they are maintained, the amount of open space provided, the care taken to provide places for large and small groups to interact, the priority given to space for students, and the amount of control students have over their setting can be viewed as demonstrating the institution's commitment to community and student life. (Kuh et al., 1991, p. 91)

While the customary approach is for colleges and universities to have distinctive architecture (e.g., ivy covered buildings, immaculately maintained campus greens), higher education institutions of the 21st century are using a wide variety of physical forms. Campus configurations now include virtual spaces absent of traditional classroom spaces and accouterments. The sprawling space and multiple campus arrangement of a research university, accessible buildings of community colleges, and tightly packed buildings of an urban college each speak to a distinctive sense of place by aptly communicating institutional goals and purposes. For-profit campuses, community colleges, and institutions with highly specialized curricular offerings often rent space in office buildings, schools, and other settings that do not resemble traditional colleges. While these spaces are often erroneously called "nontraditional," the "non-campus-like" physical space communicates the message that all students—adult, first-generation college students, returning learners—are welcome. In this way, students become connected to the campus and link their purposes to an entity larger than themselves (Manning, 2000). Regardless of the style of the college or university, campuses evoke a sense of place that remains with students for years after graduation (Bott, Banning, Wells, Hass, & Lakey, 2006; Clemons, McKelfresh, & Banning, 2005; Gruenewald, 2003).

In addition to institutional values and purposes, campus architecture defines managerial expectations about power dynamics, communication habits, and authority. Faculty and administrators' offices—their size, whether they are shared, how well they are appointed—may shape the communication patterns that emerge among colleagues and with students (Bess & Dee, 2008). In some institutions, student affairs staff may occupy egalitarian-imagined cubicles while faculty have private offices occupied for only a few hours a week. Separate dining spaces for faculty are a campus staple and fodder for debate. The presence of students in faculty space can spark discussion and resolutions at faculty senate meetings. The nature of work, individual or group, can be determined by a quick perusal of that person's space. Conference space available for group work conveys one style of work; individual offices walled off for independent, autonomous activities convey quite another.

MULTICULTURAL LEADERSHIP AND ORGANIZATIONAL DEVELOPMENT

A significant aspect of organizational culture is the presence of a wide diversity of cultural, ethnic, and racial groups among faculty, students, staff, and administrators. Higher education, from an international perspective, has always been a diverse enterprise. With the exception of the later incorporated women's colleges, Historically Black Institutions, Hispanic-Serving Institutions, and tribal colleges, U.S. higher education was founded for the education of White Christian males. Higher education in the U.S. includes a history of limiting education to White males, a practice that was challenged by the founding of women's colleges. The founding of Historically Black Institutions was enabled by the 1890 Morrill Act and specifically intended to provide education for African Americans who were barred from entering Predominantly White Institutions, including White institutions funded with federal incentives through the first Morrill Act in 1862. The more recent establishment of Hispanic-Serving Institutions and Native American colleges was driven by the objective to establish institutions with a cultural perspective different from Predominantly White Institutions. The predominantly white perspective continues to be challenged on college campuses in favor of egalitarian, inclusive, and socially just values.

Taylor Cox (1993; 2001; Cox & Beale, 1997; Cox & Blake, 1991) was an early multicultural organizational theorist who focused his efforts on transforming corporation structures to be more inclusive (see also, Blake-Beard, Finley-Hervey, & Harquail, 2008). Cox's work, controversial at the time given the prejudice against researching diversity and organizations, established the field in the corporate context and advanced the idea that diversity, as it was called then, could enhance organizational functioning. The multicultural organizational development perspective continues to expand and develop with more sophisticated and complete explanations of workplace diversity, the importance of inclusion, and the need to eliminate exclusionary structures (Jamieson & Vogel, 2010).

With the passage of the Civil Rights Act and affirmative action in the 1960s, corporations and for-profit businesses have pursued "diversity initiatives" with varying degrees of commitment and success. Initiatives have included recruitment and training programs, hiring and promotion efforts, grievance policies, training, mentoring opportunities, family-friendly programs, and sexual harassment programs, among others. Unlike higher education efforts, which entail a moral purpose, corporations are motivated by increased workforce productivity and better market penetration.

> [The] benefits include increased profitability … learning, creativity, flexibility, organizational and individual growth, and the ability of a company to adjust rapidly and successfully to market changes. The desired transformation, however, requires a fundamental change in the attitudes and behaviors of an organization's leadership. (Thomas & Ely, 1996, p. 79)

Colleges and universities, particularly through student affairs divisions, have worked to dismantle oppressive structures within the institution (Hurtado, Milem, Clayton-Pedersen, & Allen, 1999; Pope, Reynolds, & Mueller, 2014). The increasing diversity of student populations, continuation of traditional higher education purposes such as access and increased social mobility, and the goal to create equitable institutions warrant inclusive, socially just approaches to higher education leadership and management. Traditional models using the "diversity as good" approach to organizational change are insufficient to address the challenges to higher education institutions in the 21st century.

> This "diversity as good" approach … falls into one or more of the following pitfalls: increasing staff self-awareness about issues of race and racism without significant skill development to create racially equitable and inclusive programs, policies, and services; focusing on increasing knowledge without a parallel emphasis on affective elements crucial to unlearning racism and developing staff as change agents; and locating the responsibility for organizational change with staff of color without an intentional strategy to develop whites as allies in creating inclusive campus environments. (Obear & Martinez, 2013, p. 79)

When discussing multicultural organizational development and diverse leadership styles, it is important for practitioners and theorists to avoid racial, gender, or ethnic stereotypes. To avoid talking about a specific group's leadership or organizational style, one can consider the characteristics of what Bordas (2012) called, respectively, multicultural and mainstream leadership styles. She suggests that multicultural leadership is collective, other-centered, and works for the community good. Mainstream leadership, by contrast, is competitive, individualistic, lives in the present, and embraces capitalism. Using non-dominant foundational principles upon which to build her leadership concepts, she outlined a leadership approach that was inclusive, community oriented, and pluralistic. Although Bordas ill-advisedly excluded Asian American styles of leadership and framed her work solely in the context of African American, Latino/a, and Native American communities, her framework provides some insights into the ways leadership can be applied when inclusion, collaboration, and justice are prioritized. Table 4.2 details the differences between these two different styles of leadership.

Addressing the omission left by Bordas (2012) through the exclusion of Asian Americans, identifiable leadership characteristics can be garnered from a review of the history of Asian American activism, student organizations, and campus leadership. Facing isolation and prejudice which led to lower numbers of college and university administrators, faculty, and role models from this group, Asian American student organizations were established within colleges and universities to encourage "opportunities for companionship, service, breaking down linguistic and cultural divisions, working together toward a common goal, influencing local communities, and developing leadership skills" (Ko, 2012, p. 124). These organizations became a pipeline for leaders in larger communities as well as a locale through which to learn social change leadership. Given the challenges of living in communities rife with alienation, these organizations provide support, community, and advocacy (Ko, 2012). Study of the

Table 4.2   Characteristics of Multicultural and Mainstream Leadership

Multicultural Leadership	Mainstream Leadership
Collective orientation.	Individualistic orientation.
Leadership as community action and social activism.	Leadership as command and control with vision emanating from the top.
Seeks egalitarian pluralism.	Values meritocratic approaches.
Addresses the social structures that hinder people's progress.	Creates hierarchy.
Embraces public values.	Embraces private virtues.
Privileges community and justice concerns including widespread participation.	Privileges power elites as more knowledgeable and able to lead.
Seeks the good of the whole.	Seeks individual advancement and achievement.
Relies on moral authority.	Uses legitimate and positional authority.
Encourages active, visible citizenship.	Isolates leaders from the public.
Builds interdependency.	Sustains rugged individualism.
The group enlists the leaders.	Individuals seek out leadership positions or are appointed by a small group of elites.
Builds community capacity and group empowerment.	Concentrates privileges and power in the top group.
Seeks full participation and consensus building.	Top down, command and control style of decision making.
Engages people to find community-oriented solutions.	Profit and individual or limited institutional advancement as main concerns.

Source: Bordas, 2012.

literature of Asian American experiences on campus, including experiences with the model minority myth (Ching & Agbayani, 2012), can urge campus participants to move beyond monolithic treatment of the diverse Asian American population and stereotypes about their leadership capabilities and roles on campus.

STRENGTHS AND WEAKNESSES OF THE CULTURAL PERSPECTIVE

The cultural perspective, like all the organizational perspectives offered in this book, contains strengths and weaknesses regarding its implementation within higher education (see Table 4.3).

NEXT STEPS: BRINGING THE CULTURAL PERSPECTIVE INTO CURRENT USE

Critical race theory (CRT) is suggested as a contemporary application of the cultural model (Crichlow, 2015; DeCuir & Dixson, 2004; Delgado & Stefancic, 2012; Solórzano, Ceja, & Yosso, 2000). This theory, first advanced in the 1990s in the legal studies literature (Bell, 1992; Matsuda, Lawrence, Delgado, & Crenshaw, 1993), was further articulated in K–12 and higher education settings (Ladson-Billings, 1998, 2013; Patton, McEwen, Rendón, & Howard-Hamilton, 2007). The theory, which takes the cultural, political, and philosophical contexts of educational settings into consideration, has significant relevance for higher education organizations. Concepts such as the permanence of racism, Whiteness as property, color-blindness, and counterstorytelling are discussed as a means to update ideas about culture in organizational literature.

Critical Race Theory

Derrick Bell, a law professor at Harvard University, first introduced CRT in his book, *Faces at the Bottom of the Well* (1992). The following principles define the theory, which can be used as a powerful interdisciplinary analysis and critique of the cultural, social, and political contexts of educational settings.

Table 4.3 Strengths and Weaknesses of the Cultural Perspective

Strengths	Weaknesses
Provides understanding of intangible aspects of organizational life.	May conflict with the budget- and enrollment-driven emphasis of today's higher education institutions.
Enables organizational participants to infuse meaning into their daily lives.	May not appeal to students who view rituals, sagas, and other cultural artifacts as unnecessary, off-putting, or corny.
Fits well with the pomp and circumstance of higher education.	May give the impression that higher education emphasizes the superficial at the expense of substance.
Creates meaning beyond the expediencies and bureaucratic aspects of organizational life.	May seem frivolous or unnecessary to organizational members who value efficiency and expediency.
Provides alternative views of leadership that create more equitable environments for a wider range of people.	A more diverse and open view of leadership may clash with board of trustee members' and stakeholders' views of institutional leadership style.

1. Critical race theorists acknowledge that racism is normal and endemic to U.S. society. These theorists and the practitioners whose work is guided by CRT expect to see expressions of racism and oppression throughout the institutions, including colleges and universities, which make up U.S. society.
2. With recognition of the permanence of racism and the nature of racism as a socially constructed dynamic, CRT proponents are skeptical about legal claims of neutrality, color-blindness, and objectivity. Instead, they articulate processes through which political, economic, and social contexts, among others, are shaped by the racist dynamics early established in the United States.
3. Because racism and oppression underscore social structures, these assumptions and dynamics affect the ways that group advantage and disadvantage are meted out.
4. Counterstorytelling is a methodology used to convey the experiences of people of color and to display the stark differences from the dominant master narrative.
5. An innovative and particularly useful principle in CRT is the idea of Whiteness as property. Many people view property as only applicable to tangible or material items. In contrast, CRT theorists articulate the ways that Whiteness can be bartered, exchanged, and "cashed in" for other forms of capital. This exchange includes money as well as more abstract forms of capital—social, political, and cultural. Whiteness as property has particular application in educational settings where the color of one's skin can be exchanged for privilege, access to higher paying jobs, better neighborhoods, and higher quality schools; experiences that are then parlayed into additional property and capital.
6. CRT theorists seek to eliminate racism as a way to address all forms of oppression.

Theorists have used CRT as a powerful means to view higher education and the cultural context forged through years of practice, including a variety of practices of exclusion and marginalization.

Patton and her colleagues (Patton et al., 2007) challenged the neutrality of higher education theory. They addressed how racism produces campus inequities through policies, processes, and traditions that render students of color invisible. They address how microaggressions (Sue, 2010), prevalent within the daily life of college campuses, create a hostile environment for marginalized groups. CRT theorists discuss the ways that racism is a normal, everyday presence in U.S. society and, by implication, college campuses.

The institutional and organizational neutrality contested by CRT is most applicable to the cultural perspective through a challenge to the hypothetical unbiased theoretical positions and assumptions about objectivity. In the literature of organizational culture, cultural artifacts such as sagas, myths, symbols, ceremonies, and rituals are presented as if all within the organization homogeneously adhere to the messages and meanings conveyed. The historical and present-day oppression embodied in the artifacts, including, for example, buildings named after known racists, is inadequately addressed in the organizational culture literature. Instead, the theory and embodied cultural assumptions and values are presented as objective, neutral, and oftentimes naïvely positive.

Counterstorytelling, as told by students of color and other oppressed campus groups, is a technique advanced by CRT theories to expose the inequalities and oppression of higher education. Counterstories include student of color performances that confront their experience with campus racism; the celebration of culturally-relevant holidays;

faculty research agendas that focus on U.S. systems of oppression; student protests through social media that call out oppressive structures; activism to change building names in an effort to remove the daily and present-day celebration of racism and oppression; and residence hall celebrations that honor a diversity of nondominant culture heroines and heroes.

Although CRT was originally focused on race and racism as experienced by African and Black Americans, the theory has expanded into additional areas where oppression is evident. LatCRT (Urrieta & Villenas, 2013; Villalpando, 2004) focuses on Latino/a populations, LGBT and queer CRT explores CRT principles for lesbian, gay, bisexual, and transgender (LGBT) populations (Crichlow, 2015; Santiago, 2004), and DisCRT emphasizes differently-abled populations (Annamma, Connor, & Ferri, 2013; Han, 2016). The theoretical richness of CRT and its impact on understanding the role of oppression in organizations is an extremely promising development in education and organizational theory.

The following questions can be posed to explore how CRT provides increased understanding of higher education organizational theory and administration:

- How has racism shaped current college and university approaches to the recruitment of faculty of color?
- How do the traditional organizational models of higher education (e.g., bureaucracy, collegium) provide institutional mechanisms that enable and constrain the incorporation of cultural practices different from those upon which U.S. higher education was founded?
- Why are some college and university members (e.g., White men) viewed and celebrated as more legitimate within systems of higher education than other members (e.g., faculty of color, women, LGBT people)?

Further development of the use of CRT in the cultural perspective specifically, and higher education organizational theory generally, would yield significant analytical and theoretical power.

CONCLUSIONS

The cultural perspective, particularly when updated with CRT, offers a helpful analysis with which to view colleges and universities. Older concepts of the cultural perspective as elucidated by Burton Clark and others can be combined with the newer ideas related to multicultural organizational development and CRT to obtain a contextually rich view on organizational theory and leadership. This perspective can assist organizational members to invite all to employ symbols, shape rituals and ceremonies, build structures, create inclusive spaces, and practice leadership in ways that can better guide their institutions to be more inclusive and just.

Questions for Discussion
- What are some of the symbols that have endured throughout the history of higher education?
- What cultural artifacts (e.g., symbols, traditions, rituals) would you expect to experience within the United States?

- How has the internationalization of higher education influenced or been influenced by the traditions of U.S. higher education?
- What higher education cultures are the sources of tensions within college and university systems?
- How can the cultural perspective be used to understand complexity within higher education?
- How can the cultural perspective be used to address contemporary higher education pressures such as loss of public trust, low graduation rates, and inadequate college-going rates of certain groups of students?
- How do cultural artifacts and the historical cultural practices of higher education exacerbate allegations of elitism?

Recommended Readings for the Cultural Perspective

Barbera, K. M. (2014). *The Oxford handbook of organizational climate and culture.* Oxford: Oxford University Press.

Kezar, A. (2011). Organizational culture and its impact on partnering between community agencies and postsecondary institutions to help low-income students attend college. *Education and Urban Society, 43*(2), 205–243.

Lechuga, V. M. (2016). *The changing landscape of the academic profession: Faculty culture at for-profit colleges and universities.* New York: Routledge.

Martin, J. (2002). *Organizational culture: Mapping the terrain.* Thousand Oaks, CA: Sage.

Oliva, M., Rodríguez, M. A., Alanís, I., & Cerecer, P. D. Q. (2013). At home in the academy: Latina faculty counterstories and resistances. *The Journal of Educational Foundations, 27*(1/2), 91.

Tierney, W. G. (2008). *The impact of culture on organizational decision-making: Theory and practice in higher education.* Sterling, VA: Stylus.

Tierney, W. G., & Lanford, M. (2015). An investigation of the impact of international branch campuses on organizational culture. *Higher Education, 70*(2), 283–298.

Wolfe, B. L., & Dilworth, P. P. (2015). Transitioning normalcy: Organizational culture, African American administrators, and diversity leadership in higher education. *Review of Educational Research, 85*(4), 667–697.

CASE: WHAT'S IN A NAME? THE CONTROVERSY OVER RENAMING A BUILDING

College campuses have traditionally recognized their founders, notable alumni, and historical figures by naming buildings, programs, and endowed professorships in their honor. One can often trace the line of college presidents by walking through a campus and reading the building names (Manning, 2000). Although current practice often requires a sizable donation to obtain naming rights, past practice depended more on outstanding deeds than money. The names of the first president, the person who donated the land upon which a campus was built, or an original board of trustees member were frequent choices for building naming.

In keeping with organizational culture approaches to colleges and universities, building names tell a story, a saga as described by Burton Clark (1972). These buildings symbolically declare institutional values, boast of past deeds, and provide a model of behavior to which students aspire. Through these artifacts, history comes alive as students invoke the names of people who once occupied the campus grounds. For better or worse, the deeds, beliefs, and values of these people are not ignored but incorporated into daily campus life.

Unfortunately, names that were honored in the past can create controversy in modern times. Values and attitudes betraying racist, sexist, heterosexist, and other oppressive ideals overlooked in the past are now unpalatable to current campus stakeholders

(Svokos, 2015). As values and beliefs evolve, the names etched into buildings, stadiums, and colleges or schools become a daily signal that students, faculty, and staff from diverse identities are not welcome on campus. The name of a racist past president, for example, communicates to students and faculty of color that their status is provisional, they are not seen as rightful members of the community.

In addition to building names, mascots have been a source of controversy (Cabrera, Watson, & Franklin, 2016; Endres, 2015; Guiliano, 2015). Mascots that mimic or parody Native American tribes and supposed behavior have come under fire as culturally insensitive and offensive. Although opposition to these mascots and images can be fierce, many campus members have refused to make the change even when the institution and NCAA (National Collegiate Athletic Association) has banned such images (Ryan, 2016). In the midst of controversies over building names, mascots, and other offensive campus symbols and artifacts, colleges and universities have struggled to balance alumni/ae's, donors', students', and founders' wishes while respecting traditions and preserving institutional history. As campus attitudes evolve and student populations become more diverse across identities, campuses will continue to seek ways to simultaneously reflect current values while honoring their founders and benefactors. Unfortunately, these goals are not always congruent.

THE CASE

The following case discusses the controversy that potentially arises when an institution faces the decision to rename one of its buildings. The controversy is particularly acute when the benefactor or founder after whom the building was named no longer reflects the current values of the institution.

Institutional Context

Blue Mountain College is a small, private, competitive liberal arts institution in the southeastern region of the United States with a student population of 3,100. The university was founded in 1867, two years after the end of the Civil War. In the proud tradition of the South, the institution was founded by men and women with deep roots in that region. Blue Mountain College was segregated by race until 1960 when the university enrolled its first African American student. Women had been accepted into the university since 1954.

The first and most prominent building on campus is located on a hilltop, the highest point on campus and in the city in which the university is located. Originally called Heritage Hall, the building was renamed Alexander Hall in 1949 to honor one of the founding Board of Trustee members, John Alexander. Alexander was a Board of Trustees member instrumental in the institution's founding in 1867. Campus lore describes how Alexander convinced a wealthy land-holding friend to donate property that became the site of the college. Alexander also raised much of the original funds to found the institution. As a state senator, he used his influence to raise money from his circle of wealthy donors and arranged for a state allocation to construct the building that was originally called Heritage Hall. In fact, he helped lay the cornerstone for that building.

A product of his time, Alexander was a self-confessed White supremacist. He proudly and publicly boasted about the freed slaves he had murdered in the late-1800s. He was particularly implicated in the execution of a freed slave who was organizing Black voters. A well-known member of a White supremacist group, Alexander made no secret of his racist beliefs and murderous actions.

During the current academic year, students had organized themselves into a group called Students Concerned with Campus Racism. This student group objected to the name of Alexander Hall because the founding trustee member after whom the building was named was an unmistakable racist.

Characters

Mr. Mark Blanchard, Chair, Board of Trustees: Mr. Blanchard had been the Board chair for eight years. A man of deep tradition, Blanchard came from one of the oldest families in the state. An alumnus of Blue Mountain College, Mark Blanchard was proud that the institution had maintained its traditions for years. He had been apprised of recent student complaints about Alexander Hall and the racist history of John Alexander. Blanchard was a practical person who did not confront issues until they were in front of him. He had enough to worry about with the budget issues at the institution, the plans to build a new library, and the ongoing leadership challenges at Blue Mountain.

Dr. Jane Oak, President, Faculty Senate: Dr. Oak was chair of the history department and a veteran of Blue Mountain politics. She had served a term as Faculty Senate president five years ago and was encouraged to run again by the Faculty Women's Caucus. The institution was on the cusp of transforming from its traditional ways of operating to the more tolerant practices of a 21st century institution. These changes were in response to the student, faculty, and staff populations that were vastly more diverse than at any point in Blue Mountain's history.

Ms. Jess Seller, President, Student Government Association (SGA): Ms. Seller was in her senior year and had been a member of the SGA during her four years at Blue Mountain. An ethnic studies major, Jess was well-versed in issues regarding racism, sexism, and heterosexism. She was sympathetic to the recent demands of the newly-formed Students Concerned with Campus Racism.

Dr. Edward Spraul, History Professor: Dr. Spraul had been a professor at Blue Mountain for 15 years. Dr. Spraul was a traditionalist who believed that you did not change cultural artifacts according to the whims of the day. These artifacts were part of history and needed to remain intact, especially when they sparked conversation about institutional values and priorities. He was vaguely aware of a newly formed student group that was agitating to get Alexander Hall renamed. He was opposed to the effort. He believed in George Santayana's sentiment that "Those who cannot remember the past are condemned to repeat it." The name Alexander Hall was a perfect opportunity to engage in conversations about current and future institutional values. With an interest in student movements, Dr. Spraul had watched student opinion ebb and flow over the years. Like other student movements, Spraul assumed this one would run its course.

Mr. Ethan Coop, Education Graduate Student: Mr. Coop was in his 2nd year of a masters program. He enrolled at Blue Mountain because of its excellent program of secondary education and the generous financial assistance package he received. Upon arriving on campus, he was surprised to learn of the history of the person after whom the most prominent building on campus was named. He organized a group, Students Concerned with Campus Racism, that worked to get Alexander Hall renamed. The group was working with the Faculty Senate and the SGA to petition the Board of Trustees to restore Alexander Hall to its original name, Heritage Hall.

President John James: President James had been the CEO at Blue Mountain College for two years. He came to the institution with the understanding that future enrollment depended on diversifying the student body. The regional prospective student population from which the university drew had changed in the past 10 years with increased numbers of Latino/a and African American students. President James had directed the Vice President for Enrollment Management and Director of Admissions to re-configure the university's marketing and recruitment approach. There had been pushback from the Board of Trustees, particularly Chair Blanchard, who did not see the necessity of changing the traditional mix of the student body.

Questions to Consider
- What is a higher education institution's role in creating more socially just environments?
- How are the historical values of an institution transmitted through the day-to-day operations of a campus?
- Does a campus have an obligation to reconcile past and present institutional values?

SGA Petition

The more Ethan Coop learned about and researched the details of John Alexander and his White supremacist roots, the more appalled he became that there was a building named in his honor. As a self-professed ally to Black students, Coop and the Students Concerned with Campus Racism worked with the Blue Mountain College Faculty Senate and SGA to petition the Board of Trustees to change the name. They used principles from organizational culture and CRT as a theoretical basis upon which to build their arguments.

Questions to Consider
- What organizational and CRT tenets would you use if you were Coop?
- How is the concept of Whiteness as property perpetuated through the use of Alexander's name on a campus building?
- What counterstories could you construct regarding the legacy of John Alexander and the building that bears his name?

After meeting several times, Students Concerned with Campus Racism brought the following resolution to the SGA and asked for their vote of approval:

Resolution to Rename Alexander Hall

Presented by the Committee of Students Concerned with Campus Racism

Whereas, Blue Mountain College Student Government Association stands in support of students of color and all marginalized groups on campus,

Whereas, the current name of Alexander Hall was named after a known White supremacist and murderer of Black people,

Whereas, the honor bestowed through the building naming to John Alexander stands in opposition to the stated goals of Blue Mountain College as an inclusive and welcoming environment,

BE IT RESOLVED THAT THE STUDENT GOVERNMENT ASSOCIATION OF BLUE MOUNTAIN COLLEGE

petitions the board of trustees to return the name of Alexander Hall to Heritage Hall.

Signed, Jess Seller, President, Student Government Association

Questions to Consider

- How are the values and assumptions of a university expressed in the symbolic naming of institutional buildings?
- What impact could the historical naming of university buildings have on current students?
- In this situation, what opportunities for cultural growth may be lost when a building is renamed? What is gained?

SGA President Seller met weekly with President James to update him on student and student governance issues. Seller presented James with the resolution recently passed by the SGA and apprised him of the brewing controversy over Alexander Hall. James already knew of the resolution and the actions of Students Concerned with Campus Racism from a newspaper article that reported on the SGA proceedings. James discussed the issue with Seller but neglected to mention that he had received a call from Board Chair Blanchard who had stated in no uncertain terms that the Alexander Building would remain named as is.

Questions to Consider

- What are some positive and negatives messages at play with the name of the Alexander Building as a cultural artifact?
- How do the values expressed through the Alexander Building impact the value of an institution that is trying to be inclusive to students and institutional members with identities that are under-represented in the university?
- What would be your response to Board Chair Blanchard if you were President James? What organizational culture principles would you use to advance your argument?

Onto the Faculty Senate

Ethan Coop did not end his effort to rename the building with the SGA. He approached the Faculty Senate with a request for them to pass a resolution similar to the SGA's. Dr. Jane Oak was more than happy to oblige and placed the item on the agenda for the next meeting of the Executive Committee of the Faculty Senate. The Faculty Senate Executive Committee was in favor of the SGA resolution and crafted a similar one to be voted on at the upcoming meeting of the Senate. The wording of the resolution was as follows:

Draft Resolution on the Renaming of Alexander Hall

Whereas, the faculty of Blue Mountain College seek to provide an inclusive and socially just education for all students,

Whereas, the presence of a building named in honor of a university founder who is a known White supremacist perpetuates an oppressive campus climate for faculty, students, and staff,

Whereas, Alexander Hall was named, not during the lifetime of John Alexander, but in retrospect in 1949,

BE IT RESOLVED THAT THE FACULTY SENATE REQUESTS THAT:

Alexander Hall be restored to the original name of Heritage Hall.

Questions to Consider

- What elements of organizational culture would you consider if you were the president of the Faculty Senate?
- How might you write a Faculty Senate resolution taking into account the traditions and history of an institution?
- How do traditions such as the naming of Alexander Hall impact the educational effort of faculty?

The Faculty Senate Vote

The resolution written by the Faculty Senate was discussed and put up for a vote at the next Faculty Senate meeting. The meeting and discussion was heated. Dr. Edward Spraul of the history department was particularly vehement that the building remain as named. His points included the importance of remembering history so that it would not be repeated and the danger of sweeping negative aspects of Blue Mountain's history under the carpet. This history, negative or not, was part and parcel of who they were. Changing the name, for him, was akin to attempting to change history, an act that he could not abide. While other professors concurred with his assessment, some faculty agreed with the Executive Committee's concerns as expressed in the draft resolution, and other faculty thought the renaming effort was much ado about nothing. They voiced concern that students were being overly sensitive and politically correct. Other faculty expressed concern that this issue was taking attention from more pressing issues such as the new library and budget shortfalls.

Questions to Consider
- What do you think of Dr. Spraul's arguments?
- What are some arguments for and against the renaming of the building?
- How can the renaming of a building be achieved in such a way as to maintain historical accuracy while supporting the current inclusive values of the institution?

Time expired during the Faculty Senate before a vote on the resolution could be taken. Faculty President Oak was anxious to get the resolution on the upcoming Board of Trustees meeting agenda. Due to the time constraints, she decided to send the vote out to the Faculty Senate senators through electronic means. She did not feel that additional discussion on the Faculty Senate floor would yield any more insights. People were "dug in" regarding their positions and were ready for a vote. The vote came back from the senators with 14 to approve the resolution and 6 against.

With the SGA and Faculty Senate resolutions in hand, President James approached Board Chair Blanchard with a request to consider taking action through the Board of Trustees. Blanchard refused, citing a little known state law that historical buildings could not be renamed. In Blanchard's mind, the issue was settled.

Questions to Consider
- Where do you see some of the points of friction between old and new cultural ideas?
- If you were president of an institution that was constructing a new library, residence hall, or other structure, how would you go about naming the new building?
- What cultural values and assumptions, if any, do you feel are incontestable? Which ones are not?

Student Rally

Alarmed by the response from Board of Trustees Chair Blanchard, Ethan Coop, Students Concerned with Campus Racism, and the SGA sponsored a rally on the steps of Alexander Hall. They timed the rally to occur during the Admitted Student Visit Day. They handed out flyers outlining Alexander's history and the values embodied in the building. Their next steps were to petition the state legislature to retrospectively return Alexander Hall to its original name in keeping with the state law that restricted the renaming of historical buildings.

DISCUSSION

Although culture is dynamic and ever-changing, cultural artifacts are physical and tangible reflections of the past assumptions, values, and beliefs of a college or university's culture. Ideas that were palatable in the past—or perhaps excusable given other deeds of the founder or benefactor—are often now seen as reasons to remove recognition that was previously granted. Arguments on both sides—keep the named buildings as a way to keep the history and discussion alive; rename the buildings to better reflect current institutional values—are frequently waged. The issue of how to progress cultures to create coherence with current cultural values often conflicts with efforts to honor founders. This problem, whether enacted through the names of buildings, the features of a mascot, or the expression of a campus-wide event, promises to continue as campus cultures evolve, incorporate more current ideas, and change with the times.

5

FEMINIST AND GENDERED

The queer concept of multiple and fluid identities challenges the often used basic assumption that the normative employee is a heterosexual who can be identified as female or male. (Bendl, Fleischman, & Hofmann, 2009, p. 630)

INTRODUCTION

In 1977, Rosabeth Moss Kanter wrote her classic text *Men and Women of the Corporation*, and expressed the nascent idea that men and women view the organization through gendered, albeit binary, male and female lenses. Since that time an extensive collection of feminist and gender oriented organizational theory has developed. Although early notions of gender in organizations referred only to females, recent efforts to incorporate queer theory are expanding ideas about gender in organizations. The feminist perspective on organizational theory challenges entrenched assumptions and values that drive structure, planning, priorities, incentives, values, policies, and practices. Even the basic question "What forms of activity count as work?" is gender related (Meyerson & Kolb, 2000, p. 554).

This chapter introduces feminist perspectives on organizational theory and concludes with suggestions for ways of updating feminist approaches through the use of queer theory. The work of Acker (1990, 2006, 2009), Helgesen (1990, 1995, 2006), Calás and Smircich (1999, 2006), Benschop and Verloo (2015), and Bendl, Fleischmann, and Walenta (2008) are particularly highlighted. In addition to feminist organizational theories, female-style leadership, also called connective or relational (Lipman-Blumen, 1992, 2014) is discussed. This leadership style better fits the interrelated and global environment of the 21st century in which U.S. higher education resides. In these systems of education, a single institution may now span several locations, including countries, through branch campuses, articulation agreements, and scholarly exchanges. Interrelated approaches to leadership are coherent with the interconnectedness required in global relations.

FEMINIST THEORY AS THE FOUNDATION FOR FEMINIST APPROACHES TO ORGANIZATIONAL THEORY

Although the earliest feminist thought extends back to the late 1700s, continued through suffrage, and extended into the first women's movements, feminist theory expanded in earnest with the women's movement of the 1960s and 1970s. Assumptions that underscore modern feminist theories include the following:

- Gender is socially constructed including the idea that it is reproduced in organizations.
- All social processes are gendered.
- When viewed from a feminist perspective, transformation, democratization, and social justice are goals for organizations, systems, and other forms of public life.
- Western culture has traditionally undervalued skills and qualities (e.g., sensitivity, nurturing, emotional expressiveness, intuition) culturally defined as female. Culturally defined male skills and qualities (e.g., competition, aggressiveness, decisiveness, ambition, progress) are overvalued, particularly in organizations and leadership.
- Women, sexual minorities, people of color, and other under-represented groups are inequitably treated in organizations. (Calás & Smircich, 1999; Kark, 2004; Meyerson & Kolb, 2000)

Although the word feminist is often attributed to women, one need not be female to adhere to the assumptions of feminist theory. The privileging of male characteristics means that everyone, regardless of a preferred gender style, is pressured to express culturally defined masculine characteristics in leadership and organizational roles (Lipman-Blumen, 1992). The alienation created by the command and control leadership approach can be debilitating to men as well as women. This approach may also clash with the styles of people of color and sexual orientation minorities. The strengths and weaknesses of feminist theory as a foundation for feminist approaches to organizational theory are outlined in Table 5.1.

Table 5.1 Strengths and Weaknesses of the Feminist Theoretical Foundation for Higher Education

Strengths	Weaknesses
Allows the manifestation of connection as well as independence and autonomy.	Relationships and connection may be undervalued in public life.
Enables women's voices to become included in organizational life.	Does not speak to the necessary expression of the voices of people of all genders.
Provides a perspective where the female gender is welcomed.	Treats gender as binary, male/female, with inadequate attention to the range of possible genders.
Supplies a powerful analysis of how different styles of leadership and organizational functioning can engender trust, support, and nurturing.	May clash with traditional higher education assumptions based on the scientific method and assumptions of objectivity and detachment.
Facilitates a social justice perspective to be infused into traditional organizational life.	May be met with resistance from dominant culture members who see a new paradigm as a threat to their power and position within an organization.

The social construction of gender and the existence of gendered social relations means that all organizations reinforce and re-create the gender dynamics that exist within society. As such, organizational processes can be described as "gendering" (i.e., they create gender norms) and "gendered" (i.e., they reflect gender norms). With the introduction of feminist ideas into organizational theory, bureaucracy, capitalism, and hierarchy were particularly critiqued (Ferguson, 1985). "The feminist project was to create nonhierarchical egalitarian organizations that would demonstrate the possibilities of nonpatriarchal ways of working" (Acker, 1990, p. 14).

The consideration of gender in colleges and universities is particularly important because gender roles are not simply expressed in these settings; they are created and re-created. Charged with the transmission of cultural knowledge, colleges and universities are collectively a foremost social institution that creates and sustains gender differences. Examples of "gendering" processes include topics covered in the curriculum, symbols and images portrayed on campus, power relationships built into the organizational structure, and routine work practices where gender is explicit although often unnamed and unexamined.

METAPHOR

The metaphor of the web is used in this chapter to describe feminist organizations. Coined by Helgesen (1990, 1995, 2006) after observing several women-led organizations, this image fits the woman-centered, feminist-oriented organizations that she studied. In contrast to the organizational perspective metaphors of jungles, circles, or hierarchies describing other organizational theories, the web conveys pervasive connectedness. Like a spider web, touching one part of the organization causes systemic tremors to pass through all the other parts. Structural and procedural interconnectedness of communication, human interaction, and leadership underscore this approach.

STRUCTURE

The web of inclusion, unlike the hierarchical form long considered the norm in organizational life, illustrates a feminist-oriented form and one possible way to organize higher education institutions.

> Organizing human enterprise according to machine properties left people out of the equation—with the predictable result that they either became thoroughly wretched, or adapted and so lost their vitality and soul.... The subordination of people's skills and imaginations to the rigid architecture of the machine cut them off from their original sources, and so has thrown the human world out of balance. (Helgesen, 1995, p. 17)

Helgesen (1990, 1995, 2006) claimed that webs of inclusion are notable for their lack of a definitive and stable organizational structure. She described the web as

> roughly circular in shape, with the leader at the central point, and lines radiating outward to various points. The points formed loose concentric circles, which were bound together by an irregular interweaving of axial and radial lines that crisscrossed

the structure in a kind of filigree.... I added the term "inclusion" to the notion of the web because the women who led the organizations labored continually to bring everyone at every point closer to the center—to tighten ties, provide increased exposure, and encourage greater participation. (Helgesen, 1995, p. 20)

Anyone accustomed to other organizational forms may find the web of inclusion's structure difficult to identify. In fact, to someone with a traditional bureaucratic approach in mind, an organization with a web structure may appear in need of fixing and tightening up. As such, the web of inclusion represents a transformed and transforming organizational structure. Organizations using the web structure enlist different forms of communication, leadership, and power to change norms and ways of operating. These forms are possible only when a completely different set of assumptions, in this case feminist theory, underscores organizational functioning. The web has been described as a pattern and a process. Webs are adaptable, open, and responsive with open communication processes as part of their functioning.

Adaptable, Open, and Responsive

Tangled in the daily operations and needs of the organization, the web of inclusion is intricately linked to the daily rhythms of an institution. These rhythms include how time is used, what roles people assume, how physical space is allotted, how people talk to one another, and how decisions are made (Helgesen, 1995). As both a pattern and a process, the architecture of the web enables and is enabled by the arrangement of offices, the availability of organizational members (including the leader), and participation in decision making. The web facilitates connections, and connections allow the web to function.

The specific organizational structure that is chosen or evolves is always closely related to the environment in which an institution operates. Volatile, rapidly changing environments are inevitable parts of today's higher education landscape. Because the medieval-inspired higher education bureaucratic structure is slow to change, the web of inclusion with its adaptability and flexibility may be a better fit for today's institutions. Organizational life is more uncertain, fragmented, and fast-paced, so the challenge for today's "organizations [is] to become less hierarchical, more flexible, team-oriented, and participative" (Kark, 2004, p. 161). In contrast to stable organizational forms, "webs serve as a vehicle for constant reorganization" (Helgesen, 1995, p. 29). Administrative roles, lines of authority, communication patterns, and other organizational features are not fixed but change according to the circumstance and task at hand.

The web is notable in the way it shifts and adapts according to the rhythms and requirements of changing circumstances. Open office spaces allow the demands of projects to be addressed in highly adaptable ways. Flexible reporting lines allow people to shift among supervisors, work groups, and partners. Ubiquitous communication enables many to share their talents throughout the organization. One can imagine college or university offices (e.g., career services, honors colleges, women's centers) where the adaptability and flexibility of the web structure would work well. Other offices, particularly those with a need for confidentiality (e.g., student discipline services, human resources) would chafe against the openness of the web. The challenge of today's higher education environment is to imagine new ways of organizing that can assist faculty and administrators to address the needs of the organization in ways that were unimagined in the past.

Through its close connection to the environment, the web's edges remain open and responsive to its surroundings. This openness enables people, including stakeholders, to be continually pulled into decision making (Helgesen, 1995). Outsiders have access to the organization; insiders can get out. Inclusiveness is built through fluid membership, participative decision making, and omnidirectional communication. Through the permeable boundaries, innovation and responsiveness flows. Open communication, flexible roles, and adaptable structure enable talents and knowledge rather than position and protocol to shape organizational processes and practices. Titles are fluid; the structure shifts organically to redirect responsibility and information flow. The web's permeability is one of its most useful features for higher education institutions. Depending on the issue at hand, the edges of a college or university can more easily draw in, for example, community members (when the topic is town/gown), parents (when retention issues are foremost), alumni/ae (when fundraising is at issue), and state residents (when public funding is at stake).

Communication

Communication in web of inclusion structures emanates from all directions and across all levels. Because the silos often constructed within higher education organizations (Manning, Kinzie, & Schuh, 2014) are forsaken in lieu of a flatter, circular form, communication flows freely among departments and organizational participants. The assumptions of vertical (i.e., up and down) communication in bureaucracies or informal, disruptive (e.g., rumor oriented) lateral patterns of political organizations are replaced with the assumption that all participants benefit from the open flow of communication. "Web-style organizations are built on free-flowing community across levels, addressing real subjects" (Mahoney, 2002, p. 2). Communication is often more direct and face-to-face. In the web organizations studied, Helgesen (1995) found that spontaneous invitations by the leader to talk in "highly personal" ways were commonplace. The result was constant communication built into the architecture including debates and deep discussion that were exchanged in public places. Decision-making expertise shifted with the change in access to information.

Although not part of Helgesen's analysis, the presence of blogs and other social media now make the open exchange of information and ubiquitous flow of communication even more prevalent. Abundant access to information shifts earlier power structures built on the assumption that control over information was power. Old separations of leadership and task, thinking and doing, have disappeared with the new configurations of authority and access. A benefit of this approach is that these communication norms "made rumor and intrigue difficult to sustain and kept most traumas in the open and so under a measure of control" (Helgesen, 1995, p. 5). While this open, ever-present communication may appeal to some, others may find it chaotic and overwhelming. As with all organization styles, this model is not for everyone.

MAJOR CHARACTERISTICS, CONCEPTS, AND PRINCIPLES

Despite the presence of women in organizations since time immemorial, organizational theory was until recently strangely silent about feminism. Many theorists including Max Weber, Michael Cohen and James March, Burton Clark, and Karl Weick discuss theory and practice as if gender is not a factor in organizational life. Breaking from this silence, a number of current approaches to feminist theory characterize the organizational and leadership literature. A brief summary of four feminist theory approaches (liberal feminism, socialist feminism, social construction feminism, and poststructural feminism) that have been cited by Benschop and Verloo (2015) as having the most influence on organizational theory is provided below. Areas of interest for each strand of feminist theory are discussed to explore the main principles in each theoretical strand.

Liberal Feminism

Liberal feminism was one of the first theoretical perspectives to emerge with an interest in the numerical representation of women, particularly at the upper ranks of management; a critique of the public/private spheres; and concern with pay equity. Individual liberty and freedom are core values of this perspective. "The focus of liberal feminism is on individual women and men getting equal opportunities to develop themselves as they choose and to engage in free competition for social rewards" (Benschop & Verloo, 2015, p. 101). Actions promoted through liberal feminism include anti-discrimination legislation and workforce diversity programs.

Liberal feminism, including as represented in the classic work by Kanter (1977), possesses several suppositions that are currently refuted by post-structural and socialist feminisms. First, men and women are viewed as similar with no culturally-derived gender differences. Second, the power differences within gender relations are not explored. Third, liberal feminism reflects a "politics of optimism" in which "gender differences can be eradicated, allowing women to advance on a non-conflictual basis and inciting little response from men" (Lewis & Simpson, 2012, p. 142).

A variant of liberal feminism, neoliberal feminism, places particular emphasis on individualism. This theory departs from liberal feminism in the lack of a critique of capitalism or organizational masculine norms. The emphasis, instead, is on the entrepreneurial woman and high-powered female managers who succeed at the highest levels of corporate life. These are elite women who are told to "lean in" to the practices of the organization (Sandberg, 2013). A critique of those practices as unequal, oppressive, or elitist is neglected from neoliberal approaches to feminist theory.

The liberal feminist concepts of numerical under-representation, separation of the public and private spheres, and critique regarding gender inequality are highlighted below.

Numerical Under-Representation

Acker (2009, p. 202) defines inequality in organizations

> as systematic disparities between participants in power and control over goals, resources, and outcomes; in work place decision-making such as how to organize work; in opportunities for promotion and interesting work; in security in employment and benefits; in pay and other monetary rewards; and in respect and pleasures in work and work relations.

Organizational inequality results in women being remarkably under-represented in positions of authority including as executive officers, corporate board members, and upper managers. This trend exists in higher education where women are under-represented as presidents and executive officers (e.g., provosts, vice presidents) of colleges and universities and as board of trustee members. A major emphasis of liberal feminist attempts to change organizational gender relationships is to increase the number of women within organizations, particularly in top management. These theorists believe that increasing numbers of women will shift the norms and balance of power to more gender equitable relations.

Using the terms majority and minority, Kanter (1977) determines four group types to discuss the proportional representation of people within organizational work groups. The four group types are (a) *uniform* or groups that "have only one kind of person, one significant social type," (b) *skewed*, in which "there is a large preponderance of one type over another," (c) *tilted* or groups that "begin to move toward less extreme distributions and less exaggerated effects," and (d) *balanced* or a group with a proportion of majority and minority members in ratios of 60:40 to 50:50 (Kanter, 1977, pp. 208–209). Using the skewed group type as an example, Kanter used tokenism theory to explain the negative effects that occur when gender (seen by liberal feminists as the presence of women) becomes visible in organizations. In these groups, heightened visibility of the few people in the minority means that they are subjected to "performance pressures which require that they either overachieve or seek to reduce their exposure" (Lewis & Simpson, 2012, p. 143). These women become isolated from the majority (i.e., the men) or they may, through stereotyping, be relegated to traditionally female work roles. Only when a skewed group becomes a tilted group do the norms shift as visibility is reduced through the presence of more women.

Separation Between the Public and Private Spheres

Male/female work has long been identified according to the separation of work into public/private domains. Male work was performed in the public domain (i.e., outside the home) while women's work belonged in the private domain (i.e., inside the home). The outdated public/private, male/female configurations continue to have cultural and psychological impacts. Because childrearing, elder parent caretaking, and other domestic responsibilities remain in the female domain, lack of balance between work and home lives is inevitable. As the public domain is seen as the location of work while the private domain is not seen as valid work, women are relegated to two shifts, the first in the public domain and a second shift in the private one. Struggles with work–life balance are seen as a personal issue rather than a conflict created by the public/private split of organizational life. Such struggles to maintain high standards at work and at home are viewed as a personal problem, not one created by the gender norms of the organization.

Critique Regarding Gender Inequality

Liberal feminist theorists have been criticized for their elitist emphasis on managers and professionals at the expense of the working class. For many this theory falls short of any critique of the societally-inspired organizational mechanisms that maintain gender, race, class, and age inequalities. Liberal feminist theory focuses on changing the organizational mechanisms so women can attain the same status, pay, and other privileges as men. But, other strands of feminist theory purport that "numbers alone cannot create equality, because other social and cultural factors which privilege the masculine and devalue the feminine intervene" (Lewis & Simpson, 2012, p. 144). While the unique contributions of women are acknowledged, organizational and societal transformation to more equitable forms of work and cultural practices for all is not a goal of this strand of feminist theory.

Socialist Feminism

The second form of feminist theory with implications for organizations is socialist feminism. This strand of theory emphasizes the ways that gender inequalities are socially reproduced in organizations and society to create and maintain unequal and oppressive structures. At the base of these theories is an analysis of the ways that workers are dominated and exploited in the name of capitalism and profits. Patriarchy, the system that values male perspectives over female, is at the heart of worker domination and exploitation and is critiqued by socialist feminists for its excesses.

Socialist feminism steps beyond liberal feminism with an analysis of intersectionality, or the ways that race and class, in addition to gender, create unequal systems (Benschop & Verloo, 2015). Their analysis and goals for equality in organizations extend beyond executive management and the boardroom to include blue color workers. This is particularly relevant in today's climate of globalization and cross-national exploitation (Benschop & Verloo, 2015). The concepts of inequality regimes and worker exploitation are discussed as central themes within the socialist feminist theoretical strand.

Inequality Regimes

From a liberal feminist perspective, organizational theory uses the "glass ceiling" as a metaphor to describe how women could "see" the executive ranks in an organization but were unable to attain those positions. The glass ceiling metaphor conceals the fact that women, even those who have reached the upper levels of management, have faced inequalities along the way. They are not only blocked by the final glass ceiling but throughout their time within the organization.

Acker (2006, 2009) developed the glass ceiling concept through her discussion of inequality regimes. Present within all organizations, they are the "interlocked practices and processes that result in continuing classed, gendered, and racial inequalities in work organizations" (Benschop & Verloo, 2015, p. 103). In addition to describing an ongoing and constant process of discrimination that is not captured in the glass ceiling metaphor, inequality regimes rely on intersectionality, the ways that race, gender, and class are reproduced in organizations (Acker, 2009). The regimes persist through the presence of interrelated practices (e.g., salary structures, rewards, hiring criteria) that reinforce and enable the continuation of inequalities based on race, class, gender, and other identities. Inequality regimes

> suggest a different concept to capture complex, interlocking practices and processes that result in continuing inequalities in all work organizations, including at the top levels of management.... "Inequality Regimes" analysis incorporates race/ethnic and class processes, recognizing that gender processes are integrally involved with processes that can also be defined as having to do with class and/or race. Thus, one aspect of this analysis focuses on intersectionality, the mutual reproduction of class, gender and racial relations of inequality. (Acker, 2009, pp. 200–201)

The inequality regime concept provides an explanation for the ways that dynamics in organizations conspire to maintain the predominance of White men in top management, including president and chancellor positions within higher education. Inequality regime scholarship describes the mechanisms that concentrate power in the upper confines of the organization; perpetuate large wage and benefits discrepancies between, for example, top executives and secretaries and other staff; and define some work by gender (e.g., "women's work"). Inequality regimes are not static but fluid and ever-changing. The analysis of inequality regimes and the ways that inequality and exploitation is built into organizations has advantages beyond the benefits to individual women. When women occupy top management positions, increased wage equality and opportunities for women increase at all levels of the organization (Acker, 2009). Because gender, race, and class distinctions in organizations mimic those same divisions in the wider society (Acker, 2006, 2009), the analysis of inequality regimes in colleges and universities can further aid moves toward equality.

Worker Exploitation

Worker exploitation is a central concern for socialist feminists. In this area, the patriarchal capitalist system is examined for the ways in which it exploits workers in the name of profits and high executive salaries. Although higher education does not have shareholders who benefit from the profits, worker exploitation from a socialist feminist perspective is evident. The "low-qualified, low-valued, labour-intensive, temporary, numerically flexible jobs" (Benschop & Verloo, 2015, p. 103) in which women tend to be employed are rife with inequality and job insecurity. Socialist feminism provides an analytical tool with which to examine the different layers of bureaucracy in higher education. Top management in higher education, similar to corporations and the for-profit sector, reflects the societal configurations and inequalities by gender in terms of privilege and power.

Socialist feminism can provide insights into the organizational dynamics that impact administrative staff at lower levels of the college or university and into the practices of part-time and contingent faculty. Part-time work is the most gendered and exploited form of non-standard work (Benschop & Verloo, 2015). During the 2009–2010 academic year, the last year for which figures are available, over 50% of contingent faculty were women. The number of contingent faculty continues to grow each year. Insecurity is ever-present for contingent faculty because in the absence of multiple year contracts, their work is not assured from semester to semester. Their pay rate, including that of full-time contingent faculty, is significantly lower than that of tenured and tenure-track faculty. Consequently, their professional lives are fraught with uncertainty and insecurity.

Socialist feminism theories provide a critique of the patriarchal capitalist system and the ways in which workers in organizations are exploited and dominated. This area of feminist theory

> has inspired organization studies to look at the detrimental effects of gendered and classed divisions of labour, emphasizing the systemic and structural dimensions of capitalist inequality regimes. Furthermore, the attention for the intersections of gender and class has opened opportunities to incorporate other axes of inequality, such as race/ethnicity, sexuality, and age. (Benschop & Verloo, 2015, p. 104)

Social Construction Feminism

"Social construction feminism calls out the alleged gender neutrality of organization theory and organization processes, pointing to the persistent reproduction of gender inequalities in organizational realities" (Benschop & Verloo, 2015, p. 104). In social construction feminist theory, the gender neutrality is limited to the male/female binary. While these theorists discuss the interesting topic of "doing gender" and the ways workers "do gender" in the everyday interactions within organizations, this topic is limited to the "cultural prototypes of masculinity and femininity that are experienced as universal, natural truths" (Benschop & Verloo, 2015, p. 104). Emphasis in this area of feminist theory and research is placed on how the traditional societal norms of femininity and masculinity are reinforced in organizations. The social construction feminist theory ideas of gender neutrality and the ideal worker are discussed in this chapter.

Gender Neutrality

Like the social constructivist critique regarding the neutrality of knowledge (Lincoln, 1985; Lincoln, Lynham, & Guba, 2011), social constructivist feminist theorists have raised the issue of gender neutrality in organizations. Organizations and the workers within them have historically been conceptualized as gender-neutral, asexual, and objective (Acker, 1990). Despite the reality of male dominated practices, organizational practices and processes have been built on the assumption that the worker has no body and no gender. If any gender is assumed or implied, that gender is male. Often the male orientation of workers is assumed as the norm, even when the majority of workers are female.

Rather than acknowledging and regarding gender differences as a strength within organizations, gender has been rendered invisible and something to be ignored. When the worker is considered to be genderless, any roles socially constructed as female (e.g., childrearing, domestic work) are regarded as personal issues and the responsibility of the individual, not an issue to be taken into account by organizational practices (e.g., work hours, family leave). The introduction of affirmative action and legislation to combat gender discrimination in the workplace forced organizations to acknowledge the presence of gender and genders. Social construction feminists have discussed the ways in which gender is created, obscured, and re-created within organizations (Acker, 2006).

Ideal or Universal Worker

A second concept discussed by social constructivist feminist theorists is that of the ideal or universal worker. Rather than a gender-neutral conception, the ideal worker is imagined as male with no family responsibilities. For this organizational member, work comes before anything else. The worker's commitment to the organization prevails over any obligations to family and non-work commitments. These norms and expectations within the organization are not explicit but invisible. "The concept of a universal worker excludes and marginalizes women who cannot, almost by definition, achieve the qualities of a real worker because to do so is to become like a man" (Acker, 1990, p. 150). Through practices such as job qualifications, hiring procedures, and work hours, gender norms are built into organizations. Images of managers and leaders embody socially constructed male characteristics such as decisiveness, ambition, and strength. Without explicitly defining work roles as male, organizational practices are built around a male conception of work, private life, and ways of being. The ideal or universal worker is male.

Poststructural Feminism

Poststructural feminist theorists define an organization as a "socially situated practice with individuals involved in socially situated activities. Following this, gendered relations are understood as deeply embedded and continually acted out within organizational contexts" (Lewis & Simpson, 2012, p. 142).

The three strands of feminist theory previously discussed in this chapter assume a male/female dualism. For these three perspectives on feminist theory, gender is assumed to be fixed and essential. Poststructural feminists, however, assume that gender is not fixed but is fluid. Similarly, from the poststructural position, power is not fixed but a discourse made and remade through the relationships between genders (Lewis & Simpson, 2012). Visibility and invisibility as an aspect of gender in organizations is also discussed in the context of poststructural feminist theory.

Fluidity of Genders

"Poststructuralist feminism questions unitary notions of woman and femininity, demonstrating that everyday social relations are characterized by instabilities and differences" (Benschop & Verloo, 2015, p. 106). Unlike other variations of feminist theory, poststructural feminist theory dismisses the male/female binary and examines the notion of non-essentialized genders and sexuality. For poststructural feminists, more than two genders exist with categories that are fluid and subjective. The standard heteronormativity of organizational life is challenged with the idea that many expressions of gender and sexuality are possible. Gender is socially constructed in the performance of daily life.

Gender as a multiple and fluid concept is ever-present on college campuses. Student affairs professionals have taken the idea of gender expression as a social justice issue for students and institutional employees. The full range of gender expression including transgender, bisexuality, cisgendered, and other forms are explored. Gender, performed on campus with varying degrees of acceptance, is reaching beyond the inadequate ideas of the male/female binary of the past.

Visibility and Invisibility

Beginning with Kanter, feminist researchers have discussed the predominantly negative consequences for women who occupy nontraditional roles (e.g., top management) in organizations. Lewis and Simpson (2012) discussed two mechanisms that exist within organizations to maintain the gender dynamics of male dominance: surveillance and comparisons to a male norm of behavior. People of genders other than male are compared against a male norm which is assumed to be normal and inevitable. The male norms are made invisible through routinization in hiring, assessment, and other practices within the organization. Organizational members are "watched" or scrutinized and evaluated for their adherence to these gendered norms. Preferential hiring of men and/or people whose behavior is congruent with the male norm, and gatekeeping by men and women in upper management levels who wish to maintain their status, are two mechanisms guaranteeing the maintenance of the dominant system of male normed behavior.

Marginalization and ridicule (Lewis & Simpson, 2012) are sanctions levied against anyone who steps outside the tacitly expressed male norms. The power of invisibility intervenes as organizational actors, in an effort to avoid negative sanctions, police themselves according to the norms as they understand them. Outside influence is not necessary as the person is judged against an internally adopted norm. "The power of normalization lies in its *invisibility*, as individuals are constituted and reconstituted through discourses ... that reflect the accepted and 'taken for granted'" (Lewis & Simpson, 2012, p. 146) values and norms of the organization. In other words, anyone deemed as outside the accepted norm is made visible in contrast to the accepted norms; the norms become invisible as they are adopted by all, including the marginalized and "otherized" in the organization. The masculine norms of the organization are universal and so accepted as to be rendered invisible.

While most of the discussion about visibility and invisibility has centered on the negative consequences of these organizational mechanisms, there are positive, even subversive, consequences as well. "Individuals can use visibility and difference to challenge the status quo—rejecting the subjectivizing effects of competitive discourses to present 'trailblazing' identities that dispute current practices and champion different ways of doing ... difference can be flaunted and enjoyed" (Lewis & Simpson, 2012, p. 151).

COLLABORATIVE, CONNECTED LEADERSHIP

The leadership characteristics advanced by feminist organizational theorists are vastly different from other organizational choices (e.g., top-down authority of bureaucracy, first among equals leadership of collegiums) for higher education institutions. Web of inclusion leadership is collaborative, consultative, and non-elitist.

> Those who emerge in them [web structures] as leaders tend to be people who feel comfortable being in the center of things rather than at the top, who prefer building consensus to issuing orders, and who place a low value on the kind of symbolic perks and marks of distinction that define success in the hierarchy. (Helgesen, 1995, p. 20)

The accessibility and centrality of the leader in web structures has some unexpected benefits. In traditional organizations, managers are viewed as the thinkers (i.e., the head) while the workers are viewed as the doers (i.e., the hands). In webs of inclusion, distinctions between management and workers, leaders and followers are blurred because everyone is encouraged to accept responsibility for the conceptualization and execution of organizational practices; in other words, for leadership. Positional rank in webs of inclusion is disregarded (Helgesen, 1995). Trust, communication, and delegation are paramount as followers are empowered to exercise leadership throughout the entire organization.

This active, engaged approach to leadership was depicted by Lipman-Blumen (1992, 1998, 2002, 2014) who teased out how leadership could be culturally defined by the female gender. She demarcated connective leadership as reflecting a traditional female style and direct, achieving leadership as a traditional male leadership style. The differing leadership styles of connective and direct, achieving leadership have contrasting values and approaches to tasks and relationships (see Table 5.2).

The underlying assumptions of connectivity rather than isolation and individualism make connective leadership congruent with feminist ideas about organizations. Connected and relational leadership styles fit the "new global context [that] demands leaders who can enable parties, with distinctive, often inimical, agendas and world views, to work and live together harmoniously and productively" (Lipman-Blumen, 2014, p. 32).

Table 5.2 Gendered Approaches to Leadership

Connective Leadership	Direct, Achieving Leadership
Communal	Individualistic
Collaborative	Competitive
Persuasive	Controlling
Networking	Isolated
Interconnected	Self-reliant
Power with	Power over
Works together	Works separately
Mutuality	Egocentric
Contributes to the goals of others	Takes credit for the goals of others

Connective leadership is grounded in the female predilection for relationship (Gilligan, 1982). Direct, achieving leadership, culturally attributed to men, "emphasizes individualism, self-reliance, and belief in one's own abilities, as well as power, competition, and creativity" (Lipman-Blumen, 1992, p. 185). Both men and women can practice either style, both of which are shaped by culture, tradition, and practice. Despite ongoing developments regarding the value of diverse perspectives concerning leadership, deep cultural beliefs about the value of male-oriented leadership prevail. Organizations, including higher education institutions (with the exception of women's colleges and other nonpaternalistic organizations), are dominated by the direct, achieving leadership style. When most think of leadership, they assume the decisive, command and control of direct, achieving leadership. The gendered nature of organizations means that voices with a feminine tone (including males with this style) are heard less than voices with a traditional male tenor.

Although a positive aspect of feminist theory and approaches to organizations, the transformational assumptions and emphasis of the feminist model of organizations places an additional burden on women leaders. The weight placed on change means that women, people of color, and other under-represented people devote an excess proportion of effort and time to activities to transform the organization (e.g., diversity work, recruiting a diverse workforce).

STRENGTHS AND WEAKNESSES OF THE FEMINIST PERSPECTIVE

Each organizational perspective has its strengths and weaknesses. No one organizational structure can solve all problems, match the style of all organizational members, or seamlessly and adequately respond to the environment. As with other organizational perspectives, the feminist perspective on organizational structure has its strengths and weaknesses (see Table 5.3).

NEXT STEPS: BRINGING THE FEMINIST AND GENDERED PERSPECTIVE INTO CURRENT USE

Feminist theory has long criticized organizations for disregarding and erasing the female voice. The same observation could be made today about the exclusion of the full range of

Table 5.3 Strengths and Weaknesses of the Feminist Organizational Structure of the Web

Strengths	Weaknesses
The adaptability and flexibility of web structures makes them more responsive to profound change.	The chaotic and blurry roles of the web structure can be a source of confusion regarding who is responsible for what.
The web structure builds tolerance for mavericks and people at the margins.	More aggressive people in a web organization may overpower the voices of less aggressive members.
The downplayed power and status within the structure makes webs less demoralizing and more humane places to work.	There is some question about whether the web of inclusion can work without a strong leader.
The open structure and access to leadership increases participation across the institution.	Change can be a slow process as leaders solicit wide-ranging input and allow multiple voices to be heard.

genders under consideration in feminist organizational theories. The following section discusses queer theory, its implications for organizations, and its promise to engender a more equitable approach to organizational functioning and analysis.

Queer Theory

Queer theory is a poststructuralist approach that seeks to deconstruct identity (particularly forms traditionally represented in organizations), challenge heteronormativity, and dismantle the gender binary (Bendl et al., 2008). Although largely ignored in organizational theory, a field whose "engagement with queer theory, politics and identities has been sporadic, marginal and ambivalent" (Pullen, Thanem, Tyler, & Wallenberg, 2013), queer theory is a theoretical, academic, and social force on college campuses. Through the inclusion of sexual orientation and gender expression in non-discrimination clauses, higher education is an organizational space where a fuller range of gender and sexuality is expressed and performed. The presence of academic majors and minors in gender and sexuality studies further involves higher education institutions in the consideration of genders beyond the male/female gender binary.

Heteronormativity

Heteronormativity is a queer theory concept with significant implications for organizational life, including higher education institutions. Heteronormativity, the assumption of heterosexuality as the only legitimate and legitimated sexual orientation, "orders not only the social acceptance of certain kinds of sexuality (between man and woman) but also the division of power and the related division of labor based on the dual-gender construct" (Bendl et al., 2009, p. 627). Both explicit and implicit practices shape the organizational norm of heterosexuality in organizations. From benefits packages to family pictures "allowed" on workers' desks, heterosexuality is the norm in organizations. While many colleges and universities have expanded their conceptions of gender and sexuality, the foundational organizational norms remain heteronormative.

Heterosexuality "functions as a social regime ... setting the social rules and possibilities, regulating not only sexual practices but also social practices" (Bendl et al., 2009, p. 627). Through repetition, a process that Judith Butler (1990) calls performativity, male and female roles appear to be fixed and natural when, in reality, they are socially constructed, fluid, and malleable. Heterosexuality as a regime exists in organizational life underscoring assumptions that drive the societal dynamics of "public/private, passive/active, and man/woman" (Bendl et al., 2008, p. 385). As discussed earlier in the chapter, the public sphere has long been marked as the domain of men and the private sphere that of women. Both conceptions depend on heterosexist assumptions.

A goal of queer theorists is to dismantle systems of heteronormativity as well as add complexity to ideas about identity by incorporating other "personal dimensions, like age, class, ethnicity and religion" (Bendl et al., 2009, p. 628). Through these efforts, including actions to dismantle the heteronormatively-based power structures within organizations, a more holistic and real treatment of identities can be created. These efforts include the rejection of categorization and expansion of efforts in diversity management beyond the "Big 6" (i.e., gender, age, race and ethnicity, religion, disability, and sexual orientation) (Bendl et al., 2008).

Static Identities

Queer theorists use the phrase "heterosexual matrix" to describe how organizations and other societal structures treat people as "having one sex, one stable (over a life span) sexual orientation and one clearly defined gender, which are congruent with each other" (Bendl et al., 2009, p. 628). The primacy of heterosexuality is embedded in the power structures of organizations. This singular sexual orientation is seen as more valid than others and situated at the peak of hierarchies of value and power.

Sexual orientation, sex, and gender are treated in organizations as essentialist, an identity formed biologically or through some other external factor. Queer theorists reject the essentialist argument and view sexual orientation, sex, and gender as "fluid social practices [that are] context-dependent and situated" (Bendl at al., 2009, p. 628). Identities are not fixed but change and adapt over time.

Incorporating Queer Theory into Organizational Analysis

Numerous ways exist to apply queer theory to college and university organizations. The following recommendations represent a sample of possible initiatives.

1. Examine non-discrimination clauses for the inclusion of gender expression and the presence of heterosexist assumptions.
2. Expand institutional diversity initiatives beyond the traditional categories of gender, age, race and ethnicity, religion, disability, and sexual orientation to include gender expression and identity.
3. Scrutinize institutional practices for the presence of heterosexist norms and assumptions. Examples include residential hall room-mate assignments, health benefit allocations, and tuition benefits for dependents.
4. Perform a critical read of college and university documents for the presence of gender binary language.
5. Undertake training to orient college and university members to the queer theory ideas of non-binary sexual identities, heteronormativity, and unequal power structures privileging heterosexual workers.
6. Institute a preferred name project through the academic software system so that transgender and queer students can include a preferred name and gender on class and advisor lists (Tisley, 2010).

CONCLUSIONS

Feminist and queer theory approaches to organizations may appeal to anyone who feels outside of or alienated by bureaucratic, collegial, and other traditional approaches to organizations. The full and equitable inclusion of all identities results in more effective organizational structures through decreased absenteeism, increased productivity, distributed leadership, and empowered employees (Meyerson & Kolb, 2000). People's frustration with the inequitable power structures and disillusionment born when talents are un- or under-utilized provides an argument and justification for the inclusion of new organizational forms.

The need for increased involvement and multiple opportunities to express talent within an organization is essential for higher education. These complex institutions with their multiple goals, diverse funding patterns, ever-changing student populations, internal and external stakeholders, ongoing and historical social justice missions, and simultaneous organizational forms require flexibility, adaptability, and openness.

Feminist approaches to organizations, the web of inclusion structure, and queer theory provide ways to envision organizations as inclusive, open, and collaborative. To some, the perspective may seem utopian and out of reach; to others, it may give hope that higher education organizations can achieve a more equitable and just state. Whether embraced in total or applied in parts, feminist and queer theory perspectives, as applied to organizations, hold significant promise for higher education institutions.

Questions for Discussion

- How can feminist and queer theory principles of organizing be used to effect change within higher education?
- What are sources of support for feminist and queer ways of organizing? Sources of resistance?
- What sources of support exist for the use of queer theories in higher education organizations? Sources of resistance?
- Which aspects of an institution of higher education would have to change to incorporate feminist and queer theory principles into the organization?
- How do feminist and queer theory principles enable societal transformation? How do they constrain it?
- Could a university president's office be more effective with the accessibility and openness of the web structure?
- Can the participative decision making of the web be used during strategic planning processes?

Recommended Readings for the Feminist Perspective

Broadbridge, A., & Simpson, R. (2011). 25 years on: Reflecting on the past and looking to the future in gender and management research. *British Journal of Management, 22,* 470–483.

Eddy, P. L., & Cox, E. (2008). Gendered leadership: An organizational perspective. In J. Lester (Ed.), *Gendered perspectives on community colleges* (New Directions in Community Colleges, pp. 69–80). San Francisco: Jossey-Bass.

Eddy, P. L., & VanDerLinden, K. E. (2006). Emerging definitions of leadership in higher education: New visions of leadership or the same old "hero" leader. *Community College Review, 34*(5), 5–26.

Gibson-Graham, J. K. (2003). Poststructural interventions. In E. Sheppard & T. J. Barnes (Eds.), *A companion to economic geography* (pp. 95–110). Oxford: Blackwell Publishing.

Iverson, S. (2011). Glass ceilings and sticky floors: Women and advancement in higher education. In J. L. Martin (Ed.), *Women as leaders in education: Succeeding despite inequity, discrimination* (pp. 79–105). Santa Barbara, CA: Praeger.

Martin, J. (2000). Hidden gendered assumptions in mainstream organizational theory and research. *Journal of Management and Inquiry, 9*(2), 207–216.

Temple, J. B., & Jari Ylitalo, J. (2009). Promoting inclusive (and dialogic) leadership in higher education institutions. *Tertiary Education and Management, 15*(3), 277–289.

CASE: THE PREFERRED NAME AND PRONOUN PROJECT

In the last 10 years, transgender students have become a visible presence on college campuses. Offices serving students who are lesbian, gay, bisexual, transgender, queer, and questioning have sprung up on campus as a means to support students whose sexual identity and expression does not reflect the norm upon which institutions of higher education were built. Single sex bathrooms, residence hall rooms assigned by male and female gender, and class rosters that reflect a student's legal rather than identity-consistent preferred name and gender are a few of the issues that have arisen on college campuses.

Often the source of debate and alarm, bathrooms have become a lightning rod for opponents of transgender rights. State-legislated bathroom laws have been passed, making it extremely difficult for faculty, administrators, and staff across educational levels to support students whose gender expression differs from their gender at birth.

Many colleges and universities have expanded services and support for transgender students. Among these efforts are the inclusion of transgender and gender identity in institutional non-discrimination statements, gender-neutral bathrooms, athletic department locker rooms that assure privacy, transgender-related student organizations, mentor programs, counseling services, trans-aware health services and residence life policies. An area of concern for transgender students has been the listing of their legal versus preferred name on class rosters and advisor lists. Particularly when checking for class attendance, the public announcement of a student's legal name that does not match their gender expression causes the student to be "outed" to the professor and fellow students. This circumstance raises safety and privacy issues.

=========================== THE CASE ===========================

This case describes an on-campus process in which a task force of administrators, students, and faculty embarked on a project to change the student information system to reflect students' preferred name and gender.

Institutional Context

Eastern State University (a pseudonym) is a mid-sized public institution of 15,000 undergraduate and graduate students. Located in a Middle Atlantic U.S. state, Eastern is considered to be a politically liberal institution with a long history of social activism. The institution recently increased their efforts to support lesbian, gay, bisexual, and transgender (LGBT) students through the establishment of a dedicated office on campus and a presidentially-appointed commission that explored policy, programs, and services for LGBT students.

Characters

Mr. John James, Registrar: Mr. James has been at Eastern State University for 15 years. During that time, he has overhauled many of the registrar's systems including classroom assignments, standard class times, credits for academic minors, and cross-listed courses. Mr. James sees himself as a supporter of students with diverse identities, including LGBT students. Over the years, he has received requests from students to change the student information system to allow a student to list a preferred name and gender. He is supportive of the idea but to date has been unable to find the money and time to devote to re-programming the student information system to accommodate the change. Each year, he thinks he will carve out the money and personnel time needed for the project but each year another priority is assigned to him by the Vice President for Enrollment Management—a priority that uses up any money or time left over for the preferred name and gender issue.

Mr. David Miller, Director, Administrative and Academic Computer Services: Mr. Miller has been employed at Eastern State for over 25 years. His role at the institution includes software and programming support for academic computing, student information systems, classroom management products, payroll, and other business systems software. Mr. Miller manages several programmers and staff members who are assigned to internal "clients" in the institution. This includes a programmer assigned to the registrar's office.

Miller has the reputation as someone who "gets things done." Miller has heard of student requests to change the student information system to accommodate preferred name and gender but cannot make a move until officially requested by his client, the registrar. If asked, he can assign programming staff to make the change.

Lee Alexander, Vice President of Student Government Association: A senior at Eastern State, Lee is currently the vice president of the SGA after being an active member in the organization for the last three years. Lee identifies as transgender and has been advocating for transgender issues for years.

Dr. Pam Baker, Director, LGBT Student Services Office: Dr. Baker has been at the university for 25 years. She originally served as a counselor in the Student Counseling Office and was hired as the director of the LGBT Student Services Office when it was first established. As the founding director of the office, Baker built the program from scratch. Dr. Baker is an outspoken advocate for LGBT issues.

Dr. Melinda Santos, Professor, Secondary Education Program: Dr. Santos is a faculty member in the College of Education. She teaches in a masters program in interdisciplinary studies as well as her primary affiliation with the secondary education program. She has been active regarding diversity including a term as the chairperson of the President's Commission on Racial Justice. Because of her past work on diversity, Pam Baker asked and gained permission to nominate Santos to the President's Commission on LGBTQA Issues. Santos agreed to be appointed.

Dr. Victoria Steele, President, Faculty Senate: Dr. Steele is currently serving a two-year term as president of the Faculty Senate. A history professor in the College of Liberal Arts, Dr. Steele is an active member of the Women's Faculty Caucus. She is in tune with women's issues through editing several academic publications regarding women in history. Dr. Steele has used queer theory in the classroom and works with several students who identify as transgender. She is widely recognized as an ally to the LGBT community.

Questions to Consider

- What are the mechanisms for determining policies regarding gender on college campuses?
- How does the use of legal rather than preferred name reinforce organizational heteronormativity?
- How, if at all, can the different approaches to feminist theory provide arguments for advancing the preferred name and pronoun project?

History of the Preferred Name and Preferred Gender Issue

For the last 15 years through individual and student organizational advocacy, students had been asking the Eastern State president and provost to enable transgender students to list their preferred name and gender on class rosters and advisor sheets. Transgender students argued that having their legal rather than their preferred name on these two university documents placed them in an unsafe situation in class. When attendance was called, the legal name called by the professor may not match the gender identity or expression of the student. An affirmative answer to the roll call either entailed the transgender student "outing" themselves to the entire class or individually, if they approached the professor after class to have their presence noted on the roll.

Students further argued that gender, as a socially constructed identity, should not be assumed for any student. The inclusion of a preferred gender on the class rosters and advisor lists would make a strong statement about the institution's commitment to transgender students specifically, and gender variant students generally.

Over 15 years, through student-generated petitions, letters to the provost and president, and resolutions to the SGA, students advocated for a system of preferred name and gender. In one case, a masters student who identified as transgender wrote his thesis on the topic. Despite this advocacy and verbal support from several presidents and provosts, no action was taken by the registrar's office.

Questions to Consider

- How is gender expression and gender identity supported or not supported on the campuses with which you are familiar?
- How does the idea of fluid identities correspond with the preferred name project?
- How might gender neutrality be practiced on college campuses?

Request to a Faculty Member

After years of trying to affect the change in the student information system to use preferred name and gender, Dr. Baker approached Melinda Santos about becoming involved. Baker wanted Santos to use her influence as a faculty member to kickstart the change. Santos agreed to help with the situation and set about determining a strategy. She decided that a good option would be to approach the Vice President for Enrollment Management with evidence of the last 15 years of requests and activism by students and the Office of LGBT Student Services. To Santos's surprise, the vice president agreed with Santos who received assurances that the registrar would be directed to undertake the project that became dubbed the "Preferred Name and Pronoun Project."

Questions to Consider
- What types of inequality are emerging in this case?
- How can you apply the concept of "ideal or universal worker" to this case? In what ways are transgender students "ideal students"? Not considered "ideal students"?
- What obligations does the university have (including laws) to assure the equality and safety of transgender students?

A Task Force is Formed

The Vice President for Enrollment Management directed the registrar to form a task force to undertake the Preferred Name and Pronoun Project. Several members of the task force adopted roles to effect the change. Melinda Santos agreed to present the issue to the Executive Committee of the Faculty Senate and work with that group and others to pave the way for the change. David Miller was to free up resources and make a programmer available to make the necessary software changes in the student information system. Lee Alexander took on the task of crafting language for the LGBT Student Services' and registrar's websites to explain the policy. Pam Baker provided the expertise and knowledge about transgender issues, gender expression, and gender identity so that any change would be in keeping with student needs. John James was the chair of the task force and provided valuable information about the implications of the preferred name change. Most important was the process of considering how students' legal names were used (e.g., listed in the university directory, used to assign residence hall rooms, listed on the student's bill and grades).

The task force would need to consider the many circumstances when the preferred name and gender could be used and when a legal name would be required (e.g., diploma, final transcript). The task force members agreed that the policy and effort should remain transgender focused through the language used in the policy and other means. Although they realized that other students would use the procedure (e.g., students who used their middle name; international students), they wanted to ensure that transgender students were the focus of the effort.

Questions to Consider
- How was connective leadership used in this case?
- How was direct, achieving leadership used in this case?
- What elements, if any, of the web structure do you see in this case?

Meeting with the Faculty Senate

Dr. Santos and Mr. James met with the Faculty Senate Executive Committee to apprise them of the change and solicit their input about how this change in policy could work. Santos had met with Dr. Steele in advance to discuss the change and provide her with a summary of the last 15 years of activism and requests regarding this issue.

Santos and James summarized the Preferred Name and Pronoun Project for the Executive Committee and opened the floor to questions. Faculty Senate President Steele voiced her support of the project saying: "We want to eliminate that moment in the classroom when transgender students have to out themselves when their legal name is called. We want to use the name that reflects how they are expressing their gender." Surprisingly, the Executive Committee was wholeheartedly in favor of the change. Faculty on the committee related stories of discomfort when they outed a student. They agreed that the situation caused an unsafe situation for transgender students. One faculty member was particularly vocal about the need for the change. As a parent of a transgender son, the faculty member gave the opinion that a name is a very personal issue. This faculty member believed the institution should do all it could to enable students to express gender as they saw fit and proclaimed that the more faculty could create a just and safe environment, the better off they all were.

Shortly after their meeting with the Faculty Senate Executive Committee, Santos and James met with the Council of Deans. This group was made up of the provost, associate provosts, and college and school deans. The task force members were again surprised by the overwhelming support of the deans. In addition to expressions of support, the deans wanted to know when a similar system of preferred name could be instituted for faculty and staff. They were aware of transgender employees for whom the administrative and human resources information systems raised similar issues as those encountered by students.

Questions to Consider

- How does the change to a preferred name and pronoun reflect a traditionally feminist ethic of care?
- How does the Preferred Name and Pronoun Project work to dismantle the marginalization of transgender students?
- In what ways does the Preferred Name and Pronoun Project render transgender students visible? In what ways does it render them invisible?

A Joint Resolution

Lee Alexander worked with the SGA and Dr. Steele (a professor with whom Lee had coincidentally taken several honors classes) on a joint resolution from the SGA and Faculty Senate. The resolution was written by Lee and took the following form:

JOINT RESOLUTION WITH SGA AND FACULTY SENATE

Whereas: The Eastern State University Board of Trustees voted unanimously to amend the non-discrimination clause to include gender identity and expression to read:

The University therefore prohibits discrimination on the basis of unlawful criteria such as race, color, religion, national or ethnic origin, age, sex, sexual orientation, marital status, disability, or gender identity or expression, as those terms are defined under applicable law, in admitting students to its programs and facilities and in administering its admissions and educational policies, scholarship and loan programs, athletic programs, and other institutionally administered activities made available to students at the University.

Whereas: The Faculty Senate and Student Government Association recognize and honor members of the Eastern State University community who advocated for a change in preferred name procedure over the last 15 years.

Be It Resolved:

- *The Student Government Association and Faculty Senate demonstrate support for the preferred name and pronoun initiative as administered through the Registrar's Office,*
- *Urge faculty and administrators to embrace these changes, and*
- *Work in concerted fashion and with all due haste to change the policy and academic systems to accommodate transgender students who choose to express their preferred name and pronoun.*

Questions to Consider

- How does the Preferred Name and Pronoun Project enact the sentiments of Eastern State University's non-discrimination clause?
- What evidence of collaborative and connected leadership do you see in the actions taken by the SGA and Faculty Senate?
- Discuss the non-discrimination clause. What issues of identity does it include? What issues does it exclude? What would you change?

Implementation of the Change

As with any policy change of the magnitude of the Preferred Name and Pronoun Project, a variety of issues were raised with its implementation. Numerous questions were asked that needed to be resolved in order for the change to take place.

- Where should the web page summarizing the policy be housed? The Office of LGBT Student Services or the registrar's page? How would students find this page during a search on the university's website?
- What name, legal or preferred, would be used by the Student Health Center?
- How would residence life integrate these changes into their computer information systems?
- Would the preferred name be automatically used on the data chip or magnetic strip on the student's ID card? If not, would the student's legal name come up when they used the recreation center and other facilities?
- Would the student's legal name continue to be used on documents accessed by the college and school student services staff?
- What about gender-specific student awards and honors, leadership awards, and other items through the Office of Student Activities? Would a student's preferred pronoun be listed on the gendered student lists generated to determine the awards?

Questions to Consider

- How might you go about tackling the issues raised in the questions listed above? What other issues can you anticipate during this type of policy change?

- What other institutional policies reflect heterosexist norms and assumptions?
- What policy issues and concerns might be raised if a preferred name and pronoun system were instituted for faculty and staff?

Safety and Symbolism

After months of deliberation, computer programming, editing, and decision making, the preferred name and pronoun policy was implemented in the student information system. The task force celebrated with a reception during which they invited transgender students to attend. Several students were present; they expressed their gratitude for the change, and emphasized the safer classroom environment that was created through implementation of the policy. In addition to the practical elements of the policy change, symbolic elements were also evident. Students noted that the change indicated support for the LGBT community as a whole, and transgender students specifically. The allocation of resources through staff time and effort symbolically and practically indicated the importance of the transgender community to Eastern State.

Despite its successes, several problems remained that blocked the implementation of a complete system of preferred names and pronouns. The residence life computer information system, which received data from admissions records, was out of sync with any name changes effected after the data upload. Although the preferred names could be used internally on course rosters and advisors' lists, "official" documents such as diplomas and transcripts were required to indicate a student's legal name. The policy was often confusing for students who found it difficult to navigate and use.

CONCLUSION

The civil and human rights of transgender students continue to be recognized by many institutions. While many states and jurisdictions continue to denounce the rights of transgender people, other institutions such as colleges and universities are continuing their efforts to include this population as full members of the community. A change to include the preferred name and pronoun in the student information system may be a first but important step in signaling the eventual full acceptance of this historically marginalized group into college and university life.

6

INSTITUTIONAL THEORY

If one would change the rules of the game ... the choices made by the players would be different. (Immergut, 1998, p. 13)

INTRODUCTION

According to institutionalization theory, institutions (e.g., the state, family, international political orders, democracy, capitalism) are "supraorganizational patterns of activity rooted in material practices and symbolic systems by which individuals and organizations produce and reproduce their material lives and render their experiences meaningful" (Thornton & Ocasio, 2008, p. 101).

This chapter discusses institutional theory (also called institutionalization theory) in the context of college and university functioning and structure. Emerging from political science, the institutional theory topics of interest to higher education include isomorphism, organizational choice and decision making, human agency, and the influence of larger institutions (e.g., state governments, higher education coordinating boards, federal government). The historical role of institutional theory

> has been to explain the powerful capacity of the environment to promote the similarities among organizations, and implies that the isomorphic process increases the stability of organizations over the long term and thus improves their odds for survival. (Bastedo, 2004, p. 3)

In higher education, institutional theory can explain how colleges and universities come to resemble each other even when the organizations under comparison are notably different. Over-arching institutional factors such as state licensure requirements, credit hour rules, federal policies, and cultural norms drive higher education organizations to adopt similar programs, majors, and practices.

In the context of the institutional theory discussed in this chapter, the word *organization* describes colleges and universities. The word *institution* describes larger entities, external to the organization, that exert influence through policies, rules, and cultural norms. In other words, "institutions are broadly understood as 'the rules of the game' that direct and circumscribe organizational behavior" (Kraatz & Block, 2008, p. 2).

POLITICAL SCIENCE AS A FOUNDATION FOR INSTITUTIONAL THEORY

Institutional theory was introduced by political scientists to explain the ways that broader cultural, political, social, and environmental factors shaped organizations. Institutionalization defines a process through which patterns set by forces external to the organization are adopted as taken-for-granted patterns or ways of being.

DiMaggio and Powell (1983) outlined external institutional forces that reproduced structures in coercive, normative, and mimetic ways. Coercive forces in a higher education context include political pressures and state regulation. Normative forces include the influence of the professions and the cultural force of education. Mimetic factors include the "habitual, taken-for-granted responses to circumstances of uncertainty" (Powell, 2007, p. 2). Institutions such as governments, state coordinating boards, foundations, or public opinion reproduce patterns that become normative (Powell, 2007). Three forms of institutional theory, old, new, and neo, have evolved since the introduction of the theory in the 1970s and 1980s (Powell, 2007).

Old Institutional Theory

Old institutional theory held that institutional influence could be understood through the data point of organizational behavior (Immergut, 1998). The observable behavior of a university's board of trustee members, for example, could provide insight into the influence of extra-organizational institutions (e.g., state coordinating boards). Old institutional theorists analyzed behavior to explain how organizations are influenced by their external environment. The term "isomorphism" was used by these theorists to explain how organizations are influenced by institutional forces and come to resemble one another. Colleges become universities. Student life innovations are adopted across institutions. Management practices become ubiquitous across higher education systems. Universities within state systems have characteristics notably recognizable as belonging to that system of education.

New Institutional Theory

New institutional theorists explored the ways that organizations are shaped by, and operate with, competitive and cooperative exchanges with other organizations and institutions (Powell, 2007). Rejecting the old institutional theory idea that organizations fashion a homogeneous response to institutional pressures, new institutional theorists sought to account for the diversity of responses observed in organizational studies. The old institutional concept of isomorphism was rejected because theorists no longer believed that organizations simply responded in homogenous ways to institutional forces. Instead, organizations with differing histories, resources, and approaches could respond in disparate ways to the same institutional forces. Because "institutions change over time, are not uniformly taken-for-granted, have effects that are particularistic, and are challenged as well as hotly contested" (Dacin, Goodstein, & Scott, 2002, p. 45), new institutional theory expanded ideas beyond isomorphism and homogeneity.

The awareness that organizations respond differently to the same or similar institutional pressures ushered in the concept of institutional pluralism. Organizations may respond differently to the same external institutional pressures because they are shaped by actors of different identities who then shape a pluralistic environment. This concept is particularly apt for U.S. higher education that has, for example, numerous racial and ethnic identities, diverse gender identities, a multiplicity of programs, and wide-ranging degrees of quality.

New institutional theorists rejected the old institutional theory idea that observed behavior was the basic data point for organizational analysis. Organizational change became a fruitful source of analysis and research; a place where the dynamics of institutional pressures, including power, could be readily observed.

Neo-Institutional Theory

Neo-institutional theorists returned to the isomorphic and homogenizing ideas of old institutional theory to posit that organizations are embedded in wider social and political environments that shape practices and structures. The normative demands from those extra-organizational environments were theorized to be influential, even coercive.

> Neo-institutional theorists proposed that formal organizational structure reflected not only technical demands and resource dependencies, but was also shaped by institutional forces, including rational myths, knowledge legitimated through the educational system and by the professions, public opinion, and the law. (Powell, 2007, p. 1)

ASSUMPTIONS OF INSTITUTIONAL THEORY

From a political science perspective, institutional theory includes several assumptions.

- Context is an essential consideration for the analysis of organizational action and change.
- Institutions in which organizations are embedded will exercise influence that enable and constrain action.
- Institutions are created, shaped, and re-shaped through human action.
- Uni-causality has insufficient explanatory power to understand decision making and policy making.
- Choices regarding decision making and policy making in organizations cannot be traced to one cause.

Greenwood, Oliver, Sahlin, and Suddaby (2008) suggested several ways that institutional theory can explain the behavior and similar characteristics of organizations. They posited that institutional contexts influence organizations including beliefs about appropriate conduct. This characteristic is evident in higher education when colleges and universities adopt practices congruent with viewpoints from society in general as well as the national system of higher education about what colleges and universities should look like and how they should be organized and administered. These authors also suggested that organizations with unclear technologies and difficult to assess outputs are particularly affected by institutional pressures. As advanced by the organized anarchy model (see Chapter 7), colleges and universities are characterized by unclear technologies. The ongoing debate about how to measure students' educational gains points to the difficulty of accurate assessment. In order to obtain social approval, legitimacy, and eventual survival, organizations, including colleges and universities, become congruent with their institutional context. Higher education observers can see this mechanism at work as institutions establish honors colleges, residential learning communities, and other programs and services that engender approval and legitimacy. Without these initiatives, many of which are done in the name of successfully competing with rival and aspirant institutions, the college would not survive. Greenwood et al. (2008) further suggested that if conformity to institutional pressures conflicted with beliefs about efficiency, ceremonial gestures could give the appearance of compliance.

As with any theoretical foundation, political science in the context of institutional theory has its strengths and weaknesses (see Table 6.1).

The institutional theory used by higher education theorists and discussed in this chapter derives predominantly from old and neo- institutional theory including the topics of institutional logics, homogeneity and isomorphism, organizational choice, human agency, deinstitutionalization, and the influence of suprainstitutional organizations.

METAPHOR

A metaphor to envision institutional theory is a bull's eye made up of concentric circles. The college or university is at the center of the bull's eye embedded in a number of nested institutions (see Figure 6.1). A community college, for example, may be located in a city that exerts pressure on the college through local ordinances, fees in lieu of taxes, or zoning restrictions. The next circle could be occupied by the state coordinating board that issues rules about accreditation. The state could inhabit the next circle and exert its influence through budget allocations and licensure regulations for education, counseling, and various academic programs. The federal government could occupy the final circle and exert influence through Department of Education financial aid, sexual assault, and civil rights policies. The circles are not equal in size or influence but relative to others as circumstances change and shift.

Table 6.1 Strengths and Weaknesses of the Political Science Perspective for Higher Education

Strengths	Weaknesses
Enables institutional actors to understand societal forces that enable and constrain action.	Can imply determinism and lack of ability to exercise choice.
Defines human agency and inspires action toward organizational transformation.	Power differences at various organizational and institutional levels can engender hopelessness.
Provides an in-depth explanation of power.	Can overstate the influence of supraorganizational institutions such as state governments, non-governmental institutions, and cultural institutions.

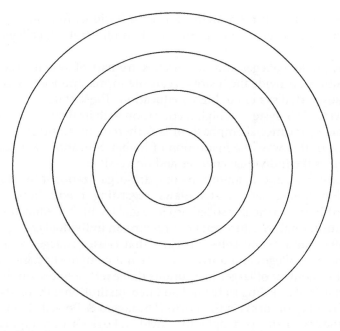

Figure 6.1 Concentric Circles Structure

STRUCTURE

As a theory rather than a model or frame, institutional theory does not adhere to or suggest a particular structure. Any organizational structure, hierarchy, web, or circle could be influenced by the institutions in which the organization is embedded. Because county, state, and federal governments are organized as hierarchies, that pyramid structure may provide inspiration regarding some structural elements at play when considering institutional theory. In hierarchies, power is progressively concentrated in fewer people as one moves up the levels in a hierarchy. Organizational actors at the higher levels of the hierarchy (or external circles in the bull's eye metaphor) have more opportunities to exert their influence on a college or university.

MAJOR CONCEPTS, CHARACTERISTICS, AND PRINCIPLES

Institutional Logics

People in organizations respond to their understanding of the rules: rules about identity, structure, and decision making. These rules are the institutional logic upon which action, decision, and basic aspects of organizational function are based. Institutional logics relate to organizational fields which are, in the context of this discussion, "those organizations that, in the aggregate, constitute a recognized area of institutional life" (DiMaggio & Powell, 1983, p. 148). U.S. colleges and universities exist within an organizational field circumscribed by societal expectations and cultural norms shaping what a genuine college looks like, how academic quality is judged, and what a family can expect from their investment of tuition dollars. These institutional logics made up of expectations and norms shape the structures available for organizational functioning (e.g., presence of a board of trustees, bureaucratic approach for administrators, collegial approach for faculty).

For example, public colleges and universities are part of systems (i.e., institutions). States, as institutions, provide the history, requisite forms, and ways of operating across a public, state-supported system of higher education. Those state systems shape and are shaped by the wider U.S. system of higher education with its distinct characteristics (e.g., funding tendencies, vocational emphasis or lack thereof, meaning of a college degree in society at large). In this way, the institution of higher education, writ large, becomes a pattern that shapes the individual colleges and universities.

The rules, meanings, and assumptions of extra-organizational institutions (e.g., the higher education public sector, state laws regarding credit hours) become self-reproducing within the particular social order (e.g., U.S. higher education system). This superseding institutional structure applies pressure on individual colleges and universities through laws, culture, and rules; pressure that causes colleges and universities to conform to a norm. Colleges and universities are not completely stand-alone organizations but exist in a context of larger institutions that exert pressure on them to conform to certain standards. According to the old and neo-institutional theorists, isomorphism rather than a diversity of forms is the norm (DiMaggio & Powell, 1983). "Institutional logics provide the organizing principles for a field.... Logics are an important theoretical construct because they help to explain connections that create a sense of common purpose and unity within an organizational field" (Reay & Hinings, 2009, p. 629).

Colleges and universities, as a long established organizational form with extensive networks of internal and external stakeholders, are particularly prone to the institutional contexts and subsequent logics concerning structure, identity, and action. These organizations must conform to the externally applied pressures or risk significant resistance, even closure. If a college does not obey the institutional rules about what it is to look like, students may not recognize it as an institution of higher learning, trustees may urge administrators to take a more conforming course of action, and external funding sources may reject the organization as a fitting place in which to invest.

Homogeneity and Isomorphism

Institutional isomorphism is a "phenomenon by which organizations lose some of their distinctive characteristics in terms of behavior, structure, and culture, and come to resemble one another" (Oliveira, 2004, p. 18). Colleges and universities come to resemble each other more and more as time and norms influence the organization. Institutions of higher education, like any organization within a particular field or area, move toward homogenization. Homogenization is driven by isomorphism defined as "a constraining process that forces one unit in a population to resemble other units that face the same set of environmental conditions" (DiMaggio & Powell, 1983, p. 149). Three types of isomorphism are discussed in institutional theory and drive organizational change: coercive, mimetic, and normative.

Coercive Isomorphism

Applied through force, persuasion, or invitation, coercive isomorphism achieves homogenization by, among other mechanisms, conforming to regulations, standard practices, and staff advocacy for particular ways of operating. "Coercive isomorphism results from both formal and informal pressures exerted on organizations by other organizations upon which they are dependent and by cultural expectations in the society within which organizations function" (DiMaggio & Powell, 1983, p. 150). Coercive isomorphism occurs when state coordinating boards and accreditation agencies establish criteria, standards, and expectations that drive institutions to look more alike than different.

A significant isomorphic mechanism for colleges and universities in any country is the presence of a common legal system and shared language. Some efforts to conform may be ritualistic or ceremonial yet still yield the result of shaping the institution toward the norm. Similar requirements for tax reporting and obtaining funding drive common methods that then become institutionalized within the organization (DiMaggio & Powell, 1983).

Mimetic Isomorphism

The second type of isomorphism is mimetic. Modeling is the most common method used to drive the mimetic form of isomorphism. Colleges seek to become universities, universities look toward their aspirant peers for inspiration, and less competitive colleges turn to Ivy League institutions for meaning. Modeling an institution after a more successful one reduces environmental uncertainty. Borrowed practices can be obtained from direct observation of the modeled institution, advice from a consultant, or through educational professional associations. The modeled institution need not realize it has been copied for the mimetic isomorphism to occur.

Normative Isomorphism

The third type of isomorphism, normative, works primarily through professionalism. Through formal education and feeder institutions, professional association involvement, and the development of professional networks, faculty and administrators in higher education institutions adopt practices consistent with other professionals in their field. As the norms upon which these professionals act become established, they come to resemble others in the field. A good example of this are student affairs professionals in higher education who informally adhere to standard titles, a common language, and other behavior norms. DiMaggio and Powell (1983) argue that these professional norms lead members of an organizational field to become nearly interchangeable. Normative isomorphism can work, in particular, through hiring decisions that use professional norms to define positions and select candidates. While professionals in the same organization (e.g., student affairs staff and faculty) may differ significantly from one another, they resemble professionals employed in similar roles at other institutions. A vice president for student affairs may fill a very different role than an English professor but both have significant resemblances and roles to professionals in the same position at another college.

Organizational Choice

Isomorphism and the pressures it exerts on organizational structure and ways of operating are closely related to organizational choice. A university may respond to coercive, mimetic, and normative sources of isomorphism to guide institutional choices. These choices may be motivated by efforts to reduce uncertainty, increase efficiency, spur growth, achieve institutional aspirational goals, and raise the institution's status. Organizations such as colleges and universities that include a large professionally trained labor force will be driven primarily by status competition. Organizational prestige and resources are key elements in attracting professionals. This process encourages homogenization as organizations seek to ensure that they can provide the same benefits and services as their competitors. (DiMaggio & Powell, 1983, p. 154)

The institutional structure, whether formed through isomorphism or as a result of a process resulting in a unique structural form, simultaneously enables and constrains action (Giddens, 1979, 1984). In one sense, larger societal institutional structures (e.g., language, rule of law, bureaucracy) enable action upon which choices are made. At the same time, societal and institutional values, mores, and ways of operating constrain or limit the range of choices. Because structures such as institutional logics enable and constrain, institutional theorists are often optimistic about the potential for humans to change and transform their organizations. Human agency, imagination, and existing structural forms are resources available for that transformation. "While institutions constrain action they also provide sources of agency and change. The contradictions inherent in the differentiated set of institutional logics provide individuals, groups, and organizations with cultural resources for transforming individual identities, organizations, and society" (Thornton & Ocasio, 2008, p. 101).

The resources provided by institutional logics contain significant material that can be used during organizational choice and decision making. Driven by competition and cooperation, colleges and universities use models and norms provided by institutional logics to change their ways of operating. Originally thought of by theorists as a way to improve bureaucratic efficiency in organizations, organizational change, from an institutionalization perspective, can improve the institution so that it can successfully compete with both similar and different higher education institutions. "Organizations in a structured field ... respond to an environment that consists of other organizations responding to their environment, which consists of organizations responding to an environment of organizations' responses" (DiMaggio & Powell, 1983, p. 149).

And on and on the process proceeds.

Human Agency

Organizations, including colleges and universities, change and develop through actors' actions as they make choices within the context of the institutions in which the organization is embedded. Through human cultural action, institutions as archetypes convey the rules, assumptions, and classifications upon which organizational structure is built. Commitment to and interaction with these institutional social structures and beliefs create stability and integration. Organizations are "institutionalized" when interaction, adaptation, and ways of operating coalesce into structures modeled after the all-encompassing institutional structures that exist in the environment. Through institutionalization, organizations take on a particular character, reach a certain competence, or, unhappily, adopt practices that interfere with their ability to perform. According to Selznick (1996), leaders must monitor the costs and benefits of institutionalization within organizations including organizational structure, institutional norms and ideologies, and myths and rituals.

Although human action within organizations is theoretically unfettered and open to the imagination, organizational actors rarely perform in entirely new and inventive ways. Instead, they fashion their actions on the existing examples of what behavior is acceptable, what has been used in the past, and the tried and true approaches to success.

Despite ideas about adherence to institutional logics and isomorphism that moves an organization closer to practices that advance its survival, institutional theorists reject the assumption that people are rational actors. Rationality is not assumed to be an explanation for organizational structure or action (Thornton & Ocasio, 2008). Rather than efficiency or some other rational goal, actors instead exercise their agency based on who and what they believe themselves and the organization to be (Olsen, 2001). Seen in this light, higher education faculty, stakeholders, and practitioners can better understand why some practices in organizations seem "right" albeit irrational. When organizational processes are not ordered as conventionally assumed, it does not mean that those processes are without logic (Olsen, 2001). The logic may be identity-based, cultural, or formed by habit rather than by rationality.

Deinstitutionalization

Although institutionalization drives homogeneity and change in the ways described above, organizations also go through a process of deinstitutionalization. Processes within the organizational field decay over time. Colleges and universities challenge institutional norms set by, for example, accrediting agencies as they begin "to question the legitimacy of a given practice" (Dacin et al., 2002, p. 46). As members and leaders within professional associations and other groups, they lead efforts to change norms and standard practices. When accepted practices no longer work with new generations of students, colleges and universities adapt. For U.S. higher education, student market demands, demographic shifts, economic changes, and environmental pressures cause norms to change from the bottom up. This process of adaptation filters into the larger institutional structure and deinstitutionalization occurs.

Deinstitutionalization of norms and practices may also proceed from adaptation of practices from other institutional fields such as business practices from corporations.

> Institutional change and deinstitutionalization may also be influenced by social pressures associated with differentiation of groups (for instance, increasing workforce diversity), the existence of heterogeneous divergent or discordant beliefs and practices ... and changes in laws or social expectations that might hinder the continuation of a practice. (Dacin et al., 2002, p. 47)

Without deinstitutionalization, organizations and their larger institutions would stagnate and fail to adapt to environment challenges.

STRENGTHS AND WEAKNESSES OF INSTITUTIONAL THEORY

Institutional theory has been criticized for what has been viewed as an overemphasis on homogeneity and the mechanisms that drive isomorphism (Dacin et al., 2002). "Organizations and managers are not sponges or pawns, but actors responding to challenges under the guidance of existing institutions" (Dacin et al., 2002, p. 50). From the perspective of this critique, human beings are not "cultural dopes" (Giddens, 1984) but agents capable of making decisions outside the realm of existing institutional structures. Humans exert their agency to adapt institutionally driven practices. They adapt the processes required by larger institutions and use their agency to modify practice for the local context. Entrepreneurship and innovation are alive in organizations as college and university faculty and staff use the resources provided to make change and shape practice.

But legitimacy must be a consideration when an organization seeks to change or innovate in ways different from the accepted institutional norms. "The creation, transformation, and diffusion of institutions require legitimacy, a condition whereby other alternatives are seen as less appropriate, desirable, or viable" (Dacin et al., 2002, p. 47). A college or university must have the organizational resources created through legitimacy to stray from the path provided by accepted practices sanctioned by the larger institutional structures. Institutions with legitimacy can experiment, challenge, and defy. Colleges and universities with less status usually conform to institutional forms that convey legitimacy.

The application of institutional theory to higher education contains strengths and weaknesses (see Table 6.2).

NEXT STEPS: BRINGING INSTITUTIONAL THEORY INTO CURRENT USE

The extensive literature of institutional theory in higher education (Bastedo, 2006a, 2006b, 2007, 2009a, 2009b, 2011, 2012) is ripe for a consideration of the work of Anthony Giddens (1979, 1984, 1993) as a way to expand the application of institutional theory to higher education.

The institutionalist perspective could be greatly enlarged if it were ready to make more than passing reference to Giddens. The structurationist conception of structural rules and resources offers a common framework for analyzing the disparate social influences—political, ethnic, domestic and professional—on managerial action. (Whittington, 1992, p. 703)

Table 6.2 Strengths and Weaknesses of Institutional Theory

Strengths	Weaknesses
Places higher education in the full context of institutions, which shape organizational forms.	Overstates the power of institutional influences and understates the power of human innovation.
Allows identification of elements that enable and constrain action.	Provides a more rational explanation of organizational change than is currently warranted with the fast pace of technological innovation.
Provides a model with which to understand organizational change and adaptation.	Implies a homogeneity of action among organizational members that may understate the power of individual thought and action.
Illustrates why colleges and universities are so driven by measures of reputation, status, and legitimacy.	Can imply determinism due to the over-reaching influence of larger institutional structures and systems (e.g., the state, social class).

Space does not allow for a complete discussion of Giddens' extensive and complex theories. Three concepts, structuralization, human agency, and choice, are discussed here with suggestions for their application to higher education organizations. The intention is to pique the interest of readers who can explore his theories in more detail.

Structuralization

According to Giddens, structure is not a concrete, tangible entity but an intangible entity formed by humans through their dynamic action and present only for a moment in time. Structure is not concretely real but built and made "real" through human action. Although structures appear concrete, in reality they exist only in temporarily fleeting moments. Through mutually shaping means, the human action that builds structure and the resulting structures *"presuppose one another"* (Giddens, 1979, p. 53, italics in the original). Action and structure exist in a chicken-and-egg dialectic such that one cannot assume that action came before structure or structure before action. This dynamic, ever-changing, ever-recreated process is called structuralization.

Through human action, structure is reproduced, recreated, and reformed. Rarely, if ever, perfectly reproduced, slight to extreme adaptations in reproduction mean that structure is never precisely replicated. This imperfect reproduction introduces dynamism and change into the structuralization process. The rules and resources—including the traditions and customs of culture—that are employed through human action to recreate structure, appear real and fixed. In reality, human action created structure; human action can transform structure.

While, theoretically, humans can alter structures through their action, realistically the rules and resources within the structure simultaneously enable and constrain human action.

> Social systems are constituted by the activities of human agents, enabled and constrained by the social structural properties of these systems. These structures define both the rules—techniques, norms or procedures—guiding action, and the resources—authoritative and allocative—empowering action. (Whittington, 1992, p. 695)

Socio-economic classes, prevailing attitudes, laws, and cultural traditions are among the rules and resources within a structure. These provide models upon which human action is enabled or constrained. As a model, structure provides the resources with which human actors can act. Their action replicates existing structures and builds new ones. These same rules and resources embody constraining forces. They provide the authority to restrict human action and correct and even punish those who do not adhere to the structure. The existence of structure upon which humans act can limit the imagination and, at worst, perpetuate attitudes and beliefs (e.g., racism, sexism, homophobia) that limit human potential.

While the mechanism of action and structure creates possibilities for human life, one must be careful to avoid determinism, a criticism launched at institutional theorists. If structure is immutable, then these social mechanisms determine human action. Human agency has no place in a society where structure is pre-determined and action conforms to the rules of those pre-existing structures. In this sense, humans are taken out of the process of building structures because the structures are set in advance by nature or some other external mechanism.

Caution must also be exercised when speculating about the infinite potential of human action. If the constraining forces of structure (e.g., oppression, poverty, lack of educational opportunity) are not included in the analysis, it could seem as if any limitations on a human being are due to the individual's shortcomings or lack of agency. When reliance is placed on human agency to shape and re-shape structure, seemingly at will, it can be assumed that all human action is possible. In reality, forces such as oppression limit human action. Giddens was not so naïve as to think that human agency was unfettered by power, class, and other influences. Not all human action is possible and not all individuals are afforded the full range of human agency.

If one applies the theory of structuralization to organizations such as colleges and universities, one can imagine that these organizations fashion themselves through human action using structural properties borrowed from the wider society (Whittington, 1992). The hierarchical structure of a college administration may be "borrowed" from the bureaucratic configuration of the class system in society. The class structure and resources available to different classes is reflected in higher education financial aid policies, scholarship allocation, and admissions procedures. The long-established structure of public/private control, state regulation of degree requirements, and other rules and techniques define and limit the available structural configurations of colleges and universities. Although dramatic change does occur (e.g., the introduction of for-profit institutions, virtual campuses), humans tend to reproduce the prevailing structures.

Human Agency and Choice

Human actors are not confined to the influence of only one structure (e.g., the national system of U.S. higher education) but live within and are identified through a plurality of structures (e.g., personal identity by race and class; values advanced by their chosen professional field or discipline). Humans make choices about which of the many available rules they will follow. Because these rules and techniques are constructed by human action, human agency can be exerted to transform the rules and build different configurations of institutions under different sets of rules. Human agency can be exerted through deliberate and knowing ways that subvert the rules. But, humans are agents only insomuch as they have the power to make a difference. "So long as actors retain the capacity to refuse ... they remain agents" (Whittington, 1992, p. 696). In other words, human agents have the ability to exercise choice.

Whittington describes two forms of human agency. The first emanates from the many rules that exist within a particular social system or organization (e.g., the higher education rule about institutional control defines public and private affiliation—both are choices). The second form of human agency emanates from the contradictions and possibilities that arise through the many organizations to which actors are affiliated (Whittington, 1992). Organizational members may take on rules and traditions based on class, ethnicity, academic discipline, and a myriad of other associations. Reconciling the different rules results in human agency and choice.

Choice is increasingly evident in modern life due to the expansion of participation and increased media exposure. Modern living provides increased opportunities for human agency through the proliferation of organizations in which all humans are involved. Even when individuals feel powerless to create change within society, collective action through organizations creates numerous opportunities for structural and systemic change. Democratic voting is an excellent example of this dynamic. While one individual vote may not have the power to change the direction of a government, the collective action of many voters can have that effect.

The promise of Giddens' work lies in his theorizing that additional structures exist in contrast to the Western management structures that prioritize capitalist goals. Through the contradictions introduced by human agent participation in structures (e.g., religious institutions, groups with a social justice mission), the possibility exists that capitalist rules and structures need not be entirely dominant. Art, social change, cultural growth, and other goals may exist simultaneously alongside profit, growth, and the overuse of environmental resources. This approach is particularly important in higher education where, for example, growth versus non-growth, corporate approaches versus traditional academic priorities, and vocationalism versus liberal arts present contradictory approaches to college and university management. College and university members' participation in their academic disciplines and professional fields, personal experiences, diverse backgrounds, and other social structures present a myriad of choices regarding priorities and management. Overarching institutions such as higher education coordinating boards and state governments need not be deterministic but can be shaped by human actors who may oppose recommendations, rules, and approaches they judge as incongruent with, and detrimental to, the goals of higher education generally and a college or university in particular. Giddens' theories on structuralization, human agency, and power provide a framework within which those choices can be considered.

CONCLUSIONS

Institutional theory can be used to explore the ways in which wider societal structures influence the makeup and functioning of colleges and universities. Particularly by incorporating Giddens' theory of structuralization and human agency, theorists can explore the ways in which higher education both changes and remains the same. The theory provides substantial theoretical insights into why colleges and universities take actions resulting in isomorphism. In a closely aligned system of higher education such as the one that exists in the United States, understanding the mechanisms as to how institutions come to resemble one another is essential. An aspect of this examination can include the ways in which this isomorphism both expands and limits opportunities for students regarding access, academic programs, and future success.

Questions for Discussion

- "How do organizational actors manage the rivalry of co-existing and competing institutional logics?" (Reay & Hinings, 2009, p. 629)
- What institutional structures drive organizational change in colleges and universities?
- How do institutions that are external to the college or university exert coercive influence on the institutional structure and practices?
- How does institutional theory help to explain the inclusion and exclusion of various cultural groups within U.S. higher education?
- How does institutional theory help to explain the retention rates of students of color and marginalized groups on college campuses?

Recommended Readings for Institutional Theory

Cai, Y., & Mehari, Y. (2015). The use of institutional theory in higher education research. In M. Tight & J. Huisman (Eds.), *Theory and method in higher education research* (pp. 1–25). Bingley, UK: Emerald Group Publishing.

Cheslock, J. J., Ortagus, J. C., Umbricht, M. R., & Wymore, J. (2016). The cost of producing higher education: An exploration of theory, evidence, and institutional policy. In M. B. Paulsen (Ed.), *Higher education: Handbook of theory and research* (pp. 349–392). New York: Springer International Publishing.

Dacin, M. T., Goodstein, J., & Scott, W. R. (2002). Institutional theory and institutional change: Introduction to the special research forum. *Academy of Management Journal, 45*(1), 45–56.

Fumasoli, T., & Huisman, J. (2013). Strategic agency and system diversity: Conceptualizing institutional positioning in higher education. *Minerva, 51*(2), 155–169.

Laden, B. V., Millem, J. F., & Crowson, R. L. (2000). New institutional theory and student departure. In J. Braxton (Ed.), *Reworking the student departure puzzle* (pp. 235–255). Nashville, TN: Vanderbilt University Press.

Tight, M. (2015). Theory development and application in higher education research: The case of academic drift. *Journal of Educational Administration and History, 47*(1), 84–99.

CASE: THE STATE VERSUS GRAND LAKES UNIVERSITY

This case demonstrates the ways in which institutional theory can be used to understand budget and policy priorities emanating from a state government. Any university or college is nested in a number of institutions that influence its operation, academic programs, and hiring practices. Laws and policies from state and federal governments, budgets determined by the state for public institutions, accreditation practices for the institution and its programs, and policy recommendations from academic non-profit organizations are a few examples of the ways that institutions influence one another. Institutional logics emerge from these institutions and shape the practices of colleges and universities. When institutional logics conflict, competition for control of the budget, curriculum, and mission is bound to result.

Current higher education reporting is filled with examples of the ways institutions (e.g., accreditation agencies, state and federal governments) exert influence on and power over the choices available to higher education institutions. In a time of budget cuts, competing priorities, and social change, the institutional logics from external institutions may be in opposition to organizational values and established ways of operating. "*When competing logics co-exist in an organizational field, actors guided by different logics may manage the rivalry by forming collaborations that maintain independence but support the accomplishment of mutual goals*" (Reay & Hinings, 2009, p. 645, italics in the original). To build collaborations in an attempt to manage competing institutional logics, Reay and Hinings (2009) suggest several strategies, which are adapted here for higher education.

1. Differentiate curricular decisions from other university decisions that may involve different institutional logics.
2. Seek informal input from faculty through faculty governance structures, college and school curricular committees, and faculty unions as part of decision making.
3. Encourage on- and off-campus groups to form coalitions to combat a common foe.
4. Combine forces with institutions outside the college or university to jointly innovate in experimental programs such as new majors and programs and research opportunities.

Through strategies that enable competing institutional logics to co-exist, disparate groups can keep their separate and distinct identities while finding common ground upon which to negotiate organizational choice.

========================= THE CASE =========================

The following case examines how faculty may discover common ground upon which to provide the business stimulation required by the state while simultaneously retaining their established role of controlling the curriculum.

Institutional Context

Grand Lakes University (a pseudonym) is a flagship university in a state well-known for its long-established and excellent higher education system. Grand Lakes enrolls 31,000 undergraduate and graduate students and boasts a highly developed research mission and close ties to the state. Having recently fallen on hard times, budget cuts over the last five years have taken their toll on the once great university. The current governor is a proponent of small government and has taken steps to change many long-standing higher education policies across the state. These include policies regarding state funding of higher education, tenure and tenured appointments, the Board of Regents, and faculty primacy over the academic mission.

Characters

Mr. Mark Patterson, Governor: Mr. Patterson became Governor after several terms as a state senator during which he served as chair of the Budget Committee. Entering his second term as Governor, Patterson was elected on a platform of reducing state government spending, increasing jobs within the state, and reforming several state-supported systems including health care, corrections, and higher education. Upon election to his second term, one of his first actions through his budget proposal was to support policies that called for the elimination of university programs that did not relate directly to job generation. Patterson vowed to redefine faculty tenure within the state system, decrease reliance on unions within the state's colleges and universities, and curtail faculty input in academic program and curricular decisions. His budget called for state colleges and universities, particularly the flagship Grand Lakes University, to become more actively involved in workforce training. Many in the Grand Lakes community decried the policy initiatives, believing that it meant a profound change in the university's mission and purposes.

Ms. Cheryl Mills, Board of Regents Member: Ms. Mills is a recent governor-appointed member of the University Board of Regents. Prior to her role on the Board, she was a staff member in the Patterson administration. Mills is widely viewed as being a proxy for Patterson on the Board of Regents. She is expected to follow his agenda and push for deep cuts in higher education spending and radically curtail faculty authority over the curriculum. Ms. Mills is an alumna of Grand Lakes University where she studied business administration. An outspoken critic of her alma mater, Mills believes that state higher education institutions should be run like the businesses they are. As multi-million dollar operations, business practices should guide the finances and policies of these institutions which are funded through state tax dollars. She has stated publicly that there is no place at state-funded higher education institutions for what she has dubbed "wasted majors." If academic programs are not associated with the governor's jobs initiation program, those programs should be eliminated.

Dr. Maxine Powell, Chancellor, Grand Lakes University: Dr. Powell has been Chancellor at Grand Lakes for 12 years. A veteran of the state's budget cuts, Dr. Powell has worked closely with faculty, the provost, and academic administrators to build a curriculum that has elements of the traditional liberal arts as well as professional education. As a result of the budget cuts, Grand Lakes has expanded its certificate, two-year degree, and online offerings. This approach has generated much needed tuition revenue but put them at odds with the three two-year colleges located within a 25-mile radius of Grand Lakes. Although Dr. Powell is concerned about mission drift from Grand Lakes University's research mission, the revenue is necessary for them to offset the budget cuts from the state.

Dr. Alton Carr, Professor, Ecological Engineering, and President, Faculty Union: Dr. Carr is a highly celebrated professor who has spent his entire career at Grand Lakes University. A recipient of numerous awards, Carr has a large and enthusiastic following of graduate students who work on his research projects. An activist by nature, Dr. Carr stepped in to be the faculty union president when the former president retired. Carr had been on the contract negotiation committee for the faculty union and had an excellent command of the intricacies of Grand Lake's budget. During the last round of contract negotiations, Carr was the primary spokesperson and advocate for concessions regarding increased faculty salaries to meet market rates, restoration of several tenure-track faculty lines, and contract language concerning academic freedom and tenure. Carr believes faculty are the only people able to judge the worthiness or unworthiness of academic programs. He is fond of saying, "the faculty own the curriculum," and defends his position resolutely.

Questions to Consider
- In what ways does the state influence a public university?
- What are some examples of the ways that state colleges and universities influence each other?
- What are some enablers and constrainers regarding faculty control of the curriculum?

The Governor's Budget

The latest budget proposal from Governor Patterson has Chancellor Powell concerned. She does not feel that the institution can sustain any more cuts. The strong workforce development approach of the budget is at odds with the traditional research mission of Grand Lakes. She believes that the research mission can be an incubator for businesses within the state. But no matter how often she makes this argument to the governor and state legislators, they do not seem to believe her. Dr. Powell has had the most difficulty convincing Board of Regents member Cheryl Mills. Mills believes that most of the research conducted at the University falls into the category of wasted effort and money. She believes that all research should be connected to the technology industry in the state, which is where growth is predicted to occur in the future. Mills argues that theoretical and basic research may be good for other institutions but not for Grand Lakes, which has more immediate issues.

Powell is due to return a phone call to Alton Carr. She knows that Dr. Carr has seen the budget proposal and will want to raise the concerns he has with the retrenchment of tenure and tenured positions.

Questions to Consider

- What actions could the Chancellor take to position the University in the eyes of the state and the state's Governor?
- How can you use the concept of coercive isomorphism to explain Governor Patterson's actions to change Grand Lakes University?
- What, in your eyes, would be an optimal relationship between a flagship university and the state in which it is located?

The Faculty's Position

Alton Carr's phone has not stopped ringing since the Governor released his budget proposal two days ago. Recently hired as well as long-standing faculty members are voicing their concern over the provisions regarding tenure in the Governor's budget proposal. Many consider this one more blow from a Governor and legislature intent on dismantling the tenure system within the University and across the state. They fear that their academic freedom will be in jeopardy from an administration that has expressed contempt for faculty.

In addition to the fears about tenure, faculty are concerned that the research mission of the University is shifting to a vocational one. Many believe that state jobs are important but feel their research is an incubator for jobs. Even the most basic research has industry and practical application. Unfortunately, those applications are not immediately obvious, a point lost on the Governor and some Board of Regents members.

Questions to Consider

- What measures of status and legitimacy exist for institutions of higher education?
- What choices are available to Dr. Carr and the faculty he represents?
- What factors enable and constrain the available choices?

Recruitment of New Faculty

The word is out about the Governor's plan to change the policy regarding tenure at the state's colleges and universities. Dr. Carr received several emails and phone calls about faculty candidates who have pulled out of searches due to uncertainty about their tenure status. Many candidates expressed concern that even if hired for tenure-track positions, any continuing erosion of tenure would threaten their academic freedom, create more reliance on contingent faculty, and place the institution's self-governance and policy mechanisms at risk. Deans suspended several faculty searches until more information is gained from the Governor and state legislature. There are rumors the Governor wants to build incentives into the higher education budget that reward contingent faculty hiring over tenure-track hiring. Until this situation is resolved, they do not want to hire a new faculty member who they cannot support.

In addition to the threats to tenure and academic freedom, deans are concerned that the ongoing budget cuts limit their ability to allocate start-up research dollars for new faculty. Without these incentives, they cannot compete for faculty with other state and private institutions which have a more favorable higher education climate.

Questions to Consider

- How does the concept of isomorphism relate to tenure?

- In what ways could (and would) you use coercive, mimetic, or normative isomorphism to explain faculty expectations regarding tenure?
- Explain the structural mechanisms that enable and constrain faculty searches in a time of contracting budgets.

Board of Regents Meeting

During a meeting of the Board of Regents, Dr. Carr saw an opportunity to take action against the policy recently handed down from the Governor in his budget proposal. By lobbying for time on the agenda, Carr offered a five-minute presentation on the importance of tenure and the social good including business opportunities resulting from research. Carr asked a number of faculty and students to attend the Board of Regents meeting as a show of support. Fifty people attended the meeting, held signs, and applauded when Carr made points about the importance of higher education. He took a few minutes of his presentation to discuss societal values related to higher education, how these values impact Grand Lakes University, and what the institution gives back to the state and society in general. He talked about the choices being made by the state regarding the institution, choices that effect the mission and goals of the University. He read testimony from faculty search committee chairs who related the difficulty they were having recruiting junior faculty members. Carr expressed concern that these promising new faculty would be unwilling to apply for positions at the University if their research, teaching, and service opportunities were limited. In fields that were highly competitive, fields directly related to state business opportunities, the difficulty in recruiting qualified faculty was particularly acute.

Questions to Consider

- What local, national, and international processes drive homogenization regarding faculty hiring?
- How might state policies regarding funding and support of the institutional mission impact faculty hiring?
- In what ways did Carr exercise human agency during his presentation to the Board of Regents?

Following Dr. Carr's presentation, Cheryl Mills requested that the Board of Regents go into executive session to discuss the personnel (i.e., faculty) issues raised through Carr's presentation. Behind closed doors, Ms. Mills expressed grave concern about the tenor of Carr's presentation, the actions taken by the faculty and student guests, and the veiled threats about future faculty hires. She saw the actions taken by the Governor and the Board of Regents as being in the best interests of the state and Grand Lakes University. Rather than being a threat to the institution, she saw the re-crafted mission as being more current. In her mind, new faculty would flock to an institution with such a forward-looking mission.

Questions to Consider

- What supraorganizational institutions are informing Mills' point of view?
- How can you use the concept of deinstitutionalization to describe the mission change being suggested at Grand Lakes University?
- How can institutional theory be used to understand the change occurring at Grand Lakes?

CONCLUSIONS

Higher education institutions do not exist in a vacuum but are embedded in institutions that impact their values and operations. Institutions such as state and federal governments and values adopted from the history of higher education, including tenure practices, shape the operations and choices made within any institution. Values gained from institutions external to a college or university have the potential to cause conflict regarding the choices being made within the institution and the pressures exerted from without.

Questions to Consider

- What are some examples of isomorphism that you have experienced in higher education?
- What behaviors continue in higher education that may be at odds with values promoted through larger institutions (e.g., governments)?
- What are the ways besides budget that institutions exert influence on a college or university?

7

ORGANIZED ANARCHY

The American college or university is a prototypic organized anarchy. It does not know what it is doing. Its goals are either vague or in dispute. Its technology is familiar but not understood. Its major participants wander in and out of the organization. These factors do not make a university a bad organization or a disorganized one; but they do make it a problem to describe, understand, and lead. (Cohen & March, 1986, p. 3)

More than one author has used the above quote by Cohen and March to poke fun at institutions of higher education. Colorful metaphors and tongue-in-cheek phrases aptly describe these organizations that many have found confusing. Though playful, Cohen and March put their finger on essential elements of modern higher education institutions. These organizations are paradoxical: familiar yet hard to describe, unpredictable though at times oddly rational, rooted in the past yet optimistically gazing into the future, traditional though educating many to anticipate change.

Organized anarchy is a theory outlined by Cohen and March (1986) in their book, *Leadership and Ambiguity.* These authors conducted their research on college presidents in the 1970s—research that yielded a particularly helpful perspective from which to understand higher education institutions. Several authors and theorists conflate Cohen and March's ideas about organized anarchies with the organizational concept of loosely coupled systems. The latter is an organizational theory with a set of theoretical characteristics (i.e., causation, typology, effects, compensations, and organizational outcomes) that are different from organized anarchies. The stance advanced by Orton and Weick (1990, p. 203) that "the concept of organizations as loosely coupled systems is widely used and diversely understood" is adopted here. Organized anarchies as structural forms may be loosely coupled but are not loosely coupled systems as defined by Weick. Readers are directed to Weick (1976, 1989) and Orton and Weick (1990) for an explication of loosely coupled systems. While this organizational perspective cannot describe all characteristics of organizations in all circumstances, the organized anarchy perspective provides a unique way to view the paradoxical yet uniquely normal institutions of higher education. "This picture of universities as 'organized anarchies' was a far cry from Weber's bureaucracy" (Gumport, 2012, p. 25).

POLITICAL PHILOSOPHY AS A FOUNDATION FOR ORGANIZED ANARCHIES

The idea of anarchy is perhaps one of the most misunderstood concepts in the constellation of organizational theories. A discussion of political philosophy can assist higher education faculty, administrators, faculty, and students to better understand the organizations in which they learn, live, and work. As opposed to popular ideas about anarchy as violence, chaos, and disorder, political theorists discuss anarchy in the context of community, mutual respect, and cooperation. Emma Goldman (1910, p. 68) said of anarchy:

> Anarchism ... really stands for the liberation of the human mind from the dominion of religion; the liberation of the human body from the dominion of property; the liberation from the shackles and restraint of government. Anarchism stands for a social order based on the free grouping of individuals for the purpose of producing real social wealth; an order that will guarantee to every human being free access to the earth and full enjoyment of the necessities of life.

Rather than the absence of order, anarchies rely on community among human beings for organization. Within anarchies, everyone is expected and urged to participate. In a twist that may seem ironic, the individualism upon which U.S. democracy is based, according to the anarchists, interferes with the human tendency to form communities. The point of anarchy is not chaos; "rather lack of community is chaos" (Walsh, 1992, p. 5). Political theory assumptions about anarchy include the following:

- Humans must form communities to survive.
- Anarchy provides freedom and places responsibility on organizational members.
- Libertarians are concerned with individual rights, anarchists with community obligations.
- Affinity groups form the basis of organizational structure in anarchies.

There are significant differences between authentic anarchy as discussed above and the organized anarchy discussed in this chapter. The term *anarchy*, as used by Cohen and March, is congruent with the popular (and largely misunderstood) view; one of chaos, disorder, and lack of control. Yet, the political theory ideas underscoring anarchy have utility for understanding higher education organizations, especially those that value the goals of community, mutual cooperation, and shared responsibility. The strengths and weaknesses of anarchy as an underlying philosophical perspective are outlined in Table 7.1.

METAPHOR

Of the organizational perspectives discussed in this book, organized anarchy is the most richly metaphorical. Using anarchy as a metaphor and means to view organizations, Cohen and March (1986) attached the modifier "organized" as a good-humored way to convey the paradoxical nature of higher education.

Table 7.1 Strengths and Weaknesses of the Political Philosophy Perspective for Higher Education

Strengths	Weaknesses
Provides a foundation for the community activities often found on college and university campuses.	May be incongruent with the individualistic values of Western cultures, particularly the United States.
Creates an expectation of individual responsibility in the context of community-oriented behaviors.	Anarchy may imply violence and confusion, particularly when associated with historical forms of higher education activism.
Provides a helpful alternative to the mechanized approach of bureaucracies.	Does not provide adequate explanation for the autonomy of higher education faculty members.
May be congruent with the community of scholars value within higher education.	May not adequately account for the professional and legitimate power present in higher education organizations.

> In a university anarchy each individual ... is seen as making autonomous decisions. Teachers decide if, when, and what to teach. Students decide if, when, and what to learn. Legislators and donors decide if, when and what to support. Neither coordination ... nor control ... [is] practiced. (Cohen & March, 1986, p. 33)

Although the rich and colorful metaphor of organized anarchy communicates dynamism and complexity, it risks overstatement and confusion. The metaphor overstates because it exaggerates higher education's irrational and sometimes absurd side at the risk of understating its well-managed, cogent aspects. This confusion is particularly at risk among external stakeholders such as legislators and parents if the modifier, "organized," is omitted or underemphasized. While it may be playful or clever to think of colleges and universities as anarchistic, the "organized" descriptor introduces and establishes balance.

STRUCTURE

From the perspective of organized anarchy, an organization

> is a collection of choices looking for problems, issues and feelings looking for decision situations in which they might be aired, solutions looking for issues to which they might be the answer, and decision makers looking for work. (Cohen & March, 1986, p. 81)

Departing from the assumptions of rationally based organizational approaches, organized anarchies adopt a nonorthodox approach to theorizing. Simplicity, determinism, linear causality, and objectivity are supplanted by complexity, indeterminism, mutual causality, and perspective taking (Clark, 1985). This paradigm shift results in newer, postmodern approaches that better match reality as lived in organizations. There is some order (many argue, through a loosely coupled structure) in organized anarchies. Referring to change, a central feature of organized anarchies, March (1981, p. 564) speculated that "change takes place because most of the time most people in an organization do about what they are supposed to do; that is they are intelligently attentive to their environments and their jobs."

ASSUMPTIONS

The organized anarchy perspective assumes multiple realities. Faculty experience the organization from their various disciplinary points of view, administrators from their different understandings, students from yet others. The situation is further complicated by the presence of internal (e.g., boards of trustees) and external (e.g., state legislators) stakeholders. No one person, regardless of power or position, fully understands the many realities and perceptions present in the organization—a situation that introduces uncertainty into the organizational structure. Though tempered by culture, history, and tradition that shape beliefs in some particular directions and away from others (Manning, 2000), the presence of multiple realities within organized anarchies is undeniable.

MAJOR CONCEPTS, CHARACTERISTICS, AND TERMS

Three properties define organized anarchies: problematic goals, unclear technology, and fluid participation (Cohen & March, 1986).

Problematic Goals

The fact that higher education institutions have unclear, contested, and often ambiguous goals makes these organizations profoundly different from other organizational forms. Corporations, hospitals, schools, and nonprofit organizations normally have a clearly focused purpose guiding their work. They may, for example, raise money to eradicate cancer, treat the sick, or assist refugee resettlement into the local community. A cancer association may raise money to eradicate cancer but also produce events that entertain while they raise those funds. A hospital may add to the professional workforce and city tax base while healing the sick. The refugee resettlement program may introduce diversity into a community while assisting people fleeing their homeland. While multiple goals and purposes exist within any organization, the full constellation of higher education organizational goals rivals the goals and purposes present within non-higher education organizational types. The difference with higher education is the number of ambiguous goals, the conflicting nature among the primary goals, and the vehemence with which institutional members may object to goals that, all the same, remain central to the college or university's purposes. Universities, for example, focus on teaching, research, and service as their three-part primary purpose. Despite the long-standing presence of these goals, heated arguments rage over whether or not teaching and research are mutually exclusive; how central service should be to faculty life; and whether teaching assistants, adjunct professors, or full-time faculty should bear primary responsibility for the teaching mission.

Conflict about the appropriate goals for a higher education institution occurs via internal and external stakeholder involvement. A municipal council or city mayor may view serving the community as the major purpose of a college or university. While a substantial number of university members may agree with this priority, others may see themselves serving a worldwide disciplinary or professional community, far beyond the scope of the local community. Conflict and complexity regarding the unclear, ambiguous, and conflicting goals or purposes is expressed most vividly with respect to board of trustee members. This stakeholder group often struggles to understand the voracity with which members of colleges and universities cling to their individual goals; for example, research that is important to a discipline but less relevant to the institution. Faculty and researchers may remain committed to goals that board of trustee members view as unrelated to institutional business.

Baldridge et al. (1978) claimed that the unclear and contested goal structures of higher education institutions mean that nearly anything can be justified and almost anything could be attacked as illegitimate. Some may find it hard to imagine how any organization could survive with its basic purposes so unclearly defined and executed. Birnbaum (1991), however, argued that this characteristic of higher education is a strength not a weakness. He contended that several institutional purposes could be achieved simultaneously because multiple, even conflicting, goals exist within the same institution. These organizations are more adaptable because they distribute their efforts in several areas rather than just one, allowing numerous societal purposes to be achieved at the same time. Perhaps the presence of multiple goals is in part responsible for the fact that colleges and universities are among the oldest existing organizational structures in the world. Colleges and universities have, in many ways, maintained the structure conceived in medieval times. Though notable innovations such as academic departments, elective courses, and electronic technology have been introduced, the underlying structure of faculty–student interaction, faculty governance, knowledge generation, and administration–faculty relationships remains medieval.

Recent trends drive the issue of problematic goals perhaps more dramatically than in the past. "During the last decade, technology, globalization, and competition have caused the ground to shift under higher education, defying national borders and calling into question honored traditions and long-held assumptions—creating a brave new world for higher education" (Eckel et al, 2015, p. 2). Among other developments and demands, reductions in state funding of public institutions, increased student debt, technology-fueled transformations in course delivery and administrative service provision, internationalization and globalization of higher education, "professionalization of the undergraduate curriculum" (Martinez-Saenz & Schoonover, 2015, p. 68), intensified influence of the market on student majors and courses offered, and increases in contingent faculty have substantially added to the number of goals embraced by U.S. higher education institutions. This situation makes the mission(s) of colleges and universities increasingly ambiguous and the reconciliation of sometimes congruent, other times conflicting, goals difficult if not impossible.

Unclear Technology

A second characteristic of organized anarchies is their use of unclear technology. This concept refers to the fact that "although the organization manages to survive and even produce, its own processes are not understood by its members" (Cohen, March, & Olsen, 1972, p. 1). As client-serving institutions (Baldridge et al., 1978), technologies must be employed to meet the needs of various participants. Students learn differently; community members have diverse needs; and research requires a variety of methodologies and approaches. As professionals, faculty and administrators use approaches which may, to the uninitiated or unfamiliar, seem strange, incomplete, or ill advised. A fundamental purpose of higher education, teaching, is at best an inexact science. Some teaching methods work well with some students but not others. Certain faculty successfully execute teaching methods that elude other professors or instructors. In the end, any measurement of what an educated person looks like is open to debate and disagreement.

Higher education does not have the luxury of clear technologies. The unclear technologies of higher education, particularly with its primary tasks of teaching and learning, have been the source of significant public criticism (U.S. Department of Education, 2006). When organizations cannot clearly prove that they have achieved their foremost mission, public trust, benefactor funding, and community support are difficult to maintain and cultivate.

When Cohen and March wrote about unclear technology in the 1970s and 1980s, they were most likely talking about the administrative and academic processes driving the curriculum and administrative practice. In particular, they may have been referring to the unclear technology of teaching, the challenge of truly assessing student learning, and the difficulty of measuring administrative effectiveness. In the current higher education climate, the term "unclear technology" takes on a broader meaning than might have previously been imagined. "Technology is reshaping pedagogy and teaching, calling into question traditional beliefs about the role of the professor. It is also spurring the development of new institutional offices and requiring innovations concerning strategy and resource allocation" (Eckel et al., 2015, p. 2).

The technology that Eckel et al. are referring to is the information technology driven changes in distance and online learning, technology-aided changes in teaching due to learning management software, and the advent of "borderless" education. Competition among institutions is no longer limited to the traditional aspirational and peer institutions. Students can now access courses from an international array of choices. The financial and strategic choices are currently less about the time-honored debate about whether lecture classes are effective. Students are exercising tremendous latitude about how and where (and from how many institutions) they pursue their degrees.

Fluid Participation

The third primary characteristic of organized anarchies is fluid participation; the idea that the involvement of organizational members "varies from one time to another" (Cohen et al., 1972, p. 1). Students occupy the institution for a limited period of time (e.g., four to six years for full-time students, longer for part-time participants, adult learners, and students with outside institutional responsibilities). Some faculty spend an entire professional career at a single institution while others advance their careers within multiple institutions. College presidents, the CEOs of these institutions, also exercise fluid participation. The average tenure for college presidents was seven years in 2011, the last year for which data are available (American Council on Education, 2012).

Fluid participation extends beyond institutional members' duration within an institution. The committee and meeting structures of colleges and universities are predicated on the reality of fluid participation. Faculty who were highly involved at one stage of a decision-making process are often uninvolved in later stages. Seen as a secondary or tertiary responsibility after teaching and research, administrative service is relegated by faculty to a lesser role. Meetings are missed, sabbaticals interfere, and professional judgment regarding the importance of attendance intervenes in a system that tolerates, or perhaps promotes, fluid participation.

The characteristic of fluid participation introduces dynamism, unpredictability, and complexity into higher education organizational structures. Participants carry less knowledge about the history and culture of the organization when movement into and out of the organization is the norm. Rather than being possessed by individuals, history, tradition, and stability must be carried by the organizational structure, among other institutional mechanisms. Unfortunately, the structure does not have the capacity to carry institutional memory in the same ways or to the same degree to which participants do. While the structure has some concrete aspects, it is always malleable; subject to change and interpretation. With fluid participation, mistakes are remade, history repeated, and decisions forgotten or overturned.

History and institutional knowledge are currently complicated with websites, social media, and the reality of ubiquitous and constant communication. Information circulates within and outside the institution at a pace that makes being informed difficult. Organizational members comfortable and proficient with social media and technology hold an advantage over those less knowledgeable about these means of communication. This circumstance, which promises to grow and become more complicated, presents new challenges to the goal of informed participation.

Higher education institutions have traditionally been places where multiple voices are expressed: the faculty through self-governance structures, students through their governance structures and representation on administrative and academic committees, and administrators through formal processes. Higher education differs from corporations in the way that participants' voices are given substantial freedom of expression. This circumstance means that communication comes from many sources and directions. Depending on where you are located in the organization (e.g., the provost's office, a dean's office, a student's home), it may feel as if communication, feedback, and opinion are originating from everywhere. The omnidirectional nature of communication in organized anarchies has introduced a layer of complexity into colleges and universities. One can never predict or assess where communication will come from, what form it will take, and which aspects of that communication will be judged most valuable. In organized anarchies, it can be difficult to separate personal disputes from informed, professional judgment. Each voice is given an opportunity to be heard, sometimes with excellent results regarding consensus building and informed decision making and at other times with disastrous results such as damaging rumors and skewed expectations of leadership capabilities.

The fluid participation in organized anarchies often results in missed and intermittent communication. Organizational complexity and the demands of a professional's responsibilities interfere with effective communication. Due to uncertainty, unintended consequences, and unanticipated circumstances, one can never fully communicate all aspects of a decision or circumstance because the full range of those circumstances can never be known. In a postmodern context, reality is not objective, stagnant, or static. Even if one could communicate the aspects of the transitory reality in that moment in time, that reality changes in the next moment. In this way, communication is always incomplete and dynamic. The best one can hope for is to collect and communicate an adequate amount of pertinent information to make an informed, effective decision. Tolerance for ambiguity and nimbleness in response are more appropriate goals than attempts to obtain and communicate comprehensive information. Administrators who understand the dynamics of organized anarchies should always be prepared for an accusation of inadequate and incomplete communication. By its very nature, the fluid participation and unclear technology of higher education make this situation a reality.

Because communication in an organized anarchy is intermittent, omnidirectional, and incomplete, expectations about what can and cannot be accomplished are likewise affected. This situation has, ironically, been exacerbated with the advent of electronic communication through e-mail and the internet. The presence of readily available information increases the number of stakeholders, introduces complexity into already multifaceted decision-making processes, and raises expectations about the availability of widespread communication.

Technology-enhanced communication has increased the pace and volume of the information received by and sent out from the institution. Processes bounded in the past are now permeable. Institutional messages are no longer closely governed by the college or university. Students use social media to transmit their position and negative messages about the institution. Websites such as Rate Your Professor and Facebook provide uncensored information to parents and students. While the benefits of technology arguably outweigh the disadvantages, the reality of its impact on increasing the uncertainty in organized anarchies is indisputable.

Client-Serving, Professionally Populated, and Environmental Vulnerability

In addition to the three characteristics of problematic goals, unclear technology, and fluid participation introduced by Cohen and March (1986), Baldridge et al. (1978) proposed several additional characteristics to the organized anarchy model. Organized anarchies serve clients who demand input into the decision-making process; they are peopled with professionals who demand a large measure of control over the institution's decision processes; and they are highly vulnerable to their environments (Baldridge et al., 1978, p. 25).

Client-Serving

The client-serving nature of higher education institutions introduces complications into the structure in ways absent from other types of institutions. Stakeholders often have conflicting ideas about who the clients are, how they are to be served, and what they are to be served. When stakeholder groups differ about whether students should be considered clients, customers, or learners, the sheer number of opinions and ways of operating introduce confusion. This circumstance makes it difficult to determine the basic nature of the higher education client.

Professionalized Organizations

The problematic nature of the client served by higher education institutions interacts with high professionalism, particularly among faculty. In contrast to bureaucratic structures that rely on positional authority, expert authority is a significant dynamic within higher education institutions. The positional authority of administrators (e.g., presidents, provosts, department chairs) often conflicts with the professional or expert authority of faculty. Administrators lack the authority to convince faculty to accept certain definitions (e.g., students as customers), the best technology to be used (e.g., distance learning), or the best way to do a particular task (e.g., bureaucratic expediency). Each professional has beliefs, informed by professional practice and experience, about the best approach to be taken. Professionally informed opinions about organizational life and its technologies abound: how decisions should be made, how teaching is undertaken, what courses should be taught, and how relationships with colleagues should progress. This belief in the veracity of professional opinion often extends to decisions made and policies set by college and university administrators. Regardless of the extent to which a faculty member may or may not be informed about those decisions and policies, that person may hold tenaciously to a professionally defined right to exercise an opinion. This includes the right to exercise a vote of no confidence if the faculty member(s) believes that institutional leaders are making or have made ill-conceived decisions. Opposition based on professional opinion also occurs if a faculty member believes that the traditional purposes of the institution or higher education are being compromised.

The expression of professionally informed, but potentially conflicting, opinion is another source of complexity and anarchy in higher education organizations. Administrators, legislators, students, and other higher education stakeholders should not view the exercise of these voices as interference or misinformation. For example, faculty, particularly those with a long-term commitment to the institution, have significant institutional history and memory. Their opinions are informed by past experience within the context of the institution. Their long-range view, though sometimes debatably anachronistic, represents a knowledgeable historical view. These points of view can often be more richly informed than administrators with less institutional history. Both views are necessary for effective management in higher education. Faculty voice and prolonged deliberation on decisions can slow or stop an overly ambitious administrator from making decisions that ultimately have a negative impact on the organization (Birnbaum, 1991). In this way, the dynamic tension between faculty and administrators introduces structure and organization to the anarchistic nature of organized anarchies.

Environmental Vulnerability

The last characteristic of organized anarchies proposed by Baldridge et al. (1978) in addition to the original three proposed by Cohen and March (1986) is environmental vulnerability. Organizations exist in systems that are exposed to and are affected by the external environment. "Organizations are remarkably adaptive, enduring institutions, responding to volatile environments routinely and easily, though not always optimally" (March, 1981, p. 564). Higher education, because of its strong dependence on tuition dollars, national and international economies, reputational measures of quality, and fluidity of the client group served, is particularly affected by environmental change. Students are a transient population in the way they attend multiple institutions, sometimes simultaneously. They frequently postpone or interrupt their college attendance or enroll in college in a variety of ways (e.g., full-time, part-time, online). The 24-hours-a-day, seven-days-a-week circumstance of many higher education institutions' operations exposes these institutions to variations in utilities, food, and maintenance costs. Environmental factors exact a heavy toll on higher education. Increased competition for students, introduction of learner-focused education, internationalization of higher education, demands for better connection between higher education and the job market, and shifts due to the knowledge economy combined with the repercussions of global economic shifts, government-mandated requirements, and market-driven pressures have intensified the impact of the external environment on higher education organizations (Conley, 2016; Miller, 2014; Newman, Couturier, & Scurry, 2004). Because these institutions are tuition dependent with relatively few sources of income, changes in the environment can have a harsh and rapid impact. Higher education institutions have minimal to no safety cushion with which to ease the impact of these environmental influences. This vulnerability introduces complexity and anarchy into the organizational structure.

STRENGTHS AND WEAKNESSES OF ORGANIZED ANARCHIES

The organized anarchy model, like all the organizational theories summarized in this book, possesses strengths and weaknesses (see Table 7.2). As with any organizational theory, this approach cannot be implemented without attention to these features.

To provide direction on ways to manage and administer organized anarchies, Cohen and March (1986) presented several helpful rules.

- "Spend time" (p. 207). Because time and energy are scarce resources within organizations, those who can dedicate time to decision and policy making will have influence.
- "Persist" (p. 208). Decisions are made over time and through multiple attempts. Because higher education organizations are constantly changing, a defeated idea one day may find champions the next.
- "Exchange status for substance" (p. 208). Cohen and March warned of the dangers of administrators becoming embroiled in their own importance. They recommended concentrating on substance to avoid the pitfalls of this self-importance trap.
- "Facilitate opposition participation" (p. 209). By drawing in people from outside an administrator's customary circles, different voices can be heard, assorted ideas shared, and a more democratic process achieved. Although the goal of coopting others can be an outcome of facilitating opposition, that is not the purpose here. One can hope that all sides of the debate can be informed by increased contact and communication.
- "Overload the system" (p. 210). If many programs and ideas are proposed, some of them must, through persistence, be enacted. "Someone with the habit of producing many proposals, without absolute commitment to any one, may lose any one of them ... but cannot be stopped on everything" (Cohen & March, 1986, p. 210).

Table 7.2   Strengths and Weaknesses of the Organized Anarchy Model

Strengths	Weaknesses
The professionalized nature of higher education institutions means that there is a system of checks and balances regarding institutional power and authority.	The organized anarchy perspective is descriptively rich but practically incomplete.
Organized anarchies are more democratic because the multiple, even conflicting, goals create more opportunities for disparate points of view to be expressed.	The rationale and recommendations for practice concerning organized anarchies fly in the face of accepted bureaucratic and rational management procedures.
Higher education organizations, which are organized anarchies, better prepare students for a complex, postmodern world.	Because ambiguity is central to organized anarchies, administrators, faculty, and students with little tolerance for uncertainty may struggle in an organization functioning in this manner.
There are more opportunities for critical thinking and multicultural perspective-taking in organized anarchies.	The organized anarchy perspective cannot adequately explain all parts of a college or university.

- "Manage unobtrusively" (p. 212). Higher education organizations are difficult to manage. If one forces solutions or aggressively directs the organization in particular directions, failure is likely. Cohen and March (1986, pp. 212–213) suggested that leaders are more successful when they "let the system go where it wants to go with only the minor interventions that make it go where it should." An aspect of this approach is to make small adjustments in a range of places rather than a concerted and large effort in one place. The chances of success, through these multiple means, are increased.

Leaders, including college and university presidents, believe in their capability to effect organizational change. The organized anarchy perspective, while paying homage to the facility of leadership, explains why and how organizations operate even in the presence of weak leadership. The fact that higher education institutions have a life of their own despite the efforts of presidents and other organizational leaders may be disconcerting for those seeking to control and manage these institutions.

NEXT STEPS: BRINGING THE ORGANIZED ANARCHY MODEL INTO CURRENT USE

The organized anarchy perspective was proposed in the 1970s and continues to be used as a metaphor for colleges and universities. The theory can be brought into current use by considering the writings about change in the higher education literature. Adrianna Kezar is a leading scholar in the area of higher education organizational change. Through a number of publications and research projects (2001, 2013, 2014a, 2014b), Kezar expanded and synthesized the change literature to add to this important area of organizational life.

Understanding change is crucial given the national and international calls to innovate in higher education. National commissions, international associations, local and regional accrediting boards, government officials, board of trustee members, and corporate officers are among the many asking higher education to change. Suggestions include better preparing students as future members of the workforce, instituting more affordable costs, eliminating tenure, and introducing business-oriented practices. Higher education as a system is unique in the number of stakeholders invested in its outcomes and practices. This characteristic means that change, like communication in an organized anarchy, is omnidirectional and ever present.

Change in Higher Education Systems and Institutions

Kezar offers several definitions of change but recommends caution about adhering to a static, out-of-context version. Because change must be viewed in the context of the organizational model being considered (e.g., organized anarchy, bureaucracy, collegium), one must reflect on the context in which the change is taking place. One definition offered by Kezar and based on Burnes (1996) sees change as "understanding alterations within organizations at the broadest level among individuals, groups, and at the collective level across the entire organization" (Kezar, 2001, p. 12). A second defines change as "the observation of difference over time in one or more dimensions of an entity" (Kezar, 2001, p. 12). Kezar notes that change is complicated in organized anarchies due to the presence of ambiguity, multiple authority structures, and the presence of numerous perspectives on the organization and its functioning.

Diffusion of Innovations

Early scholarship by Everett Rogers (1962) sheds light on change in organizations. His original work was called *Diffusion of Innovations* and was based on research on change in agricultural practices. He outlined a process through which innovations circulate among people, are adopted, and subsequently change the organization. Rogers originally speculated that it took approximately 20 years for an innovation to circulate through an industry. Diffusion of innovations has sped up significantly with the advent of the internet and modern communication. The five-step process proposed by Rogers included a First Step, Knowledge, when an organizational member, in this case, becomes aware of an innovation and comes to understand how it functions. In the Second Step, Persuasion, the person forms a positive or negative impression about the innovation or change. In the Third Step, Decision, the member takes actions that lead to adoption or rejection of the innovation. The Fourth Step, Implementation, begins when the member uses the innovation. The final and Fifth Step, Confirmation, occurs when the member evaluates the merits of the decision to innovate (Rogers, 1962/2003).

Rogers summarized the characteristics of various members and their reactions to the introduction of change or innovation into an organization by describing five types of behavior: Innovators, Early Adopters, Early Majority, Late Majority, and Laggards. In reading these different characteristics, one can imagine college or university colleagues who fit these categories.

Innovators make up the smallest percentage of the population at 2.5%. They are the first people to adopt the innovation. They take risks, tend to be young, and with upper class social standing. They have the financial means to take the risk on a new product or innovation. They have high risk tolerance because many of the technologies they adopt will most likely fail but their financial standing allows them to tolerate the financial and social consequences of these failures. On campuses, innovators are the first people to try a new computer software, device, or organizational practice. They attend conferences and interact with people who are on the cutting edge of their field. They are often enthusiastic about the innovations they discover and are very willing to talk about them.

Early Adopters make up 13.5% of an organization or population and adopt the innovation after innovators but at early stages of the introduction. These individuals are well-connected and carry high opinion leadership with others in the organization. Like Innovators, they are typically younger, have higher social status, financial means, and advanced education. They are social with links to a variety of groups within the organization. Although they are more cautious about their innovation adoption than Innovators, they are invested in adopting innovations as a way to maintain their social status within the organization.

The Early Majority make up 34% of the organizational population. They adopt innovations and embrace the change but across a period of time, which is significantly longer than the Innovators and Early Adopters. They tend to have average social status but their contact with Early Adopters exposes them to the innovation. Unlike the Innovators and Early Adopters, they are rarely opinion leaders in the organization.

The Late Majority also make up 34% of the population. They tend to adopt the innovation later in the diffusion process. They are skeptical about change and wait until others have tested out the innovation before they commit. They tend to have below average social status, limited financial means, and are rarely opinion leaders in the organization.

Laggards, making up 16% of the population, are the final category to be considered in the diffusion of innovations. They are the last group to embrace an innovation. Unlike previous categories, individuals in this category show little to no opinion leadership. Older and averse to change, they focus on traditional aspects of the organization. They possess the lowest social status, have very limited financial means, and concentrate their contact primarily with family and close friends. They have no role in opinion leadership within the organization.

When one considers the various organizational roles regarding change and adoption of innovations, one can imagine the motivations of administrators, faculty, students, and stakeholders. Long-term members of the college or university may be more adverse to change (e.g., Late Majority, Laggards) with more connection to the past and the "way things were." Recent hires, particularly those with experience from other institutions, may be motivated to introduce change into the organization with goals to increase effectiveness, market share, and curricular improvements. Without stereotyping faculty and administrators into the various categories, one can see how different positions and vantage points within the institution may drive the adoption process regarding change.

Kezar makes an important point regarding change within higher education. While change is certainly warranted in many areas, unexamined change is dangerous and unnecessary. "What needs to be preserved may be just as important to understand as what needs to be changed" (Kezar, 2001, p. 9). Well-established traditions in higher education such as the value of liberal arts education, the importance of critical thinking, and the social change mission of higher education, for example, cannot be discarded in the name of the latest innovation.

Disruptive Change

Traditional models of change, including Roger's diffusion of innovation and the change literature specific to higher education, can now be considered in the context of the disruptive change affecting higher education and other sectors such as health care, technology companies, and service industries. All modern organizations and systems are affected by disruptive technologies, which can be defined as "products, services, processes, or concepts that disrupt the status quo" (Meyer, 2010, p. 1). These innovations are compelling, resulting in organizational members giving up their accustomed way of acting and adopting a new way using the introduced technology (Lucas, 2014). Disruptive technologies and the changes they catalyze are, by nature, only disruptive for a short period of time before they are either incorporated into our lives or passed over for the next technology. Their disruptive nature becomes commonplace as the innovation is absorbed within an organization, system, or society.

While the following list of disruptive technologies (Afshar, 2014) will decay before this book is published, the items on the list are examples of past, present, and future disruptive technologies; technologies that can cause faculty and administrators to rethink their ways of operating. As you read this list, consider the campus character before these technologies changed teaching, administration, and student life:

1. campus Wi-Fi and the changes it has brought to communication, access to information, and workplace portability;
2. social media and its ability to transmit information quickly, connect people across distances, and occupy people's time;

3. digital badges awarded for online course participation and the ways that this innovation could displace college diplomas;
4. analytics for business applications, admissions targeting, data mining, and other areas;
5. wearable technology and its potential for live-streamed lectures, virtual field trips, and self-guided campus tours;
6. drones and their ability to transform campus tours, sporting events, and campus maintenance;
7. 3D printing and the possibilities for art, design, and engineering;
8. digital courseware and the changes it is bringing to adaptive learning and personalized education;
9. small private online courses, as opposed to massive online open courses (MOOCs), and the possibilities for access to higher education;
10. virtual reality and the opportunities for remote instruction and virtual classrooms.

The most important aspect of disruptive technologies in higher education is their potential to change systems that have been in place for millennia.

> Perhaps ... technology derives its potentially disruptive power from interrupting our usual practices and policies.... Technology prompts a pause in the usual thought patterns, encouraging reflection. Eventually a new understanding of how learning happens and what a course could be emerges. (Meyer, 2010 p. 1)

Disruptive Technologies and Organized Anarchies

The organized anarchy model is a useful perspective to consider when thinking about disruptive technologies. Administrators and faculty must be nimble in organized anarchies to cope with the uncertainty, fluidity, and problematic environment of these organizations. Because organized anarchies are by nature unstable, they provide an ideal platform from which to consider the dramatic changes that may occur due to disruptive technologies. The presence of multiple institutional goals means that there may be a corner of the organization poised to respond to a disruption. Fluid participation positions change agents to introduce innovations and disruptions in a variety of settings. The unclear nature of technology means that new methods may be tested out as a way to better define successful learning and teaching. The client-serving nature of organized anarchies means that disruptive technologies may be introduced from students and stakeholders on the margins of the institution. The professional nature of the members within an organized anarchy means that their educational backgrounds may push them to be more innovative regarding the disruptive technologies.

CONCLUSIONS

When administrators, faculty, and students use the organized anarchy perspective to understand organizations, there is a shift in traditional expectations about communication, decision making, and participation. In contrast to a traditional top-driven approach to organizational communication, leadership, and decision making, all members within an organized anarchy can imagine a role they may play within the institution. Intermittent communication means that influence can be exerted from a number of sources.

Fluid participation means that pressure, power, and influence can be exerted at any point of the decision- or policy-making process. The reality of multiple goals means that the institution can adopt a new direction without fundamentally changing the college or university's mission and purpose. The newly adopted purpose may have been lingering as a subgoal for years, waiting for the right external or internal institutional context. Rather than being a weakness, the flexibility of organized anarchies provides strength and opportunity to higher education institutions.

Higher education's pace, including the degree of change and the need for response, has increased significantly over the past 20 years. Despite the fact that higher education institutions have been chronically and historically under-resourced and staffed, the imperative to do more with less is now amplified. The survival and health of higher education institutions and systems depend on rapid and flexible responses to internal and external changes. This pace has a significant negative impact on higher education participants' ability to communicate fully, adequately collect information, and satisfactorily vet decisions. The increased pace and amplified environmental and organizational complexity has made the organized anarchy perspective a useful metaphor for today's higher education institutions.

Effective leadership requires that administrators and faculty operate from the viewpoint of several organizational perspectives. The organized anarchy perspective provides a helpful approach to managing higher education institutions in ways that are more congruent with and accommodating to their unique structures and approaches. Uniquely to higher education and other client-serving organizations, the organized anarchy perspective provides a way to think about colleges and universities that can result in the achievement of a wide variety of institutional goals and societal purposes.

Questions for Discussion

- How might multiple goals and purposes increase the effectiveness of higher education institutions? How might they decrease the effectiveness?
- How does the unclear technology of higher education institutions leave these organizations open to public criticism?
- How does the presence of multiple professional communities increase the complexity of a college or university's organizational structure and operating procedures?
- What aspects of organized anarchies make higher education more adaptable or less adaptable?
- How can the organized anarchy perspective help faculty, stakeholders, and practitioners make sense of the traditional tensions in higher education?
- What are some of the origins of change for institutions of higher education? Are these from internal leadership? Are they from external societal factors?
- Which is more sustainable—revolutionary change that occurs in a short period of time or evolutionary change that involves a long-term process occurring in stages?

Recommended Readings Related to Organized Anarchies

Daft, R. L. (2007). *Organization theory and design* (10th ed.). Mason, OH: Cengage Learning.

Gillett-Karam, R. (2013). The future-shaping function of the governing board. In G. Myran, C. L. Ivery, M. H. Parsons, & C. Kinsley (Eds.), *The future of the urban community college: Shaping the pathways to a multiracial democracy* (New Directions for Community Colleges, No. 162, pp. 37–44). San Francisco: Jossey-Bass.

March, J. G. (1981). Footnotes to organizational change. *Administrative Science Quarterly, 26*(4), 563–577.

March, J. G. (1994). *A primer on decision making: How decisions happen.* New York: Free Press.

March, J. G., & Shapira, Z. (2007). Behavioral decision theory and organizational decision theory. In G. R. Ungson & D. N. Braunstein (Eds.), *Decision making: An interdisciplinary inquiry* (pp. 293–345). Boston: Kent.

Mintzberg, H., & Westly, F. (2010). Decision making: It's not what you think. In P. C. Nutt & D. C. Wilson (Eds.), *Handbook of decision making* (pp. 73–82). Hoboken, NJ: Wiley.

Peterson, M. W. (2007). The study of colleges and universities as organizations. In P. J. Gumport (Ed.), *Sociology of higher education: Contributions and their contexts* (pp. 147–184). Baltimore: Johns Hopkins University Press.

Trondal, J. (2015). Ambiguities in organizations and the routines of behavior and change. *International Journal of Organizational Analysis, 23*(1), 123–141.

CASE: A CHANGE IN MISSION GENERATES DISRUPTION

Every higher education institution has a mission, vision, and set of goals. Colleges and universities have historically been asked to fulfill a herculean task for society. They are to transmit, preserve, and create knowledge through teaching and research while simultaneously enacting social change. Colleges and universities provide an analytical view on societal issues, whether through well-practiced and historically justified student activism or via the public intellectual and social critic roles exercised by faculty. Their physical and virtual libraries house the most significant knowledge known to human beings. The intellectual riches contained on college campuses are virtually unimaginable. Traditional college students come of age on college campuses; nontraditional students gain an education to change careers and get a second chance in life.

The responsibilities and societal tasks as described above dictate that colleges and universities are among the most complex institutions in society. This is as true for U.S. institutions as it is for universities across the globe. The case outlined below describes the complexity of higher education decision making through the processes of curricular change. The competing demands, high expectations, and individual and group preferences that exist within a curricular change process create an apt circumstance to discuss organized anarchies and the garbage can model of decision making.

Decision Making in Organized Anarchies

Cohen and March (1986) described decision making as a fundamental activity of organized anarchies. Using the metaphor of a garbage can, a model intended to "encourage colleagues to play with the basic ideas" (Olsen, 2001, p. 192), decision making in these organizations is an opportunity to make choices.

> The garbage can process is one in which problems, solutions, and participants move from one choice opportunity to another in such a way that the nature of the choice, the time it takes, and the problems it solves all depend on a relatively complicated intermeshing of elements. These include the mix of choices available at any one time, the mix of problems that have access to the organization, the mix of solutions looking for problems, and the outside demands on the decision makers. (Cohen et al., 1972, p. 16)

Choices are constrained by the time, energy, and resources available, as well as by the circumstances of the decision and choice situations. Originally conceived as a way to describe university governance (Olsen, 2001), Cohen et al. (1972) outlined the garbage can model of decision making as one of many ways that participants choose options within organizations. Through their research, these theorists concluded that the decisions made and choice opportunities available were less rationally obvious and more detached from the organizational structure than previously imagined.

During decision making, organizational members attend "to the strategic effects of timing (in the introduction of choices and problems), the time pattern of available energy, and the impact of organizational structure" (Cohen & March, 1986, p. 81). The model acknowledges the contextual nature of organizational life as well as the ways that timing and coincidence drive choices. Decisions are more about the ways that problems, solutions, choice opportunities, and decision makers come together at any point in time than they are about a rationally and objectively determined "right" answer to a particular problem (Olsen, 2001). Taking into consideration the temporal and coincidental nature of events, circumstances, and people leading to a decision, higher education administrators can better understand the complex nature of decision making.

The knotty politics of participation in strategic planning and other decision-based activities are more comprehensible when one abandons the idea of an objective and rational "right" choice. Decision making is more than "simply" a matter of rationally defining the problem, determining alternative solutions, choosing among the options, and implementing the decision. Whereas the rational decision model defined choice as a decontextualized "given," an aspect of organizational life where a "correct" response can be identified, the garbage can model of decision making acknowledges the role of participants and other circumstances integral to the context of the choices available and decisions made. In fact, in this model four independent streams influence the decision made: problems, solutions, participants, and choice opportunities (Cohen & March, 1986; Cohen et al., 1972; Olsen, 2001).

In addition to the mix of the four streams, the specific choices made also depend on what other "garbage" is present at the time of the decision. If decisions could be "placed" in garbage cans, then:

> The mix of garbage in a single can depends partly on the labels attached to the alternative cans; but it also depends on what garbage is being produced at the moment, on the mix of cans available, and on the speed with which garbage is collected and removed from the scene. (Cohen & March, 1986, p. 81)

A decision and its attendant choices cannot be taken out of context from the other "garbage" surrounding it. Figure 7.1 illustrates a case in which the independent streams of problems, solutions, participants, and choice opportunities influence strategic change at an institution.

Types of Decisions in the Garbage Can Model

Decisions using the garbage can model are made by oversight, flight, and resolution. In oversight, choices become available when a problem at hand is "solved" by becoming attached to a choice at hand. In flight, unsuccessful choices become attached to a problem until a more attractive choice presents itself. The problem then "leaves the choice" and a more fruitful decision is possible. In this decision-making mode, decisions are not so much made but avoided. The final decision approach within the garbage can model is by resolution. Using this approach, problems are resolved when time allocated to the

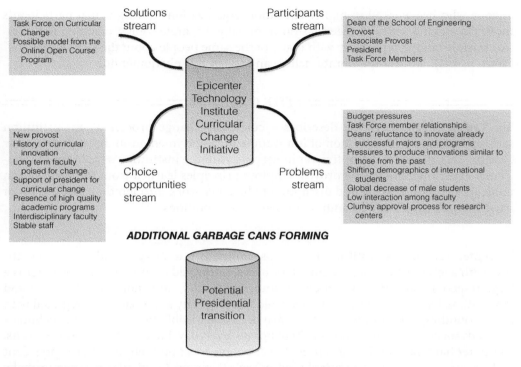

Figure 7.1 Epicenter Technology Institute's Garbage Can Model of Decision Making

selection or identification of choices leads to a solution (Cohen & March, 1986). Because problems can be independent from solutions in the garbage can model, these elements of organizational life are often elusive, may combine in unexpected ways, or may result in surprisingly original answers to persistent difficulties. A solution, rather than a rational choice discovered through deliberation, could be "an answer actively looking for a question" (Olsen, 2001, p. 193).

Cohen et al. (1972), with their innovative model, elaborated on five decision-making properties that partially explain why making choices is so often difficult to accomplish.

1. Most issues have low salience for most people.
2. The organizational system has high inertia.
3. Any decision can become a garbage can for almost any problem.
4. Processes of choice are easily subject to overload.
5. Organizations have weak information bases. (Cohen & March, 1986)

Because issues have low salience for most people, participation in decision making "is not always stable ... there is unresolved conflict, and ... authority relations are ambiguous or shifting, not organized into stable hierarchies" (Olsen, 2001, pp. 193–194). In this way, the model explains why some problems persist year after year, why some choices look good but fail to solve the problem, why choice is so contentious among participants, and why decision making is so difficult. Olsen described a familiar experience for anyone who has worked in higher education organizations during which participants move "through a series of meetings on nominally disparate topics, reaching few decisions, while talking repeatedly with many of the same people about the same problems" (2001, p. 192). No amount of rationality can explain this phenomenon.

THE CASE

The organized anarchy case describes a curricular change process at an institution seeking to maintain its tradition of innovation and experimentation through curricular change. This change is disruptive yet in keeping with the institution's tradition of intellectual experimentation. The provost employs principles learned from the garbage can model of decision making and disruption to help her work through the complexities of participation, choice opportunities, problems, and solutions.

Institutional Context

Epicenter Technology Institute (ETI—a pseudonym) is a 200-year-old private institution with a long history of experimentation and cutting-edge approaches. Epicenter is a large research institution which draws students, faculty, and staff from domestic and international locales. The Institute is located in a large city and is closely integrated with its surroundings. Its research centers have been responsible for many of the technological advances that people use in their homes everyday including microwave ovens, computer hardware, and solar power. Never people to sit on their laurels, the president and provost of ETI recently established a Task Force on Curricular Change to make recommendations for the curriculum of the future.

Questions to Consider

- What external pressures influence the curricula of higher education institutions?
- How is the overall mission of U.S. higher education fulfilled through the specialized niches of institutional types?
- In what ways does the research mission of universities create the forces that drive organized anarchies?

Characters

Dr. Frank Lincoln, President: Dr. Lincoln has served as ETI's president for four years. He came to Epicenter from a large research university in the Midwest. As provost of his previous institution, he led the effort to update the curriculum by developing academic programs that reflected the most cutting-edge technologies of the time. Lincoln plans to bring that experience to bear on curriculum reform at ETI. With four years' experience of building an administrative team, Lincoln believes now is the time to assess and modernize the curriculum at ETI. The institution has always been on the cutting edge and Lincoln is dedicated to keeping it there.

Unbeknown to his staff, particularly the provost, President Lincoln is being courted by his old institution to assume the presidency. Although he had planned to stay at Epicenter for the remainder of his career, the opportunity to go "back home" is extremely tempting.

Dr. Julie Kimball, Provost: Dr. Kimball, appointed provost at ETI six months ago, had moved up through the ranks of academic administrators at the institution. Currently in her honeymoon period, Dr. Kimball recognizes that action taken now would likely meet less resistance than if it were taken when the honeymoon was over. Provost Kimball is in agreement with President Lincoln that the curriculum at ETI needs to stay cutting edge by taking a probing and creative look at the future.

Dr. Ann Royce, Dean, School of Engineering: Dr. Royce has been a faculty member at ETI for 20 years. She is a veteran of new administrators and their plans. An activist by nature, Dr. Royce was involved in the movement 10 years earlier to establish a faculty union. Although she is still interested in union activities, she feels her voice could best be heard through work as a dean. She had lobbied for and been appointed to the position of dean of the school of engineering. At a recent deans' council meeting, Dr. Royce and the other deans were apprised of President Lincoln's and Provost Kimball's plans to convene a Task Force on Curricular Change. She is supportive of the Task Force's work but is concerned about how it will impact her very successful academic programs and majors.

Dr. Warren Norton, Chair, Task Force on Curricular Change: Dr. Norton has been a faculty member in the computer science department for 20 years. He is committed to ETI's cutting-edge mission regarding technology and is not afraid of major upheaval. He believes that true innovation can only come when the system is shaken up and new possibilities emerge. For the past five years, Norton has taught through the open course online program established at ETI. This internationally known program makes ETI courses available to the public worldwide. He can talk for hours about the obligation of higher education institutions such as ETI to make their curricular content available to the general public. As a way to test new content, Norton views the open course system as a mechanism that could introduce innovation into the ETI curriculum overall. Norton has been appointed as chair of the Task Force on Curricular Change and he looks forward to using the task force as a way to shake things up.

Dr. Dana Briggs, Associate Provost: Dr. Briggs is a bit of an anomaly at ETI. A traditionalist by nature, Dr. Briggs sees her role as slowing processes down so more deliberation can take place. She is not one to change for change's sake. ETI is an established institution with a long and distinguished history. She does not want that tradition to be jeopardized by "flash in the pan" ideas. Considered a "laggard" by ETI standards, Briggs knows how expensive disruptive change can be. Even ETI, with its vast resources, does not have endless amounts of money to expend. She believes that one has to balance innovativeness and creativity with the cost and consequences of disruption and anarchy, even an organized one.

Questions to Consider

- How does the increasingly short tenure for presidents add to the problematic goals, unclear technologies, and fluid participation of colleges and universities?
- What factors affect the shortened tenure of college presidents?
- What is the relationship between the president and provost regarding decision making?

Curricular Change

Provost Kimball was optimistic about today's meeting of the Task Force on Curricular Change. An advocate of inclusive processes, Kimball invited Warren Norton, Ann

Royce, and Dana Briggs to be on the task force knowing that each brought different, often opposing, perspectives. She took seriously her commitment to build task force participation that considered different perspectives. Kimball believed that true innovativeness could only occur if different positions were considered and debated, regardless of the conflict and uncertainty that often resulted. Kimball knew organized anarchies were inherently unstable and she did not expect anything less from the task force. President Lincoln was joining today's meeting to charge the group with their task. Lincoln and Kimball were in agreement about the need for the institution to remain cutting edge through bold curricular innovativeness.

The lively discussion among task force members stopped as Kimball and Lincoln entered the conference room. The first order of business was introductions followed by the president's charge (see below). Although Kimball remained optimistic about the group's ability to complete the charge, she sensed tension and potential conflict in the room. Upon entering the group, she heard Norton and Briggs arguing about balancing organizational change and disruption. Kimball was hoping that involvement on the task force could harness conflicting ideas and perspectives, engendering ownership for the curricular change process.

Text of the President's Charge to the Task Force on Curricular Change

The Board of Trustees tasked me to undertake a process that crafts the future of the curriculum at Epicenter Technology Institute. It is their hope that this plan will guide our educational efforts to 2025 and beyond. I have directed Provost Kimball to assemble and subsequently chair a representative task force of college faculty, students, and staff to complete this responsibility. Within six months, the task force will present a plan to my office. Upon review of this plan and vetting by the institution's governance groups, I will determine the next steps regarding presentation of the plan to the Board of Trustees. This process will involve extensive discussions within the task force and among the governance groups about available options and potential directions for ETI's curriculum. ETI will always remain at the cusp of innovation, inventiveness, and opportunity. We appreciate your service and dedication and trust you will map out a bright future.

Questions to Consider
- If a participants stream is one of the factors in the garbage can model, what are ways that participation can be managed? Should it be managed?
- Who gets "a seat at the table"? What implications does this have for the participants and solutions streams?
- What messages in President Lincoln's charge helped build momentum for his desired changes? What messages worked against his desired changes?
- What are the garbage cans forming around the curricular change?

Following the reading of the charge, the President left the task force meeting and Provost Kimball opened the floor to questions. The first question was from a business management faculty member who had been at the institution for three years: "Does this mean that we are going to change the curriculum to include only content that is cutting edge? What about traditional practices about which students must be knowledgeable?" Not being one to avoid a question, Provost Kimball replied, "Placing a premium on innovativeness is one option on the table. The world is changing and we have to change with it. President Lincoln and I are committed to maintaining ETI's tradition of innovativeness and experimentation."

Theory to Practice

Provost Kimball had recently read a book by Govindarajan and Trimble (2010) that helped her put theory behind her assumptions and practices regarding change and innovation. Kimball was struck by the quote that: "Organizations are not designed for innovation. Quite the contrary, they are designed for ongoing operations" (Govindarajan and Trimble, 2010, p. 10). The authors offered the following insights regarding change, innovation, and disruption:

- Since innovation is neither repeatable or predictable, rules that are unpredictable are necessary for innovation to occur. Innovation rules are unpredictable but not unmanageable.
- Though always and inevitably in conflict, mutual respect between performance engines (the ongoing organizational mechanisms that coordinate processes and activities into repeatable, predictable forms) and the unpredictable innovation processes was essential.
- Innovation does not simply equal ideas.
- Innovation equals ideas plus execution.

Kimball had considered Cohen and March's garbage can model of decision making as she composed the task force. She knew there would be fluid participation, that the technology (teaching and learning) they would be employing was unclear, and that the goals for higher education were problematic. Cohen and March's ideas about organized anarchies could be considered alongside Govindarajan and Trimble's ideas about innovation and disruption to enact the curricular changes required. Kimball asked the task force to identify several resources that could enable curricular innovation in the university:

- The presence of several high quality academic programs (e.g., business management, computer science, electrical engineering) with historically robust enrollments and a penchant for experimentation and invention.
- Recent interdisciplinary faculty hires designed to create collaboration and innovation.
- An average staff tenure of 15 years, that provides stability in the system—stability that can be useful as the faculty innovates.
- The presence of a president whose tenure was longer than the national average and a provost who understood their institution.

Questions to Consider

- How does stability simultaneously enable and constrain innovation?
- What managerial tools exist that executive administrators can use to effect innovation?

- What limits innovation within a higher education institution? What enables innovation?

Following the identification of stable processes, Kimball asked the task force members to identify demographic, economic, social, and political forces acting on the curriculum that required innovation by the institution. Several of the forces identified were:

- Shifting demographics of international students away from higher education institutions like ETI and toward universities in Europe and other parts of the world.
- The global decreases in male enrollment that may particularly impact engineering, math, and science programs.
- The tendency of ETI faculty to remain cloistered in their programs and departments, limiting the opportunities for interdisciplinary and cross-department curricular innovation.
- The clumsy approval process for new research centers that has a dampening effect on creating "skunk works" to generate innovation and experimentation.

The processes and forces identified would serve as internal and external environmental scans upon which they could build their innovation process.

Questions to Consider
- How do loose and intermittent connections between and among academic units affect organizational change efforts?
- How does ambiguity affect change and innovation?
- What are some of the ways in which negative trends can be turned into positive opportunities?

Leveraging the Margins

With great enthusiasm, Warren Norton convinced many on the task force that the greatest source of innovation could be found in the open course online program at ETI. This program contained elements that promised to disrupt the traditional ways that knowledge was disseminated in higher education institutions. Online open course systems are asynchronous, transcend borders, and offer educational opportunities to people not served by courses traditionally taught on campus. Norton had long believed in intellectual engagement independent of institutional physical spaces and even ability to pay.

Ann Royce and Dana Briggs thought Norton's ideas were interesting but naïve. Someone had to pay the bills and keep the lights on. They agreed that the online open course program was an important intellectual experiment. But they did not see it as a model upon which to transform ETI's curriculum. Because higher education was a global enterprise, the open course program offered an easily adaptable way to experiment with new ideas and content. Curriculum developments could be "tested" with less risk than within traditional programs that were more expensive. But Royce and Briggs did not see this program as a model for the curriculum of the future.

Questions to Consider
- What are the sources of disruption in the current higher education climate?
- What aspects of higher education institutions are pockets of innovation? Pockets of resistance to innovation?

- What pathways exist for curricular innovations to be brought into the traditional curriculum?

A Change in Participants

After several meetings of the Task Force on Curricular Change, it became clear that the group was not working effectively. Dr. Royce rejected every suggestion made, regardless of how benign or innovative. Kimball decided that she must make the difficult decision to ask Royce to leave the task force. She was hoping that a change in the participants stream would yield different results regarding strategic change. Although Royce was furious about being asked to leave the task force, she looked at the change in participation as a way to exert her influence as a dean to resist elements of the curricular change that she felt were dangerously disruptive.

In addition to changing the participants, Kimball also decided, based on the ideas expressed in the garbage can model of decision making, to change the solutions stream. If she introduced a new person with new ideas, novel and different solutions would present themselves. With Royce, the only solution was to keep the current curricular structures of the institution. Kimball was interested in expanding, not contracting, the options.

Questions to Consider

- How does changing the mix of participants alter the dynamic of a task force?
- What solutions may be attached to a different dean, administrator, or faculty member than Royce?
- What are some ramifications of the provost asking a dean to resign from a task force?
- Could adjustments in the other streams be made in lieu of changing the participants stream?

Strategic Choices

After several additional months of meetings, a plan emerged from the task force. While some suggestions were conservative, others had the potential to disrupt the curricular offerings at ETI. The plans included the following:

- Increase flexibility in student time and requirements toward their degrees. This included an increase in the self-designed majors that spanned programs and departments.
- Increase the number of "just-in-time" courses through more online offerings. Without the physical restrictions of classrooms and scheduling, online courses could be more flexible than on campus, real-time options.
- Change the business management and computer science graduate degrees into modules. This configuration would enable different pathways to a degree.
- Allow students to "bundle" the modules into new ways of thinking and learning.
- Increase intellectual connections through the disaggregation of academic departments into new configurations that could be adapted with the needs of the curriculum. New configurations were expected to emerge on an ongoing basis.
- Use the lessons learned through the online open course project to make further advances in the use of technology in on-campus course options.

- Decouple space from learning by increasing the options for learning that were mediated through technology—including technologies that had not yet been invented.

New Garbage Cans Form

As Kimball worked with the Task Force on Curricular Change, two developments occurred that threatened to disrupt the process. First, ETI was changing its financial model to a revenue-centered management approach. The change was instituted to (a) manage changes in the external environment, (b) balance academic prerogative and financial accountability, (c) encourage entrepreneurship, (d) accurately measure quality, cost, and administrative growth, and (e) understand the actual costs of academic programs and relate them to courses, credits, and research dollars generated (Curry, Laws, & Strauss, 2013). The change in the budget model required significant effort by executive leadership, deans, and several task force members. It served as a garbage can in the decision-making process regarding curriculum change.

A second garbage can was forming over the announcement by President Lincoln that he was a finalist for the presidency at his old institution. He was apologetic about breaking his pledge to Provost Kimball to remain at ETI for the first three years of her tenure as provost, but explained that this was an opportunity he could not pass up. Kimball was amazed to realize how relevant the garbage can model of decision making was to the situation she faced.

Questions to Consider

- How does the presence of additional "garbage cans" influence the curricular change process?
- How might a provost disentangle curriculum change planning from the additional garbage cans forming?
- How are choices enabled and constrained by the presence of additional garbage cans?

Disruptive Forces

The task force plan promised to profoundly re-shape ETI's curriculum. Most significant was the fact that the innovation could be responsible for self-disruption. While disruption often has an external catalyst (e.g., a new and unanticipated technology, the introduction of a new business model, the occupation of an educational niche by a new competitor), few institutions choose to disrupt their curricular model through internally-generated catalysts. The curriculum changes at ETI did just that, making the proposal particularly remarkable.

Questions to Consider

- What examples of disruption in higher education can you identify?
- How can an institution of higher education stay ahead of disruptive forces?
- What environmental scans can one stay attuned to in order to remain aware of potential disruptions?

CONCLUSIONS

Understanding the garbage can model of decision making and disruptive innovations may assist administrators to manage the complexities of organizational functioning.

However, this understanding may leave all involved longing for the confident feeling that progress on measurable goals and anticipation of disruption is possible. Higher education institutions have traditionally been complex organizations with multiple and often conflicting purposes and goals. They have always struggled to better understand the technologies (i.e., teaching and learning) upon which they depend. Fluid participation among students, staff, and faculty characterizes these institutions. And, their client-serving nature and use of highly professional staff has introduced uncertainty. The current circumstances that further introduce uncertainty and complexity through disruptions from a variety of internal and external sources add to the complexity of these traditional yet completely modern institutions.

Questions to Consider
- Do you agree that administrators can decrease the complexity and uncertainty within higher education institutions? If so, why? If not, why not?
- What is gained in terms of innovativeness and creativity by the presence of disruptive forces upon higher education as a system?
- What disruptions have you witnessed and what was their effect on your work as a faculty member or higher education administrator?

8

POLITICAL

This place is more like a political jungle, alive and screaming, than a rigid, quiet bureaucracy. (Baldridge, 1971b, p. 9)

INTRODUCTION

The birth of the political model in higher education is unmistakably identified with the early 1970s writings of J. Victor Baldridge. Baldridge observed that the then widely accepted perspectives of bureaucracy and collegiums did not adequately explain university administration or faculty life: "we see neither the rigid, formal aspects of bureaucracy nor the calm, consensus-directed elements of an academic collegium" (1971c, pp. 19–20). The lack of fit of the bureaucratic and collegial models was particularly evident regarding organizational change and decision making. Higher education organizational theorists suggested that the political model might better explain higher education organizations than other choices available (Baldridge et al., 1978).

Regardless of any cultural beliefs about the rationality or serenity of college campuses, higher education history—including the social unrest of the 1960s, intense public scrutiny of the 1990s, and economic crisis and political uncertainty of the early 21st century—shapes these organizations as contested political ground composed of stakeholders, power elites, conflicting priorities, and strategic maneuvering. Although public institutions with governor-appointed board of trustee members, public funding, and close connections between the institution and state are most obviously political organizations, private institutions are strongly affected by policies regarding federal financial aid, the effects of public opinion regarding tuition and fees, and government and foundation funding for research and initiatives. "In an era of declining resources, increasing competition for students, and conflicting demands … [higher education institutions] are becoming arenas for coalition building, win–lose games, ambiguous goals, and uneven power distribution" (Amey, Jessup-Anger, & Tingson-Gatuz, 2009, p. 17). Similar to the ways that feminists in the 1960s declared that the "personal is political," higher education institutions can claim that their existence is political.

Although his work has been criticized as not adequately explaining the pluralistic nature of higher education decision making, Baldridge opened the discussion about the political nature of higher education including the strengths this model brings to an analysis of higher education institutions. Baldridge's political approach positions executive administrators as the primary decision makers with faculty, students, and others playing a consultative rather than principal role. The contest and conflict inherent in Baldridge's model places non-elites in roles opposing or supporting rather than initiating and determining decisions. This chapter shares Baldridge's work on the political aspects of decision making and discusses theories that expand and enrich those original conceptions.

SOCIOLOGY AS A FOUNDATION FOR THE POLITICAL MODEL

In any organization, relationships are key to understanding behavior, structure, and interactions. At its basic level, the political model is about relationships as it accounts for interactions, connections, and exchanges among people, organizational levels, and social and cultural capital. Decisions are not made in isolation but in relationship to others who are invested in the outcome to some degree (Ellis, 2016). Viewing an organization as an interacting set of relationships embraces the view of leadership advanced by Rost (1993, p. 102; emphasis in the original): "*Leadership is an influence relationship among leaders and followers who intend real changes that reflect their mutual purposes.*" In this chapter, the sociological theoretical perspective is used to consider the interacting relationships within higher education institutions. As with any theoretical perspective, the sociological one brings strengths and weaknesses to bear on its use as a point of analysis (see Table 8.1).

Baldridge's theory, interest convergence from critical race theory, and positive theory of institutions (PTI) are introduced and discussed in the context of the political model and decision making in higher education.

METAPHOR

Though apt in many ways, the jungle metaphor, commonly used to describe political organizations, overemphasizes the negative and underemphasizes the positive aspects of the political model. If the negative side of political organizations—the power plays, gamesmanship, and deal making—is the primary consideration, political organizations are seen as competitive, treacherous, and suitable only for the most fit. The positive side of the political model—the richness of constituent involvement, potential for goal

Table 8.1 Strengths and Weaknesses of the Sociological Theoretical Foundation for Higher Education

Strengths	Weaknesses
Explains interconnections among different campus groups and constituencies.	Over-explains group behavior while it under-explains individual behavior.
Provides a potent analysis of power.	Views power struggles as a central component of organizational life.
Draws connections among coalitions, interest groups, and power elites.	Places an emphasis on competition at the expense of adequate analysis of cooperation.

achievement, and possibility of change through policy making—go unremarked when institutions are pictured as environments teaming with danger and conflict. Without a view that embraces a balanced approach to politics in organizations, the negative features of the model (e.g., rivalry, backstabbing, and competing goals) overpower the positive features (e.g., attention cues, relationship building, and goal clarification).

Knowledge about colleges and universities as political organizations assists administrators, faculty, and students achieve their goals in an environment containing conflict, interest groups, and divergent points of view. The ideas presented in this chapter can help administrators, faculty, and students recognize when they are already, or becoming, embroiled in a political situation, particularly one they would rather avoid. "To dismiss or avoid political dimensions is a mistake. *Mastering the connection between politics and decisions is key*" (Ellis, 2016, p. 458, emphasis in the original). With knowledge about the political model, institutional members can choose to participate, take action to manage the situation, or bow out gracefully.

STRUCTURE

The political model has a more amorphous structure with relationship rather than structural principles defining its form. Using relationships among individuals as an organizing principle, Morgan (2006, p. 161) stated, "the political metaphor encourages us to see organizations as loose networks of people with divergent interests who gather together for the sake of expediency." The dynamics and relationships among people are areas where the political model is most explanatory and insightful. Coalitions form and dissolve, depending on the issue, task, or conflict; bedfellows are exchanged, subject to the goal; and conflict ebbs and flows with the passage of time and experience.

The political model can be applied to or combined with other organizational forms. Any organizational structure can include elements of a political system. It can be used to understand decision making, relationships, and power dynamics in a bureaucracy, collegium, or organized anarchy, for example. The purpose of political systems is to make decisions that achieve the goals of the political actors and influence parts or the whole of an organization. "Members of political systems interact with one another to influence the meeting of desires and objectives through decisions that allocate resources, give approvals or denials, move agendas forward or delay their progress" (Ellis, 2016, p. 468).

CHARACTERISTICS OF THE POLITICAL MODEL

The political model has several characteristics that make it unique among possible higher education organizational choices. These features include conflict as normal, interest groups and coalitions, interest convergence, inactivity, fluid participation, and attention cues and privilege. Particularly applicable during times of intense change, an ongoing circumstance for higher education institutions, the political model provides insights into policy making, change, and strategy.

Conflict as Normal

From the political model perspective, conflict is natural and to be expected in dynamic and complex organizations such as higher education institutions (Baldridge, 1971b). Whether explicit or implicit, conflict is always present in organizations. It identifies allies, empowers under-represented groups, and motivates organizational members. "Conflict may be personal, interpersonal, or between rival groups or coalitions. It may be built into organizational structures, roles, attitudes, and stereotypes or arise over a scarcity of resources" (Morgan, 2006, p. 163). In contrast to perspectives that view conflict as dysfunctional (Pettigrew, 2014), from a political model viewpoint conflict exposes institutional priorities, focuses commitment to goals, and connects people to goal achievement. Rather than avoid conflict, organizational members are encouraged to embrace and work with conflict (Ellis, 2016).

Morgan (2006) borrowed from Thomas (1976, 1977) to discuss five styles of conflict management: collaborating, compromising, accommodating, avoiding, and competing (also summarized in Coburn, 2015). *Collaborators* seek win–win situations and use this style when learning, integration, and relationship building are necessary to meet a goal. Negotiation is at the heart of collaboration and involves exchanges of favors, services, or future commitment. "Negotiation is a dialogue between parties to reach an understanding, resolve a difference, or gain an advantage in the outcome" (Ellis, 2016, p. 469). *Compromise* is an often-used style and involves give and take. Organizational members *accommodate* when they submit to or comply with the demands at the heart of conflict. This approach may alleviate the conflict in the short term, but does not prevent it from arising later. Higher education administrators and faculty use *avoidance* when they wait out or ignore conflicts. An avoidance tactic is to deflect attention to other priorities in the institution. Over time, the conflict may fade or it may become a lingering, tolerated aspect of organizational life. Avoidance is useful when the conflict is trivial and one must pick one's battles. *Competing*, because it creates win–lose situations, is to be avoided completely or perhaps used judiciously in higher education settings. This approach has its usefulness during emergencies or circumstances when immediate action is needed but there are always adverse consequences with this approach to managing conflict. Because "conflict arises whenever interests collide" (Morgan, 2006, p. 163), a discussion of interest groups and coalitions can aid one's understanding of conflict.

Interest Groups and Coalitions

A major characteristic of higher education organizations and systems is the presence of stakeholders who often band together to form interest groups.

> These groups articulate their interests in many different ways, bringing pressure to bear on the decision-making process from any number of angles, and using power and force whenever it is available and necessary. Once articulated, power and influence go through a complex process until policies are shaped, reshaped, and forged from the competing claims of multiple groups. (Baldridge, 1971a, p. 8)

Whether directly associated with the institution (e.g., students, faculty, alumni, parents) or not (e.g., neighbors, state legislators, government officials), interest groups are concerned with the actions and decisions of colleges and universities (Bok, 2015). Whether demanding lower tuition, the increased teaching of employable skills desired by corporations, or providing services to local communities, interest groups and the stakeholders who comprise them lobby and exert their influence on higher education institutions. Skilled decision making involves relationship building, coalition building, alliances, and partnerships (Ellis, 2016).

Coalitions form among internal and external institutional members who share common beliefs and goals. While coalitions enable those with limited power to increase their influence, these groups can also form among those who already have sufficient positional or institutional power. Organizational members can combine and increase their power base by joining forces. When interest groups form among those at the top of the hierarchy (e.g., presidential cabinet members), or those with power (e.g., senior faculty), they become power elites.

While a power elite such as the president's staff is responsible for a wide range of major decisions (Baldridge, 1971b), no one group makes *all* the decisions *all* the time. Instead, several fluid and ever-changing groups determine the direction of a college or university. In higher education, the presence of faculty with professional expertise, student affairs professionals with a strong influence on student life, and trustees with fiduciary and planning responsibilities means that several power elites operate simultaneously. Faculty control the curriculum, the president and vice presidents make key budget decisions, and trustees approve or disapprove the strategic direction of the institution.

Interest Convergence

Baldridge's theory can be partially updated by considering the concept of interest convergence as advanced by Critical Race Theorists (Delgado & Stefancic, 2012). "One major tenet of CRT is Interest Convergence, which … typically compels white people to advocate for the advancement of people of color only if their own self-interest is better served" (Harper, 2009, p. 31).

In a discussion of the *Brown* v. *State Board of Education* decision, Derrick Bell (1980) first advanced the idea that civil rights and other potential gains obtained by people of color only occurred when the economic or social conditions were also advanced for Whites. The classic example of interest convergence is affirmative action as enacted by President John F. Kennedy in 1961. Although originally used to combat discrimination by race, creed, color, or national origin, subsequent laws extended affirmative action to additional groups including women. Interest converged between the original protected classes of affirmative action and White women such that the latter group has historically been the primary recipient of affirmative action programs and initiatives. The Critical Race Theorists' approach to interest convergence sheds new light on interest groups and coalitions and their role in decision making. These theorists insert race and racism into processes that could wrongly be conceived as neutral.

Inactivity Prevails

Political models assume that most organizational members will not be involved in decision making (Kezar, 2013). Although decision making is constrained by budgets, time, attention, expertise, and other factors, disinterest by most organizational members means that the majority of decisions are left to interest groups and power elites. The sentiment, "for most people most of the time … they allow administrators to run the show" (Baldridge et al., 1978, p. 35), may be truer today than when it was first written. Academic and administrative activities have increased significantly with the advent of technology, raised expectations of parents and students, and demands for accountability by state and federal governments. Whether by preference or circumstance, many members prefer not to be involved, lack the time or interest to serve on campus-wide committees, are without the power to influence, or do not have access to the decision-making processes impacting the organization as a whole. This detached stance is a particular preference of faculty (Baldridge et al., 1978) who see their primary roles as teaching, research, and service. From their point of view, management, decision making, and policy determination are the purview of administrators. This inactive stance changes when, and if, the decisions made have a direct impact on or negatively affect faculty activities.

> When resources are plentiful, few people worry about changes or come into conflict. It is when resource constraints and pending changes might impact people (or when they encounter an inability to create changes because of a lack of resources) that people mobilize. (Kezar, 2014b, p. 35)

In that case, the norms of inactivity shift to the collegial expectation of consultation and discussion. "When faculty believe collegial decision-making is valued and rewarded and when professional authority is recognized, they are more likely to engage in governance activities" (Lawrence & Ott, 2013, p. 149).

Fluid Participation

Fluid participation is a concept advanced by Cohen et al. (1972) in their organized anarchy model. Because "participants of decision-making bodies are continuously changing and their engagement strongly depends on the amount of interest and time they are willing to invest" (Kroeger, 2014, p. 4), fluid participation is closely related to the political organization characteristic that inactivity prevails. The political model assumes that organizational participants will "move in and out of the decision-making process" (Baldridge et al., 1978, p. 35). Unlike bureaucratic processes that assume fixed job responsibilities and procedures, decision making from a political model perspective occurs in fits and starts. If expectations are not met, previously uninvolved actors may suddenly become active. Seen from a political model viewpoint, it is not unusual for organizational members to expect their opinion on an issue to be considered; even on an issue previously and thoroughly vetted. Higher education's democratic practices and the tradition of consultation built into faculty culture shape expectations concerning access to decision making, the "right" to exercise one's voice, and a prerogative to intervene at any stage of the process. With fluid participation as an expectation, administrators, faculty leaders, and others must plan for an iterative and prolonged decision-making process. Newer technologies both help and exacerbate fluid participation. Anyone can build websites, send widely distributed e-mails, and write blogs that aid communication. These dynamic and accessible communications enhance democratic processes while simultaneously making the organization more politically sensitive.

Attention Cues and Privilege

While the shift from inactivity to activism by faculty and students, in particular, often feels seismic, attention cues often foretell when institutional members are moving out of their inactive stance. From faculty discussions about a vote of no confidence in the president, department chair rumblings of dissatisfaction about a dean's behavior, to student protests about campus social justice efforts, there are always advance cues to which politically astute administrators can attend. "Powerful political forces … cause a given issue to emerge from the limbo of on-going problems and certain 'attention cues' force the political community to consider the problem" (Baldridge, 1971c, pp. 190–191). While it may be difficult to accurately predict who will attend to specific goals and when they will do so, decision makers are well advised to attend to the early cues that portend political challenges.

Privilege is a consideration regarding exposure to attention cues. Access to information, expectations about consultation regarding decisions, and ability to exercise voice are examples of privilege held by selected, particularly elite, organizational members.

> Privilege increases the odds of having things your own way, of being able to set the agenda in a social situation and determine the rules and standards and how they're applied. Privilege grants the cultural authority to make judgments about others and to have those judgments stick. It allows people to define reality and to have prevailing definitions of reality fit their experience. Privilege means being able to decide who gets taken seriously, who receives attention, who is accountable to whom and for what. (Johnson, 2008, p. 117)

Faculty possess privilege accrued from the double advantage of academic freedom and expert power. Executive leaders possess privilege emanating from their access to information and experience with institutional roles that led them to the positions they hold. Their privilege also arises from the deference given to those occupying upper level positions that is dictated by cultural mores. Regardless of the dynamic of the privilege, there is no doubt that this force operates in political situations. The political model offers insights into why exercising privilege is common, frequently unwise, and often undemocratic.

PROCESSES IN POLITICAL ORGANIZATIONS

Political acumen and expertise by any institutional player requires an understanding of how political organizations work. Knowledge of how power and authority interact and are expressed is particularly essential for students, faculty, and administrators who seek to be politically astute.

Power

"Power is the medium through which conflicts of interest are ultimately resolved. Power influences who gets what, when, and how" (Morgan, 2006, p. 166). Power is a context-specific, relationship-oriented resource used to achieve goals and realize relationships. Birnbaum (1991) discussed five kinds of power: coercive, reward, legitimate, referent, and expert. *Coercive power* occurs when a person or group punishes or threatens another unless attempts at influence are heeded. *Reward power* occurs when an advantage (e.g., payment, raise, promotion) is offered or promised in exchange for an action or compliance. Reward power is also in effect when the removal of negative consequences or outcomes are promised. *Legitimate power* exists when those involved agree to a standard or set of rules through which one person or group influences the other in a specific context. When influence is gained through a relationship with another, that form of power is *referent*. When a person or group gains influence due to their special knowledge or competence, *expert power* is being applied.

Power from a political model perspective is dynamic, transient, and volatile. It has been a topic of considerable speculation and discussion over the millennia, giving rise to a thought-provoking collection of quotes (see Table 8.2). If higher education is to be a force for societal transformation, power must be understood and taken into consideration as a means to achieve that goal.

Although personal style and specific situations dictate which kind of power is to be used, understanding the different forms provides insight into organizational decisions and processes. Morgan (2006) outlined various ways that power is expressed in organizations. His ideas were adapted for higher education organizations and summarized in Table 8.3.

Scare Resources and Power

Control of scarce resources is a form and source of power (Morgan, 2006). The exercise of this power is particularly effective when the resource, for example, money, is limited. But money is not the only resource and source of power. Positions, administrators' time, and space are resources available for maneuvering and acquiring power. Knowledge is an important resource, particularly in higher education. Although controlling knowledge to gain power is a less potent mechanism with the increased access to information available through the internet, gatekeepers can still gain power by controlling, shaping, or spinning information. "Scarce resources, competing interests, and struggles for power and advantage" (Ellis, 2016, p. 468) are all related to power and the decision-making process.

Table 8.2 Memorable Sayings about Power

"The most common way people give up their power is by thinking they don't have any." Alice Walker
"Knowledge is power. Information is liberating." Kofi Annan
"Power corrupts and absolute power corrupts absolutely." Lord Acton
"A good indignation brings out all one's powers." Ralph Waldo Emerson
"A friend in power is a friend lost." Henry Adams
"When the whole world is silent, even one voice becomes powerful." Malala Yousafzai

Table 8.3 Power within Organizations

Autocracy "We'll do it this way."	Old style presidents' model
Bureaucracy "We're supposed to do it this way."	Financial aid office
Technocracy "It's best to do it this way."	Registrar's office
Codetermination "Let's decide how to do it together."	Career services
Representative democracy "How do your constituents want to do it?"	Faculty senate and faculty unions
Direct democracy "How shall we do it?"	Women's faculty caucus

Source: Adapted from Morgan, 2006, p. 156.

Uncertainty and Power

In the volatile climate in which higher education exists, the ability to cope with uncertainty is an important source of power. Postmodern theoretical perspectives such as critical theory, feminism, and critical race theory identify the inevitable uncertainty that exists within and outside higher education institutions. When administrators see uncertainty as opportunity rather than threat, power can increase as that person remains effective in situations where others are not. Institutional and individual reputation and the concomitant increase in power emerge when situations fraught with hazards are transformed into new or renewed programs and innovative approaches.

Interpersonal Power

Interpersonal power is a palatable form gained through associations and friendships. This type of power is particularly relevant to colleges and universities, because few institutions enable lifelong friendships as completely as these organizations. Networks established in colleges and universities have always been traded for power and influence to gain jobs, work connections, and favor. The more influence one has to trade, the more power is gained. Old style associations of the past (e.g., old boy and old girl networks) have recently been supplanted with social media. These newer forms of connecting with friends and others expand people's reach, which was previously limited by time and distance. Asynchronous communication and access to global linkages are dismantling physical and temporal barriers. Ease of communication, links to friends of friends, and global connections have exponentially increased the possibilities of interpersonal alliances from which influence can be gained.

The Interrelationship of Power and Authority

Power and authority, although related, are different concepts. Authority is more formal than power and emanates from one's position (Morgan, 2006). As a result of social approval, tradition, or law, administrators possess authority to act that is defined by the position they occupy. Using authority, administrators, particularly executive leaders, can, among other responsibilities, hire and fire employees, determine budgets, and set goals. Authority is exercised in the influence of supervisors over employees and the chair of the board of trustees over the president. Although an important concept in organizational structures, higher education institutions and the people within them have significant limits on their authority. The presence of faculty governance structures, student organizations, and informal elements such as charisma and non-positional power means that no one has ultimate or limitless authority. Because authority and the ability to enact decisions is distributed across interest groups, coalitions, and power elites, power from a political model perspective is limited and diffuse. Although many people assume that power is located primarily in the upper executive ranks (in other words, authority and positional power are equated), in higher education structures, "power is more diffuse, lodged with professional experts and fragmented into many departments and subdivisions" (Baldridge et al., 1978, p. 44). A college president, provost, or dean may have the authority to enact a decision, but lack the political power to make that change.

Understanding the limitations of authority and the dynamics of power can help administrators avoid naïveté about their range of influence and effectiveness. Leaders are not immune from challenges to their authority and power. In addition to the issues that occur as a result of these challenges, power is distributed throughout the organization, even at levels where there is less positional authority. "In spite of the considerable degree of power possessed by lower level employees, these employees seldom attempt to exercise their power or to resist the instructions of their managers" (Pfeffer, 1991/2005, p. 291). Employee strikes, faculty "work to rule" action, and student activism are ways that authority can be challenged and power exercised. Students, often erroneously viewed as powerless, express their voice and power through formal student governance organizations, collective action, and informal student activist groups.

DECISION MAKING

Rationality is assumed to be the basis for decision making by those who believe that colleges and universities operate in orderly, methodical ways. From a political perspective, order and rationality are not assumed. Instead, it is assumed that "political constraints can seriously undermine attempts to arrive at rational decisions" (Baldridge et al., 1978, p. 36). Political decision making depends on timing, finesse, and persistence.

Baldridge et al. (1978) devised a political model of decision making that assumed fluidity and complexity. Unlike the linear step-by-step procedures of the rational model, these higher education theorists believed that *"decision making is likely to be diffuse, segmentalized, and decentralized"* (Baldridge et al., 1978, p. 38; emphasis in the original). They outlined the why, who, how, and which of decision making including the political controversy, compromises, and bargaining likely to occur within higher education institutions. The following questions can be used to assess successful ways to pursue decision making in a political climate:

1. *Why is a decision being made?* Political forces often bring the problem to someone's attention. Those political forces could be a downward shift in enrollment, the upcoming retirement of key faculty members, a president's retirement, or a host of other issues. Because momentum and institutional procedures will carry an institution through the day-to-day decisions, it takes political pressure for larger scale decisions and change initiatives to capture the attention of administrators and faculty.
2. *Who should be making the decision?* "The right to make the decision often determines the outcome" (Baldridge et al., 1978, p. 38). Anyone can make a decision but it takes power and authority to implement it.
3. *How do you gain the advice of others?* The political model assumes that leaders will solicit input from colleagues (and foes, in some cases), gain support, and build ownership prior to making a decision. In higher education, this consultation often takes place through strategic planning committees, faculty governance bodies, and unofficial conversations.
4. *Which solutions are realistically available?* A solution may appear to be appropriate but unfeasible given the monetary, human, and time resources available. Some solutions are possible when an event, particularly a crisis, captures attention and makes a previously unpalatable decision inevitable.

The political model assumes that controversy, compromise, bargaining, and power are part of decision making (Ellis, 2016). These are particularly in play when faculty are involved in the decision. There are three types of faculty decision-making involvement: (a) *inactive*, employed primarily by faculty who concentrate their efforts on teaching and research; (b) *power elite*, used by senior faculty with the connections and longevity within the organization to unify other like-minded associates; and (c) *strategic*, initiated by faculty unions or other groups (e.g., college or school faculty groups) within the campus organizational structure (Baldridge et al., 1978). In general, a small group of faculty influences decision making while the majority of organizational members remain inactive and disinterested.

Internal and external stakeholder groups, including students, administrators, alumni, parents, and others, can carve out "spheres of influence" in which they make or influence decisions (Baldridge et al., 1978). In political organizations, it is the practice that groups outside a particular "sphere of influence" refrain from participating in decisions in that area. The character and range of the spheres shift depending on the environment, issue at hand, and type of campus. Administrators make decisions on a community college campus, for example, that would normally be executed by faculty at a liberal arts college. Administrators avoid curricular decision making; faculty eschew detailed budget decisions; student opinion is seldom exercised in long-term capital improvements. By establishing relationships, perfecting timing, and cultivating determination, faculty and administrators in political organizations can achieve their institutional purposes despite the inevitable setbacks and challenges.

Non-Decision Making

Non-decision making is an aspect of decision making that should be considered. "Non-decision making is a political space in which contest does not manifest because the issues have not reached the decision-making arena" (Pusser, 2015, p. 70). When norms (e.g., higher education as a good to be paid for by the recipient) are accepted and unchallenged, organizational functions proceed without conflict or contest. Decisions just happen in the day-to-day operation of the institution; they need not be public or even obvious. Although this economy of administrative and faculty effort has some benefits, there are certainly times when non-decision making should be urged back into the more open, democratic processes of decision making. Pusser offers three ways to urge non-decision making back into the decision-making sphere: "contextualizing norms, turning attention to historical precedents, and creatively reconstructing the debate over what is possible" (2015, p. 71). These means can be achieved, among other approaches, through engagement and discussion in governance (e.g., faculty senates, staff councils), via strategic and other long-range planning activities, as a result of lobbying and convincing stakeholder and interest groups, and through student and faculty activism.

STRENGTHS AND WEAKNESSES OF THE POLITICAL MODEL

When decisions are grounded in the values of the institution, then "each decision made builds an organizational culture in which values are communicated through consistent action" (Ellis, 2016, p. 469). Unfortunately, not all decisions are wise or grounded in a collaboratively determined set of institutional values. Skilled use of the political model requires knowledge of the strengths and weaknesses (see Table 8.4) and the ways the model can assist faculty, students, and administrators to more effectively make decisions, set policy, and avoid undesirable consequences.

Table 8.4   Strengths and Weaknesses of the Political Model

Strengths	Weaknesses
Provides a powerful analysis for decision making and policy making.	Can highlight divisiveness, competition, and other negative aspects of organizational life.
Clarifies organizational vision, mission, and goals.	Can focus institutional membership on immediate rather than long-term goals.
Provides attention cues for institutional leadership.	Can redirect attention onto tangential organizational goals.
Offers alternatives to the positional view of power and authority.	Can disempower the under-represented and those with limited access to power.
Explains the dynamic of relationships across bureaucratic levels.	Can diminish morale and healthy work environments.
Builds processes for change.	Can concentrate major decision making in the hands of an elite few.

NEXT STEPS: BRINGING THEORY INTO CURRENT USE

Current organizational theory in higher education notes the limited discussion and use of the political model and the need for more study and theorizing in this area (Pusser, 2015). The interest articulation model of Baldridge is enhanced with the inclusion of positive theories of institutions (PTI), articulated by Pusser in 2003 but yet to be fully incorporated into the political model as used in higher education. PTI "moves beyond the analysis of organizational decision making as an endogenous process, as it suggests that external influences and interests benefit from, and endeavor to influence, organizational structures and policies" (Pusser, 2003, pp. 125–126). Using PTI as applied to higher education involves considering the ways that colleges and universities are political institutions influenced by external forces. Examples of interests from such a perspective include laws enacted to influence higher education, efforts by state legislators to set the agenda for organizational action, and court judgments.

Characteristics of the Positive Theory of Institutions

PTI contains several characteristics that can enhance the political model as traditionally discussed: higher education institutions as political entities, the pluralistic considerations in PTI, and expanded dimensions of power and decision making.

Higher Education Institutions as Political Entities

Pusser (2003, p. 126) defines political institutions as: "those entities that control significant public resources; that have the authority to allocate public costs and benefits; that implement policies with significant political salience … and that stand as particularly visible sites of public contest." Regardless of where one might stand on the debate about whether higher education is a public or private good, a college education assuredly provides benefits and privileges to its recipients. The resources it controls, public dollars it commands, and benefits it provides squarely place colleges and universities in the realm of political entities.

Pluralistic Considerations in PTI

Decision making is a pluralistic process, particularly within higher education. Minority and majority preferences are expressed through internal governance structures (e.g., faculty senates, student government associations, staff councils). External political mechanisms such as voting provide opportunities for those outside the college or university to exercise their preferences for decisions (e.g., affirmative action legislation) that affect the internal operation of the institution. These pluralistic considerations provide a mechanism for the public and others less closely connected to higher education institutions to voice their opinion and exert influence over decision making. Unlike the internally focused direction of Baldridge's approach to the political model, PTI explores the ways that internal and external governance and political actions have an influence.

Although structures inside and outside higher education institutions provide people with an opportunity to voice their opinion and perhaps gain access to decision making, there are limits to this pluralistic process. Power, organizational role, and characteristics such as educational level constrain the ability of all constituents or political players to express their preferences regarding decision making.

Dimensions of Power and Decision Making

Pusser (2015) expands Baldridge's and others' conceptions of power and decision making through his discussion of three dimensions of power specific to higher education. These dimensions of power provide more nuanced approaches to political decision making and an expanded understanding of the uses of the political model in higher education institutions.

The first is the instrumental view, congruent with Baldridge's model of political decision making, understood through observations of conflicts, bargaining, and compromise. The second dimension of power considers conflict but in the context of whose interests are favored by the prevailing norms regarding the decision-making context. In other words, decision making and any accompanying conflict is grounded in the norms of the various parties. Prevailing norms may have considerable weight and precedence, both of which may be hard to overcome. The third dimension of power moves beyond the norms and assumptions of the interested parties. From this perspective "a different outcome might emerge if the unthinkable was thought, the unspoken proclaimed, and critical imagination brought to bear on the conflict" (Pusser, 2015, pp. 65–66). This third dimension is the most creative and original. The resources of the interested parties are harnessed to enact a decision with outcomes not previously imagined. This dimension of power, though difficult to imagine and achieve, carries with it considerable optimism and decision-making influence.

CONCLUSIONS

Despite the fact that the political model has been touted as particularly relevant for higher education, many may find this approach to be distasteful. Others may find information about the model useful as they avoid politically charged associations and situations. Morgan (2006) offered some advice about situations to avoid when considering the political model. If one views these political games with insight, the efficacy of the political model can be revealed.

- *Being co-opted.* Dissent can be quelled by inviting the dissenters into "official" ranks. Women faculty members with legitimate complaints about inequitable salaries are appointed as department chairs; student protesters are recruited onto presidential advisory boards.
- *Careerism.* A long-established practice in political organizations is to establish oneself on a committee or in association with a person or group to advance one's career.
- *Gamesmanship.* Some people play the political game simply for its enjoyment. For those uninterested in this approach, it is best to avoid these people and the situations in which they operate.
- *Turf protection.* The administrative overzealous defense of resources and power within a unit is a challenge to all organizations. This turf protection is particularly a problem in higher education institutions where individual colleges and schools compete for limited resources. When administrators or faculty concentrate on local goals at the expense of institution-wide purposes, all are disadvantaged.
- *Freewheeling.* Organizational participants who loosely apply the rules, disregard policies seeking fairness, and play by "who you know" principles rather than equity create a negative political climate. Caution must be exercised to avoid being embroiled in this political game.

The positive aspects of the political model have much to lend administrators, faculty, and students seeking to better understand higher education institutions. Knowledge of the negative aspects of this model can aid those seeking to improve the organization through more collaborative and equitable means.

Questions for Discussion

- Whose loose networks are you currently part of or do you think you will be part of? How do you think this will affect your decision-making ability?
- How does knowledge about colleges and universities as political systems help you understand your current and/or future situation as a faculty member or administrator in higher education?
- How does coalition building between faculty and students support activism within colleges and universities?
- How can conflict be viewed as a positive force for change in higher education settings?
- How can conflict be a negative force for change?
- How can political principles be used to effect change at the board of trustees level of an institution?
- What political, economic, and cultural implications need to be exposed to reveal the liberatory potential of higher education?

Recommended Readings in the Political Model

Bruns, J. W., & Bruns, D. L. (2007). Effecting change in colleges and universities. *Journal of Leadership Studies, 1*(2), 53–63.

Chambers, A. C., & Burkhardt, J. C. (Eds.). (2015). *Higher education for the public good: Emerging voices from a national movement.* New York: Wiley & Sons.

Hatch, M. J., & Cunliffe, A. L. (2006). *Organization theory: Modern, symbolic, and postmodern perspectives.* Oxford: Oxford University Press.

Kezar, A. (2010). Organizational theory. In J. H. Schuh, S. R. Jones, & S. R. Harper (Eds.), *Student services: A handbook for the profession* (pp. 226–241). San Francisco: Jossey-Bass.

Mendez, J. P., Bonner II, F. A., Méndez-Negrete, J., & Palmer, R. T. (Eds.). (2015). *Hispanic serving institutions in American higher education: Their origin, and present and future challenges.* Sterling, VA: Stylus Publishing.

Pettigrew, A. M. (2014). *The politics of organizational decision-making.* New York: Routledge.

Rhoads, R. A., & Liu, A. (2009). Globalization, social movements, and the American university: Implications for research and practice. *Higher Education: Handbook of Theory and Research, 24,* 273–315.

CASE: THE MERGER OF HISPANIC-SERVING AND PREDOMINANTLY WHITE INSTITUTIONS

Hispanic-Serving Institution (HSI) is a designation within the U.S. Department of Education in which greater than 25% of total student enrollment, part- and full-time and graduate students, are Hispanic.[1] The designation was codified over a period of years between 1965 and 1986 through U.S. Congressional action on the Higher Education Act (Valdez, 2015). When designated as an HSI, an institution is eligible for Title III federal grants to be used for faculty development, academic program development, laboratory equipment, and other uses. The highest number of HSIs are located in California with Texas following as the second leading state. The majority of HSIs are two-year institutions. The continuing growth in the population of Hispanic students in the United States makes the HSI designation an important one in U.S. higher education.

=========================THE CASE=========================

Institutional Context

Two-year public institution, Greenville Community College (a pseudonym), has been a designated HSI since 1990. With a student population of 2,300 students, the community college has struggled to maintain its enrollment over the past 10 years. Greenville is located in a Rust Belt state that has seen the decline of its major industries. Although new businesses have come into the region, the newer jobs have been located in the lower-paying service sector. Greenville has sought to provide training for unemployed Greenville and surrounding community residents through educational and training programs associated with the state. Many in the community of Greenville remember when the college was not an HSI but enrolled the predominantly White students who were the offspring of workers in the nearby industrial plants. With the closing of local industries, Greenville's population evolved to be predominantly Hispanic, the population of students who now attend Greenville Community College.

Questions to Consider

- In what ways does the character of a community reflect the population and mission of a local community college?
- What economic changes have impacted higher education over the last 20 years?
- What initiatives have been instituted in community colleges to retain relevance during economic and industrial changes in the United States?

Characters

Dr. Valeria Perez, President of Greenville Community College: Dr. Perez has been president of Greenville Community College for 15 years. As a long-standing president, she has seen many changes in the institution. She was president when the college served a predominantly White population. With the shift in the local population, she spearheaded efforts to increase the number of Hispanic students being served by the institution. Dr. Perez believes that Greenville has a significant role in generating innovation and jobs in the local community. She sees the college as an incubator for ideas and products. While she knows that the size and teaching as opposed to research emphasis of the institution limits its impact as a business starter, she believes the college can provide job training and academic programs that can spur job growth for the regional economy.

Zachary Daniels, State Governor: Governor Daniels was in his second term of a success-ful governorship. His administration had taken on the important task of generating business for a state that had suffered job losses with the flight of its major industries. He had attracted technology industries in addition to service industry jobs. Although the state had an otherwise bright future, there was a problem in the region surrounding Greenville Community College. That area of the state continued to experience job losses and negative economic growth. Daniels had appealed directly to the college's president, Dr. Valeria Perez, for help with this issue but she had not responded to his requests as vigorously as he would have liked. Given the inadequate enrollment at Greenville, Daniels had asked his Higher Education Commissioner chair, Melissa West, to explore the possibility of merging Greenville with a local state four-year university, Worthing-ton University. The institutions were within 25 miles of each other and the two-year programs at Greenville could be subsumed into Worthington University's programs. The research incubator programs at Worthington would be an excellent complement to the two-year job focused programs at Greenville.

Dr. Jonathan DeSaeger, President of Worthington University: Dr. DeSaeger has served as president of Worthington University for two years. With a background in mechanical engineering, Dr. DeSaeger worked during his tenure to increase the research efforts that generated business for the local economy. As a four-year state institution, Dr. DeSaeger took the institution's role as an instrumentality of the state very seriously. He worked closely with Governor Daniels to match emerging university programs with the employ-ment needs of the state. Because of these initiatives, Dr. DeSaeger had received criticism from many faculty members who felt that the institutional mission was drifting from general education and research to job training and economic development. Governor Daniels has floated the idea of a merger with Greenville Community College with DeSaeger who feels that the programs would be a good complement to the business incubator efforts of the University.

Dr. Melissa West, State Higher Education Commission Chair: West was appointed by Governor Daniels at the beginning of his second term of office. A relative newcomer to the state, West had to quickly become familiar with the state system of 15 public colleges and universities. A firm believer in efficiency, West believed it was her primary role to advance the Governor's agenda regarding higher education and economic growth within the state. West has limited to no experience with HSIs, having moved to the state from a predominantly White area.

Questions to Consider
- What is the role of public education in regional, state, and national economic development?
- Do you favor a liberal arts, vocational, or other educational approach for students? How might your approach be reflected in the academic programs at an institution?
- What are some of the advantages and disadvantages of a close connection between the state governor's office and the president's office at public colleges and universities? What is an appropriate balance between autonomy and coordination between the state and a public institution of higher education?

The Proposed Merger

Governor Daniels asked his State Higher Education Commission Chair, Melissa West, to open the conversation about a merger with Greenville Community College president Perez. West invited Perez to her office in the state capital to broach the topic with her. West explained the need to consolidate institutions within the state to achieve financial efficiencies. She explained that the merger would provide additional resources to the students of Greenville—resources not currently available within the community college. When asked about the designation as an HSI, West explained that the population of Greenville would combine with the predominantly White population of Worthington University so the HSI designation would no longer be necessary.

Questions to Consider
- What does the loss of an HSI designation mean for an institution? What are the political and cultural ramifications of such a change?
- If you were opposed to the merger, what political means would you employ to combat it?
- If you were in favor of the merger, what political means would you employ to garner support for this position?
- Whose interests are served through the potential merger?

West had a similar conversation with Worthington University president DeSaeger. DeSaeger was skeptical about the merger but decided to suspend judgment. He wanted to speak with his staff and explore the political ramifications of such a change. He considered President Perez a good colleague, someone he knew from their state-organized meetings of college and university presidents. He was conflicted about whether or not he would approach her for her opinion on the issue. While he believed that her reaction would help him gauge support or opposition for the merger, he did not want to be seen as thwarting the efforts of the Higher Education Commission Chair or the Governor.

Questions to Consider
- If you were in the position of President DeSaeger, would you have an informal conversation with President Perez? If so, what would be the nature of that conversation?
- What are some of the potential political ramifications of a conversation between Presidents Perez and DeSaeger?

- Can you suggest ways that DeSaeger could ferret out Perez's opinion without contacting her directly?
- How do the political characteristics of conflict, stakeholders, and coalitions come into play during a merger of two different higher education institutions?

Political Action

As a result of a leak from an unknown source, Greenville students, alumni/ae, and faculty became aware of the proposed merger and launched a protest at the state capital to voice their opposition. They felt that the needs of Hispanic students would be disregarded under a possible merger between Greenville Community College and Worthington University. Alumni and faculty who had previously worked to gain the HSI designation were particularly vocal in their opposition to the merger. A letter-writing campaign was launched so that constituents could attest to the education they received from Greenville and express their concerns about loss of identity and emphasis were the merger to occur.

Questions to Consider

- What insights does the theory of interest convergence add to the motivations behind the merger?
- How are the interests of Worthington advanced through the merger? Of Greenville? How are the interests of these institutions thwarted?
- Which institution stands to gain the most from the merger? The least?

DISCUSSION

Institutional mergers are riddled with political implications but a merger between an HSI and a Predominantly White Institution raises additional concerns and political questions. The HSI designation was determined to assist institutions to gain federal dollars to enable them to better accommodate underserved student populations. The merger of an HSI (or a Historically Black Institution, Women's College, or other institution serving under-represented populations) with a Predominantly White Institution must be examined with regard to whether or not such a merger is in the best interests of that underserved population. History and the legal challenges to such mergers serve as cautionary tales about such institutional change.

The political model offers both advice and caution about ways to proceed with a plan to merge two institutions. The model provides guidance about considering the interests of constituents, the potential for conflict, the role of stakeholders, the coalitions that will inevitably form, and the dynamics of interest convergence that emerge. The model further provides insights into the ways that such a change could be approached, both by those supporting and those opposing the merger. As stated earlier in the chapter, the political model provides insights for those wanting to use its characteristics as a way to advance their agenda. It offers insights for those wanting to anticipate the political ramifications present during any organizational change.

NOTE

1 The term "Hispanic" is used in lieu of the more current and accurate "Latino" to remain in keeping with the terminology used by the U.S. Department of Education designation.

9

SPIRITUAL

Organizational theories and models that ignore the spiritual dimension will remain deficient. (Oliveira, 2004, p. 19)

INTRODUCTION

Interest in religion and spirituality has seen a marked increase since the mid- to late 1990s (Briskin, 1996; Daloz, Keen, Keen, & Parks, 1996; Gunnlaugson & Vokey, 2014; Jablonski, 2001; Kessler, 2000; Small, 2015). Most attention regarding this topic has focused on students and their development as spiritual beings (Astin, 2004, 2016; Astin, Astin, & Lindholm, 2010; Chickering, Dalton, & Stamm, 2005). A complementary interest in spirituality exists in the context of organizational theory, although the collection of scholarship is a modest one at the present time. Despite its size this stream of scholarship is essential to understanding modern organizations because

> the spirituality in the workplace movement is the manifestation of a deep yearning for meaning and purpose in the work lives of individuals. People want to know that their work matters, that their efforts are in the service of something worthwhile, that their legacy is one of contributing to the betterment of humankind. (Rogers & Dantley, 2001, p. 601)

An exploration of organizations from a spiritual perspective is helpful because people within and outside of higher education institutions question the U.S. emphasis on materialism, deterioration of community, and de-emphasis of the search for something larger than the self. Writing on spirituality and organizational theory, Oliveira claimed that "when spirituality is cultivated in the workplace, a creative energy is unlocked" (2004, p. 19). Spirituality in organizations represents an organizational paradigm that considers important aspects of human existence that transcend common negative organizational practices such as downsizing, re-engineering, and outsourcing.

A renewed interest in spirituality in organizations emanates from changes such as globalization, the increased presence of workers from ethnicities that value spirituality and meaning making, the recognition that spirituality is a "critical human need" both within and outside the workplace, and enhanced understanding of the ways that expressions of spirituality in organizations better meet workers' needs. (Oliviera, 2004, p. 19)

This chapter explores the spiritual perspective in organizations and organizational theory, including implications for the work lives of faculty, administrators, and staff. The implications of spirituality, interrelationships, leadership, power, and vision in the context of higher education institutions are explored.

The differences between religion and spirituality—concepts often conflated but with vastly different meanings—are helpful to explore prior to any discussion of spirituality. Rogers (2003, p. 22) stated that "spirituality is an inner, private process while religion is an outward, public one." Chickering (2006) also teased out the differences between religion and spirituality.

Being religious connotes belonging to and practicing a religious tradition. Being spiritual suggests a personal commitment to a process of inner development that engages us in our totality.... Spirituality is a way of life that affects and includes every moment of existence. It is at once a contemplative attitude, a disposition to a life of depth, and the search for ultimate meaning, direction and belonging. (Teasdale, 1999 as cited in Chickering, 2006, p. 2)

Zohar (2010) clarified that there need not be a connection to religion to embrace the organizational spiritual perspective. In this chapter, spirituality, not religion, is the focus of the discussion.

Rogers and Dantley (2001, p. 591) noted that: "Spirituality manifests in our search for wholeness, meaning, interconnectedness, and values." One of the places where that search occurs is in higher education organizations. Spirituality is a corporate and organizational concern, not one solely related to individual growth and development. Spirituality from this perspective has substantial implications for leadership, organizational vision, and interrelationships within organizations.

PSYCHOLOGY AS A FOUNDATION FOR THE SPIRITUAL PERSPECTIVE

Organizational theorists have a long history of approaching organizations from a psychological perspective. Motivation, job satisfaction, interpersonal relations, and leadership merge with and emerge from psychological concepts. Assumptions from this theoretical foundation include the following:

- Understanding human nature and behavior can assist one's job performance and effectiveness.
- Organizations are sites where human agency is acted and expressed.
- Humans seek to become self-actualized in organizations.

- Psychological health and the lack of thereof can be expressed at both individual and organizational levels.
- Individuals' and groups' psychological and emotional health (or the lack thereof) have an impact on organizational health.

In addition to these assumptions, the spiritual perspective is particularly well suited to the assumptions of positive psychology, an arm of the discipline that challenges the disease-oriented approach of traditional psychology. "The positive psychology approach sought to bring a complementary focus to the psychology field's emphasis on remediating mental illness by attending to the study and practice of fostering human strengths and emotional well-being" (Mather, 2010, p. 158). This approach, a continuation of the work of Abraham Maslow, Carl Rogers, and other humanistic psychologists, is a particularly apt foundation for the spiritual perspective of organizational theory. Several aspects of positive psychology, as articulated by Mather (2010), include the following:

- Happiness is a goal of human living.
- Nurturing positive emotions can significantly affect individuals' sense of well-being.
- "Embracing the strengths of the heart" and telling one's healthy (as opposed to horror) story can lead to healing and growth (p. 161).
- Seeking authentic goals such as intimacy, generativity, and spirituality promotes well-being.

Psychology as a theoretical foundation has strengths and weaknesses, like the foundations of all the organizational models (see Table 9.1).

METAPHOR

Journey is the metaphor that best describes the spiritual approach to organizational theory. Journey describes organizational members' meaning-making processes as well as the path an organization takes to achieve its mission and purposes. Journey is a particularly apt metaphor for the spiritual perspective in the way it conveys enrichment, searching, and progression.

Table 9.1 Strengths and Weaknesses of the Psychological Theoretical Foundation for Higher Education

Strengths	Weaknesses
Places the enduring human search for meaning into an organizational context.	May over-estimate the impact of one individual on the complex relationships within an organization.
Brings positive elements such as wholeness, beauty, and passion into the thinking about organizations.	The inclusion of psychological concepts and practices may feel intrusive to some organizational members.
Acknowledges that people bring the whole of themselves, including emotions, into the workplace.	An over-emphasis on the emotional and personal aspects of organizational functioning may distract members from other organizational goals.
Can perpetuate individual and organizational well-being through the expression of positive emotions and a healthy work environment.	Can become a one-sided approach to examining organizational functioning.

STRUCTURE

Unlike other organizational models described in this book, the spiritual approach does not conform to one particular structural arrangement (e.g., web, hierarchy, circle). The principles and processes of spirituality can be combined with many organizational forms. Yet, some organizational structures are more congruent with the spiritual approach and its underlying assumptions. For example, the web structure of the feminist perspective works well with the spiritual perspective's emphasis on interpersonal relationships. The rigid standard operating procedures of bureaucracies would be a difficult fit with the openness espoused in organizational spirituality. The "first among equals" leadership of the collegial circle structure would fit well with a spiritual model but the isolation and separation embodied in department structures potentially works against the connection and integration preferred in the spiritual approach. Depending on the organizational form, certain underlying assumptions would necessarily shift to accommodate the spiritual model.

MAJOR CONCEPTS, CHARACTERISTICS, AND PRINCIPLES

Danah Zohar (1997) was one of the first theorists to explore how spirituality impacts organizations and the theory that guides them. In her book, *ReWiring the Corporate Brain*, Zohar explored spirituality from the point of view of quantum theory. Using postmodern perspectives, Zohar discussed vision, interrelationships, cooperation, holism, context, and uncertainty. Because organizations are not value free, an understanding of organizational functioning at the paradigm level is essential. The spiritual perspective makes organizational values explicit.

The spiritual perspective lends a unique understanding to organizations, including higher education institutions. Although people pursue higher education degrees for many reasons, including materially driven purposes (Pryor, Hurtado, DeAngelo, Palucki Blake, & Tran, 2010), students, faculty, administrators, and staff are fundamentally and developmentally changed through their campus experiences. The purposes of higher education encompass the fulfillment of human potential, social justice, and social change. The underlying individual and societal principles and assumptions of these higher education institutions make the spiritual perspective (including discussions of spirit and soul, vision, interrelationships, leadership, and power) uniquely fitting to that environment. Zohar's ideas about spiritual capital and spiritual intelligence add richness to the application of organizational spirituality to higher education organizations.

Spiritual Capital and Intelligence

Human beings have spent eons in the search for meaning larger than the individual's experience. Zohar connected this search to organizational functioning through two concepts: spiritual capital and spiritual intelligence. Spiritual capital is defined as

> the wealth, the power, and the influence that we gain by acting from a deep sense of meaning, our deepest values, and a sense of higher purpose, and all of these are best expressed through a life devoted to service. (Zohar, 2010, p. 3)

Spiritual capital, much like cultural and social capital (Dowd, Sawatzky, & Korn, 2011; Lamont & Lareau, 1988), provides resources and capabilities to the person possessing it. This resource is linked to spiritual intelligence:

> It is by seeking meaning in our lives and acting in accordance with our deepest values that we can commit ourselves to lives of service based on the capacity that we are best suited to, whatever we choose to do personally or professionally. (Zohar, 2010, p. 3)

Zohar and Marshall (2000) introduced personal qualities to people with spiritual intelligence: flexibility; self-awareness; capacity to face and use suffering; capacity to face and transcend pain; quality of being inspired by vision and values; reluctant to cause unnecessary harm; able to see connection between diverse things; tendency to ask why, what if, and to seek answers; facility to work against convention; and servant leadership (Greenleaf, 2008; Morgan, 2001). These qualities and principles were drawn from complex adaptive systems including biological systems; they are ways that people within organizations can act as complex adaptive systems to craft order from chaos. With the introduction of multiple intelligences by Gardner (1993) and emotional intelligence by Goleman (1998), among others, developmental and leadership scholars advocated for varied approaches to experiencing the world. Zohar and Marshall (2004, p. 64) elucidated spiritual intelligence as "the intelligence with which we have access to deep meaning, fundamental values, and a sense of abiding purpose in our lives." Spiritual intelligence is related to wisdom intelligence and "embraces all that we traditionally mean by wisdom, as opposed to mere knowledge acquisition or to a rather mechanistic talent for solving problems" (Zohar & Marshall, 2004, p. 64).

By linking service and meaning making to organizational functioning, Zohar raises the purposes of corporations and, by extension in this book, colleges and universities to the level of vision, legacy, and commitment. "Exploration, cooperation, self- and situational-mastery, creativity, and service" replace fear, greed, and anger (Zohar, 2010, p. 3). Business becomes higher service; jobs become callings; organizational values become linked to beneficial human purposes; and goals such as global understanding and environmental stewardship become part of everyday organizational functioning. Given the historical developmental and social change purposes of higher education, the spiritual perspective is a particularly apt approach.

Soul and Spirit

Alan Briskin (1996; Peppers & Briskin, 2000), an author who pioneered organizational spirituality, introduced the elements of uncertainty, interrelationship, and metaphor into his explanations of organizational theory. Briskin grounded his discussion on organizations and spirituality in the concepts of spirit and soul. Briskin, portraying a historical view on soul, explained that the Hebrews viewed soul as vitality; the Greeks saw this human aspect as underworld; others saw soul as containing a spark of the divine (Briskin, 1996).

> The challenge of finding soul in organizations, as in life, is to embrace not only what we see, hear, and understand but also to attend to what we don't know, what we cannot see at first glance or hear on first listening. (Briskin, 1996, p. 9)

In particular, Briskin discussed the danger of neglecting soul in organizations. When the soul is ignored, both its positive and negative elements seep out in unexpected ways.

Working from Jungian philosophy, Briskin (1996) discussed the ways that the underworld or shadow side of soul is as integral to life as the upper world aspects of soul. Abandonment, rage, despair, and shame are as much a part of human living as wonder, happiness, and joy (Manning, 2001). Shadow elements of organizations include power, hierarchy, inequality, anger, impatience, and burnout. When the upper world of soul is overemphasized and the underworld de-emphasized, organizations fail to account for these two uniquely human aspects of organizational life.

> Modern business life arises from a love of the upperworld, of material products, of order and organization; it celebrates the material, light-filled portion of existence. It is the world as we see it (or as we would like to see it) and as it most makes sense to us. But as many of us suspect in sensing the shock waves now traveling through our corporations and institutions, it is only half the story. (Manning, 2001, p. 29)

There is wisdom in the shadow side of soul, and without it the soul is incomplete. With the full embrace of the positive and shadow sides of the soul, one can live with the paradox that it is possible to be both generous and controlling, compassionate and cruel, efficient and ineffectual. Organizational members can use the creative polarity of the soul and apply this understanding to higher education administration and leadership (Briskin, 1996; Manning, 2001) (see Table 9.2). Briskin's account of the positive and negative aspects of soul and how this is expressed in organizations is a fascinating account of how these uniquely human groups reflect the best and worst part of human living. These elements should not be ignored but rather embraced as part of the sorrow and joy of working in organizations, including higher education institutions.

In addition to soul, Briskin explored spirit, which he defined as: "the wind of a divine inspiration. Different from soul, spirit comes from higher up and descends into the body…. Soul is in the middle, holding together spirit and body, lofty inspiration and physical limitation" (1996, p. 17). He discussed the fact that the spirit and physical worlds have been split off from one another. In the workplace, the remnants of spirit exist in "a thin and airy call for abstract workplace virtues such as teamwork, responsibility, accountability, and inspired leadership" (Briskin, 1996, p. 19). These thin concepts, particularly as discussed in the higher education leadership literature, fail to excavate the full depth possible when soul and spirit are incorporated into organizations through

Table 9.2   Application of Soul to Higher Education

Upper World in Higher Education	Shadow Side in Higher Education
Patient	Impatient
Fulfilled	Overworked
Visionary	Burned out
Empowered	Bored
Optimistic	Unable to set limits
Collaborative	Controlling

administration, leadership, and teaching. Materialism, profits, and inadequate relationships have become a poor substitute for matters of the soul and spirit.

Whether one embraces soul or spirit, both concepts lend aspects to organizational theory that have previously been ignored in the bureaucratic, political, collegial, and other organizational approaches. Briskin's work can assist higher education faculty and administrators realize that human beings bring all of themselves to an organization. Rather than struggling to manage the Cartesian split of mind, spirit, and body or the feminist-challenged dichotomy of public versus private, the literature about organizational spirituality provides a more holistic approach to management, leadership, and organizational theory.

Vision

Vision is inseparable from our spiritual intelligence.... Our striving, our drive toward perfection, our dedication, and our need to serve are bound up with our "spiritual intelligence." And these are the human qualities for which organizations must make room—indeed must nurture—if they want to unleash the full potential of human creativity and productivity. (Zohar, 1997, p. 14)

Briskin's work dovetails nicely with Zohar's theorizing on vision and interconnectedness. As meaning-making beings, humans long to endow their lives with meaning as well as connect our individual lives to a larger sense of purpose (Rogers & Dantley, 2001). True vision in organizations can only be enacted when the wisdom of the soul and the full impact of interrelationships are considered as legitimate aspects of organizational living. From Zohar's perspective, vision is only possible when the organization is viewed as a whole including the environment in which it exists. An organization that ignores the environment ignores the extraorganizational lives of its employees. From the corporate perspective from which Zohar and Briskin write, when profits are emphasized above people, the organization will not be as productive or successful. When these ideas are applied to higher education, budgets and administrative processes are viewed as means to the essential end of student learning. Budgets and administrative processes are not ends in themselves.

Interrelationships

Interrelationships are another aspect of organizations to which the spiritual model lends insights and understanding. Organizations are not mechanized, isolated entities, but interconnected organisms that affect one another across units, structures, and national borders. An organization, corporate, nonprofit, or otherwise, cannot act without having an impact on the political, social, and economic health of the surrounding communities. The economic crash of 2008 is an excellent example of the ways that everything is connected across borders and boundaries. One industry, banking in this example, can have devastating effects on profit and nonprofit organizations within and across countries as well as on the global economic structure as a whole.

Organizational members operating from a spiritual perspective recognize the interconnectedness of organizations, their processes, and the people within them. From a spiritual perspective organizations

have infrastructures that encourage and build on relationships, relationships between leaders and employees, between employees and their colleagues, between divisions and functional groups, between structures themselves. It will also be aware of its environmental context, human, corporate, societal, and ecological, and will build infrastructures that encourage exchange and dialogue. (Zohar, 1997, pp. 123–124)

Interconnections through dialogue, associations, and networks create opportunities for creativity and innovation. Relationship forms a wholeness that can build toward the greater purpose required by organizations to succeed and by organizational members to feel fulfilled through their work lives. Given the globalization and internationalization of higher education, the centrality of interrelationships and ability to transcend physical and conceptual boundaries are essential dimensions of organizational life.

Leadership

Leadership is in part about building purpose into our lives and creating opportunities for others to do the same. One cannot have leadership without interdependence (there is no such thing as a leader of one) and interdependency links us to the purposes and desires of other people. Rogers (2003, p. 23) emphasized the connection between leadership and spirituality by stating, "exceptional leadership incorporates the spiritual dimension"; in fact, "leadership is transformed when infused with the spiritual." Infusing leadership with spirituality has implications for a variety of forms: soul leader (Hagberg, 1994), collective leaders (Ospina & Foldy, 2015), servant leaders (Greenleaf, 2008), and stewardship (Block, 1993). This scholarship emphasizes the need for leadership to extend beyond the positional style where only those with a title deserve the designation of "leader." Spiritual leadership (also called quantum leadership) connects one's actions to meaning beyond one's individual life, creates shared purpose, and enables meaning making. "Spiritual leadership taps into the fundamental needs of both leader and follower for spiritual survival so they become more organizationally committed and productive" (Fry, 2003, p. 694).

Zohar determined the characteristics of what she called spiritual or quantum leadership. Leadership from this perspective has a subtler, more intuitive feel than the traditional command and control leadership style. It is "less goal oriented and more process-oriented" (Zohar, 1997, p. 89). Quantum, spiritual leadership is concerned with the creative process of the team, and less with the structure imposed in advance of the project, goal, or purpose being pursued. Spiritual leadership is more creative and trusting. The leaders' and followers' jobs from this perspective are to cultivate individual potential while drawing insight and inspiration from the group (Zohar, 1997). This understanding of the deeper spiritual meaning of leadership is essential, particularly in higher education, because

leaders have an unusual degree of power to create the climate in which people live. Leaders can create conditions that inspire the soul or cause despair. They can engender commitment to an emancipating vision or create a sense of isolation and fear. (Rogers, 2003, p. 20)

Leadership from a spiritual perspective contrasts sharply with conventional varieties. Bureaucratic or traditional leadership is top-down, rule bound, fixed on the one best way, slow to change, and isolated from the environmental context. This traditional style of leadership is inadequate to today's organizations, including higher education. Zohar connected leadership to vision and stated that leaders, and this includes higher education administrators, must have the ability to "lead from that level of deep, revolutionary vision" (1997, p. 146). Spiritual intelligence gives leaders a way to envision the sense of self needed to relate to others, create meaning, and exist in community: "Spiritual intelligence, in essence, represents a dynamic wholeness of self in which the self is at one with itself and the whole of creation" (Zohar & Marshall, 2000, p. 124). The ability to attain the vision essential to leadership in higher education is not a solitary activity but one rising from "a deep sense of the interconnectedness of life and all its enterprises"; leaders "must have a sense of engagement and responsibility, a sense of 'I *have* to'"; and they "must be aware that all human endeavor ... is part of the larger and richer fabric of the whole universe" (Zohar, 1997, p. 153; emphasis in the original). With leadership and vision, engagement and responsibility connect to form a whole that is larger than the sum of its parts.

As a concept related closely to leadership, Zohar (1997) postulated that genuine empowerment occurs when the organization is viewed holistically and the dichotomy between leader and follower is dismantled. The notion that everyone can exercise leadership, given their particular take on the organization and sphere of influence, supplants the disempowering leader–follower dichotomy: "Leadership, not only 'at the top' but throughout the organization, is critical" (Chickering, 2006, p. 5).

Similar to the interconnectedness of Zohar, Briskin, and organizational theorists embracing a spiritual perspective, Allen and Cherry (2000) discussed the systemic leadership of relational organizations. These organizations embody networked forms that acknowledge the interconnectedness of all organizational elements. By envisioning leadership in an organic, networked system, Allen and Cherrey (2000) used a combination of orthodox organizational theorizing and new perspectives to enable meaning making, energy flow, renewal, and organizational learning. Although Allen and Cherrey did not use the language or principles of the spiritual perspective, their conceptualization of leadership echoes Zohar's and Briskin's ideas.

Allen and Cherrey (2000) encouraged new ways of leading and relating that result in deeper understandings about the self, leadership, and the organization. In a traditional view of leadership and organizations, goals are optimal; from a relational leadership standpoint, core values are given priority. Rather than rigidly linking performance reviews to standard operating procedures and static job descriptions, organic and dynamic systems are nurtured by encouraging employees to innovatively flirt with organizational boundaries. Noticing patterns and responding to their occurrences allows the organization to remain dynamic. Either–or thinking is abandoned in favor of an approach that embraces both ends of a paradox. Tension between opposites is optimized as a way to encourage innovation and organizational and individual growth. Planned change is perhaps an oxymoron. Instead, fluctuations are noticed as opportunities (Allen & Cherry, 2000). Organizations become more nimble and adaptable to minor as well as major changes in the internal and external environment.

Allen and Cherrey (2000), Briskin (1996; Peppers & Briskin, 2000), Zohar (1997; Zohar & Marshall, 2000, 2004), and other proponents of systemic, relational, and spiritual leadership are united in their call to transform the traditional command and control style of leadership. This approach, long embraced and overdue for change, has left members of organizations tired and disempowered and leaders desperate and helpless. The traditional hero or heroine style of leadership has not worked for anyone. The spiritual organizational theorists urge us to choose a different path.

> Work is an expression of the Spirit at work in the world through us. Work is that which puts us in touch with others, not so much at the level of personal interaction, but at the level of service in the community. (Briskin, 1996, p. 143)

Rather than seeing organizational life as drudgery, these authors suggest that people use spirit as a way to find joy and balance within their employment.

Equity, Fairness, and Organizational Spirituality

The organizational spirituality movement places equity and justice as values upon which institutional behavior, policy, and leadership is based. From an organizational management perspective, equity and justice includes fair wages, equitable hiring, and equal performance management (e.g., evaluations, promotions) (Quatro, 2004). The long-standing equity movements on college campuses reflect the organizational spirituality practitioners' approach to fairness and equity.

While organizational spirituality may sound new to many, its roots are firmly planted in classical organizational theory and practice. Abraham Maslow incorporated self-actualization into his hierarchy of needs. Mary Parker Follett argued for empowerment and the higher purposes of organizational life and work (Quatro, 2004). Greenleaf (2008) argued for a humanist approach as reflected in his concept of servant leadership.

The organizational spirituality movement is congruent with ethnic and racial groups on campus who place spirituality and religion as central to their ways of being. Organizational spirituality's emphasis on empowerment and meaning making is central to human rights movements on and off campus. The appreciation for following your calling to create social good, a concept within organizational spirituality, is derived from religious traditions. Many of the emphases of organizational spirituality including journey, selflessness, and wholeness can be traced to Muslim, Judeo-Christian, Buddhist, and other faith-based traditions (Quatro, 2004). In an age where materialism, consumerism, and individualism are readily identifiable, the organizational spirituality approach to higher education administration can provide guidance and completeness.

Power

Power is a topic of organizational functioning to which the spiritual organizational theorists lend significant insight and creativity. Regardless of whether one views power as a limited or unlimited resource, power as an element of organizational life must always be considered. From the spiritual perspective, power is the

> capacity to express one's inner self, one's talent, passion, skill. The soul loves power because without it we cannot effectively negotiate the interaction between inside and outside. Soulfulness requires both inner work—finding meaning and purpose—and outer work—seeking avenues for expression. (Briskin, 1996, p. 208)

When power and spirituality are linked, it becomes a force to achieve external purposes and goals as well as an internal resource for meaning, fulfillment, and joy. Rather than a competitive approach to power (i.e., power as a finite resource), the spiritual perspective considers the ways that power can be a potent source of energy for the people working in the organization and those served by institutions such as colleges and universities. Power from a spiritual perspective is given away, not hoarded or manipulated. This perspective offers an optimistic and idealistic view of organizational life.

STRENGTHS AND WEAKNESSES OF THE ORGANIZATIONAL SPIRITUALITY MODEL

The spiritual perspective lends several helpful points of view on organizational theory. Theorists who separate the mind and spirit envision organizations as mechanical and fragmented. They act as if human beings lack the ability to make meaning of their lives, including their organizational lives. When meaning making is taken into account, the full potential of human productivity, sense of accomplishment, and satisfaction is unleashed. Like other organizational perspectives, the spiritual approach has strengths and weaknesses (see Table 9.3).

NEXT STEPS: BRINGING THE SPIRITUAL PERSPECTIVE INTO CURRENT USE

Of the various organizational perspectives offered in this book, the spiritual perspective is among the most contemporary. Despite its popularity among some corporate organizational theorists, particularly in Europe, the perspective is rarely used in U.S. higher education settings. The detached scholarly demeanor in higher education organizations makes it particularly difficult for many to embrace a spiritual approach in their practice. Both in and out of the classroom, higher education administrators and faculty divorce the public and private, the intellectual and the spiritual, the mind and spirit. Perhaps nowhere is the Cartesian split between mind and body more evident than on college campuses. Faculty are distinctly divided into disciplines, administrators are accustomed to a bureaucratic way of operating, and students, rightfully begrudgingly, know their "place" within the higher education structure. The presence of these traditional approaches to organizational life makes higher education an important location for theorists and practitioners to consider the spiritual

Table 9.3 Strengths and Weaknesses of the Spiritual Perspective

Strengths	Weaknesses
Provides hope in situations including those previously dominated by competition and control.	May be off-putting to people who see spirituality as religion or those who do not believe in a spiritual presence.
Can bring diverse perspectives into organizations.	May seem overly optimistic, bordering on naïve.
Provides a concrete means to use collaboration and cooperation within organizations.	May not express a sufficiently sophisticated analysis of followership.
Provides an alternative to bureaucracies.	Can convey a romanticized approach to leadership.
Can be empowering.	May appear too "new age" for many.
Provides a means through which marginalized and disenfranchised organizational members can voice their points of view.	May seem impractical in many organizations focused on financial expediency and conventional measures of success.

perspective. "We who are in the positions to do so have to bridge the polarity that exists in the academy. We have to welcome mind, body, heart, and soul into the learning process" (Rogers, 2003, p. 26).

The incorporation of ways to understand and operate beyond cognitive intelligence, the form most highly valued in higher education, has expanded in recent years. Howard Gardner (1993, 2003, 2006) is the most prominent theorist in this area. His elucidation of multiple intelligences includes information on linguistic, logical, mathematical, musical, spatial, bodily kinesthetic, interpersonal, and intrapersonal intelligences. Most relevant to the organizational perspectives offered in this book, Gardner (1995) relates his multiple intelligence theory to leadership and describes the ways that exceptional organizational members apply more than their brains to the task of leadership.

Tirri and Nokelainen (2008) and Tirri, Nokelainen, and Ubani (2006) adapted Gardner's theory and added an additional intelligence—spiritual intelligence—to his collection. The researchers' four dimensions of spiritual intelligence are awareness sensing, mystery sensing, value sensing, and community sensing. In addition to being an extension of Gardner's theory, their work relates to that of Daniel Goleman on emotional intelligence and to Zohar and Marshall's work on spiritual intelligence. The latter theorists claim that spiritual intelligence is our ultimate intelligence, necessary to use and integrate the multiple intelligences and emotional intelligence (Zohar & Marshall, 2000). Strange (2001, p. 59) applies Zohar and Marshall's (2000) conception of spiritual intelligence to higher education by stating that the two authors

> suggest that those most capable of addressing such concerns [of self-definition and understanding] are distinguished by advanced levels of "spiritual intelligence" … a dimension they describe in terms of certain capacities and qualities (being flexible and self-aware, having the capacity to face and use suffering, being inspired by vision and values, being reluctant to cause unnecessary harm, and tending to see connection between diverse things and to ask Why? or What if?— while seeking fundamental answers).

Further exploration of spiritual intelligence aptly fits higher education's mission of self, intellectual, and personal development.

Although space does not allow for a full explanation of multiple, spiritual, and emotional intelligences, research in this area holds significant promise for higher education. These ideas can be used to explore the personal and professional fulfillment of higher education leaders and faculty, staff, students, and administrators. The spiritual perspective provides a foundation upon which faculty, administrators, staff, and students create meaning, build community, explore the mysteries of life, and determine their deepest values. The current popularity of student learning communities, faculty-led study abroad programs, service learning, and other effective educational practices (Kuh, 2008) advances higher education's commitment to transform lives, empower through education, and create viable communities. If through using spiritual intelligence we can "address and solve problems of meaning and value" (Tirri et al., 2006, p. 39), this approach can assist higher education faculty, students, administrators, and staff as they confront the challenges that exist within these institutions. This approach could assist all who seek to fulfill the long-standing purposes of higher education regarding societal change, equity, quality of life, and social justice.

Higher education organizations are unique among modern organizations in their emphasis on individual and societal development, growth, and improvement. The products of higher education are not tangible, material objects but intangible qualities developed in individuals. The intangible nature of this "product" means that one must often take its achievement on faith; that is, faith grounded in a belief in the power of education, a force larger than oneself.

CONCLUSIONS

A powerful aspect of the spiritual perspective is its critique on the nearly normative use of bureaucracy in organizations, including higher education. The spiritual perspective theorists, particularly Briskin (1996), criticized the rational, logical, and impersonal approach of bureaucracy. Bureaucracies with dehumanizing and soulless approaches to management and administration do not take all aspects of human living into account. "Organizations are (ideally) a place to express one's intellect, and perhaps one's physical skills depending on the job, but one's emotional and spiritual dimensions are typically not welcomed or nurtured" (Rogers & Dantley, 2001, p. 592). Similar to a critique offered by Ferguson (1985), Briskin (1996) offered the following observations on bureaucracies:

- They dehumanize the people who work and live in them by reducing their actions to a routinized set of standardized procedures.
- At a certain point, humans become dispensable in the name of efficiency.
- When problems arise, the individual, not the system or structure, is seen as flawed and in need of re-training or replacement.
- Upper management in bureaucracies is seen as the brain while laborers are viewed as hands that know nothing about how organizations could be structured and managed.
- Progress and growth are major goals, regardless of the size, or sustainability of the advancement.
- Standard operating procedures and policies are intended to limit thinking, creativity, and ingenuity.

Bureaucracies are the antithesis of the spiritual perspective. Where bureaucracies limit thought and initiative, spiritual organizations seek to humanize and include all. In bureaucracies, people are urged to separate professional from private; spiritual organizations seek to consider the whole person. "People cannot simply become mechanisms of production without losing connection with their own experience: fragility, wonder, passion, and mystery. These qualities are critical to health, creativity, and compassion for others" (Briskin, 1996, p. 134). These organizational theorists support the idea that the efficiencies of bureaucracy are offset by the losses to community, beauty, and meaning.

Questions for Discussion
- To what degree would you like to work at an institution that places the spiritual perspective as primary?
- What advantages are gained from employing a spiritual perspective? What disadvantages ensue?

- How is vision used in higher education organizations?
- What traditional conceptions of power would have to change to embrace a spiritual perspective on this concept?
- What are the ramifications of ignoring the underworld of soul within higher education institutions?
- Upon reading Table 9.3, comment on the utility of the spiritual perspective for understanding higher education organizations.

Recommended Readings for the Organizational Spirituality Perspective

Briskin, A., Erickson, S., Ott, J., & Callanan, T. (2009). *The power of collective wisdom: And the trap of collective folly.* San Francisco: Berrett-Koehler.

Hacker, S. (2016). Is the workplace a zombie breeding ground? *The Journal for Quality and Participation, 39*(1), 4.

Kaur, M., & Kaur, D. (2014). The power of organizational spirituality: Its effect on job satisfaction, quality of work life and occupational stress. *International Journal of Research in Organizational Behavior and Human Resource Management, 2*(2), 356–369.

Leider, R. J. (2015). *The power of purpose: Find meaning, live longer, better* (3rd ed.). San Francisco: Berrett-Koehler.

Strange, C. C. (2001). Spiritual dimensions of graduate preparation in student affairs. In M. A. Jablonski (Ed.), *Implications of student spirituality for student affairs* (New Directions for Student Services, No. 95, pp. 57–67). San Francisco: Jossey-Bass.

CASE: THE INTEGRATIVE PEDAGOGY INITIATIVE

Teaching has been described as a calling, an art, inspirational, and complex. Some argue that being a teacher involves natural ability. Others argue that teaching is a learned art, not something into which people are born. Higher education has a long history of teacher-centered learning. In this style of teaching, the instructor is the center of attention. Students in the teacher-centered learning model primarily work independently with little to no collaborative efforts. In a learner-centered approach the direction in which the learning occurs is determined by students—the questions they ask, prior knowledge to which they can add the new learning, and the experiences gained from their backgrounds and identities. The learner-centered approach is more collaborative with students working together on projects of mutual interest.

Higher education, like other educational areas, has moved from an emphasis on a teacher-centered style to a learner-centered approach. In keeping with this, scholars and higher education associations have argued for an approach called integrative learning. Quoting from the American Association of Colleges and Universities (AAC&U) publication, *Greater Expectations: A New Vision for Learning as a Nation,* Huber and Hutchings (2004, p. iv) urged colleges and universities to

> change their practices to develop students as "integrative thinkers who can see connections in seemingly disparate information and draw on a wide range of knowledge to make decisions," students who can "adapt the skills learned in one situation to problems encountered in another." This integrative capacity characterizes learners prepared for the twenty-first-century world: who are intentional about the process of acquiring learning, empowered by the mastery of intellectual and practical skills, informed by knowledge from various disciplines, and responsible for their actions and those of society.

Ferren and Anderson (2016, pp. 33–34) also defined integrative learning "as an empowering developmental process through which students synthesize knowledge across curricular and cocurricular experiences to develop new concepts, refine values and perspectives in solving problems, master transferable skills, and cultivate self-understanding." Based on the principles and values of liberal education, the context of integrative learning is to teach students as whole persons. Through a liberal education, students are encouraged to be civically engaged, prepared to live and work in a diverse world, and view life from an inclusive perspective. Those involved in liberal education know that learning is more than a sum of its parts (Huber & Hutchings, 2004). It is from this point of view that liberal learning, integrative learning, and organizational spirituality converge.

Rendón (2009) used the term sentipensante, "a combination of two Spanish words: *sentir*, which means to sense or feel, and *pensar*, to think" (p. 131, emphasis in the original) to discuss pedagogy. Inspired by the work of Eduardo Galeano, she encourages "Sentipensante (sensing/thinking) Pedagogy, which represents a teaching and learning approach based on wholeness, harmony, social justice, and liberation" (Rendón, 2009, p. 132). Rendón (2009, p. 6) emphasizes "interdependence, connectedness, wholeness, and harmony" to build complementary processes and acknowledge the inner and outer lives of students and teachers. To disconnect the inner and outer lives of students, divide thinking and feeling, and separate teaching and learning is to do harm to learning, a human practice that is deeply spiritual.

A teaching method that decreases the split between the inner and outer lives of students involves contemplative practices including meditation, mindfulness, deep listening, reading, and writing (Barbezat & Bush, 2014). Zajonc (2013, p. 83) describes contemplative practices in higher education as a method that

> offers to its practitioners a wide range of educational methods that support the development of student attention, emotional balance, empathetic connection, compassion, and altruistic behavior, while also providing new pedagogical techniques that support creativity and the learning of course content.

THE CASE

Curricular change at any institution of higher education is often met with both excitement and resistance to change. In the 21st century, colleges and universities strive to offer curricula applicable to the needs of society while balancing past traditions and approaches. The tension between cutting edge and traditional is exposed during discussions regarding curricular change. The following case illustrates how an institution sought to incorporate the spiritual traditions of its founding through the learner-focused approaches of integrative pedagogy and contemplative practices. The goal was to create a cutting-edge curriculum that maximized student engagement and learning.

Questions to Consider
- How do the approaches of integrative pedagogy and contemplative practices compare with the traditional collegium practices within higher education?
- In what ways can integrative pedagogy and contemplative practices develop spiritual intelligence in students?

- How are integrative pedagogy and contemplative practices related to vision in organizations?

Institutional Context

West Shores College (a pseudonym) is a private, Historically Black, four-year institution with a proud history of traditional learning. Building on a foundation of professors with degrees from the best institutions, West Shores was proud of the teaching that had been a hallmark of its education for 150 years. Recently, however, challenges to West Shores' curriculum were evident. Students complained that the college failed to provide the innovative teaching practices with which they had become accustomed at their previous schools. Students familiar with collaborative projects, group and experiential learning felt stymied by classrooms characterized by lectures and assignments requiring individual rather than group work. They also felt that the arms-length approach to spirituality in the curriculum betrayed the traditions of Black Americans who had long embraced religion and spirituality as a way to combat the oppression and prejudices aimed at individuals with their racial background.

Questions to Consider

- Discuss the ways that spirituality influences Historically Black Institutions.
- How are decisions about pedagogy reached at institutions of higher education?
- What is your experience with integrative learning and learner-centered pedagogical approaches? What are the advantages and disadvantages of these curricular approaches?

Characters

Dr. Perseo Márquez Laureano, Provost: Two years ago, Dr. Laureano came to West Shores College after serving as the associate provost at a progressive Predominantly White liberal arts institution. Although he respected the teaching and learning approach at West Shores, he knew that the college needed to update its curriculum and pedagogy if it was to remain competitive.

A group organized through the faculty senate had approached Dr. Laureano urging a new initiative based on the principles of integrative learning advanced by the AAC&U. Dr. Laureano was intrigued and in response formed a group called the Integrative Pedagogy Initiative and tasked it with studying ways to institute integrative pedagogy and contemplative practices into the curriculum. The Initiative was fueled by a donation from a West Shores College alumna. The donor wanted to see the college maintain academic excellence yet incorporate a spiritual perspective into its pedagogy. Dr. Laureano was enthusiastic about the idea and gave the effort his full support.

Dr. Miriam Margalit, Chairperson, Integrative Pedagogy Initiative: Dr. Margalit had taught biology at West Shore College for 15 years. During registration, her classes filled quickly, giving her a reputation for innovative and collaborative teaching. A gifted teacher, Dr. Margalit took advantage of regional and national conferences to keep her teaching fresh. She was a proponent of integrative learning and incorporated ideas about wholeness and authenticity from her recent reading of Laura Rendón's *Sentipensante Pedagogy*. She was particularly taken with the quote, "Tension-filled spiritual moments can be learning opportunities" (Rendón, 2009, p. 11).

Dr. Margalit, a member of the faculty senate, had led the effort that resulted in the recommendation to the provost for curriculum change. Because of her interest and skill as a professor, Dr. Margalit was appointed by Provost Laureano to chair the Integrative Pedagogy Initiative. The initiative was composed of eight faculty members representing a variety of majors from the college's four academic programs and one student representing the student body.

Mr. Vincent Dawson, Chairperson, Student Government Association Curricular Affairs Committee: Mr. Dawson, a senator in the West Shores Student Government Association (SGA), was assigned to represent students on the Integrative Pedagogy Initiative. The SGA, through Mr. Dawson's Curricular Affairs Committee, had become acutely aware of student dissatisfaction regarding the traditional (some students said "old") pedagogy at the college. Students were bored with the teaching methods that favored lectures and minimal interaction between students and professors. Mr. Dawson had worked with the provost on a previous committee to update student course evaluations and looked forward to making progress on this issue.

Dr. Gabrielle Charest, Professor, History: Dr. Charest had been at the institution for only one year but was fully invested in its traditional approach to teaching. Her main reason for accepting the faculty offer at West Shore College was because of its emphasis on traditional teaching. She believed that high quality academic experiences were crucial to the survival of Historically Black Institutions and that experimental efforts to reform curricula were doomed to fail. Traditional methods of teaching had survived for centuries and would continue into the future. Although Dr. Charest had updated her lectures with Powerpoint presentations and occasional small group discussions by students, most of her content was conveyed through the tried-and-true lecture method. Having experienced a wide range of teaching styles throughout her education, she was convinced that lectures conveyed the most knowledge to students and were the most efficient way to manage the classroom. She was opposed to any effort to update the curriculum and was vocal about her opposition. Dr. Charest was particularly skeptical about the spiritual and contemplative approaches recommended in *Sentipensante Pedagogy.* Given the financial and academic credibility issues that often plagued Historically Black Institutions, she felt that traditional curricular approaches were the best way to proceed.

Given her objections, Dr. Charest was surprised by the invitation from Provost Laureano to serve on the Integrative Pedagogy Initiative. He explained that he wanted the group to benefit from a full exploration of the issue. Any curricular change, he observed, deserved a thorough vetting.

Questions to Consider
- From the perspective of organizational spirituality, where would a likely catalyst for curricular change come from?
- What are some benefits of a traditional lecture-style teaching model? What are some disadvantages?
- What are some benefits of a learner-centered curricular approach? What are some disadvantages?

Introduction to Integrative and Contemplative Pedagogies

Provost Laureano and Integrative Pedagogy Initiative chair, Dr. Margalit, knew that incorporating integrative pedagogies and contemplative practices into the West Shores curriculum would face objections from some faculty and stakeholders at the institution. But, both Margalit and the Provost believed the goal of revitalizing the curriculum and incorporating new and traditional spiritual practices demanded that both approaches be pursued.

In preparation for the first Initiative meeting, Dr. Margalit asked members to read several articles and chapters about integrative pedagogy and contemplative practices. Before the first meeting was held, Dr. Charest called Dr. Margalit to express skepticism about these approaches. The call from Dr. Charest and several other conversations with faculty members confirmed Dr. Margalit's impression that the curricular change suggested by Provost Laureano would take some convincing.

Questions to Consider
- If you were Dr. Margalit, how would you respond to Dr. Charest?
- How would you approach the first meeting of the Initiative?
- If you were Dr. Margalit, what principles from the spirituality perspective might guide your leadership?

At the first meeting of the Integrative Pedagogy Initiative, Dr. Charest voiced her objections to the proposed curricular change. Although stating that integrative pedagogy had its place, she felt the lecture style of teaching was best for her academic discipline. Other disciplines might use different approaches but she had too much knowledge to be shared in any way other than by lecture.

Dr. Charest's main concerns were with the idea of contemplative practices. To her, religion and spirituality were private, not public concerns. Charest was particularly troubled that students who were atheists would be put off by such a pedagogical approach. Atheists were a group she knew was growing in numbers and becoming more vocal. How were their preferences being considered in this change? She was also concerned about students who had experienced trauma and other life circumstances that made "going inside" difficult. She and her faculty colleagues were not counselors she argued. How were they expected to manage their classrooms using the contemplative pedagogy techniques of meditation, mindfulness, and other practices?

Vincent Dawson countered Dr. Charest's concerns with data from student surveys conducted by the SGA's Curriculum Affairs Committee. He shared that students wanted more engaged and relevant classroom material. His group was acutely aware that students wanted the classroom to be more relevant to their personal lives.

Questions to Consider
- What is your perspective on the roles of religion and spirituality in a college or university curriculum?
- How are ideas regarding organizational spirituality appropriate for a public space such as higher education? How are they inappropriate?
- What do you think of Dr. Charest's concern about students who have experienced trauma or other difficult life circumstances? Should they be asked to undertake spiritual activities in the classroom such as meditation and mindfulness?

The Initiative's Proposal

Initiative members brought a variety of perspectives to their monthly meetings. Some members were particularly interested in practices introduced from the Effective Educational Practices project. This project encouraged student-focused group projects, improved class discussions, and student input as ways to guide classroom learning (Kuh, 2008). Other members felt that education emphasizing democratic citizenship as advanced by the AAC&U could only be achieved if students' spiritual sides were encouraged to develop through the use of contemplative practices in the classroom.

Questions to Consider

- If you were Dr. Margalit, what principles of organizational spirituality would you use to effect the institutional curricular change toward more integrative pedagogy and contemplative practices?
- What are some of the ways that the traditional role of the Black Church in African American culture could impact this curriculum change at a Historically Black Institution?
- If you were a member of the Integrative Pedagogy Initiative, would you—and, if you would, how would you—include student views about spiritual practices in the classroom?

After several months of meetings and debate, the Integrative Pedagogy Initiative finalized a report that was sent to the Provost based on study, community vetting, and visits by a consultant from the AAC&U. The Initiative proposed the establishment of a pilot New Student Seminar taught by six professors from different academic departments. Seminar instructors selected via application would be guided by the Initiative proposal suggesting the use of contemplative practices including mindfulness, meditation, and reflection. The goal was for students and professors to move away from the instructor being at the center of the teaching/learning effort and to move toward learner-focused approaches. Jargon in this area of curricular development coined the effort as moving from the "sage on the stage" to the "guide on the side" (Berrett, 2014).

The Initiative proposal encouraged West Shores College's Center for Teaching and Learning to apply for a grant through the National Institutes of Health and the National Science Foundation to support this curricular change. Both organizations had taken leadership in encouraging institutions of higher education to "adopt teaching methods that have been demonstrated to bolster student learning" (Berrett, 2014).

Questions to Consider

- How do the principles of integrative learning and contemplative practices overlap with the characteristics of organizational spirituality?
- How would you characterize reactions to the proposal as being motivated from the upper world of human spirituality? From the shadow side?
- How can the organizational spiritual approach to interrelationships be instituted through this curricular change?

The Faculty Senate Vote

The Integrative Pedagogy Initiative members were ready to present their proposal to the faculty senate. As expected by Dr. Margalit and Provost Laureano, the proposal generated vigorous discussion during the faculty senate meeting. Some faculty were excited about the prospect of rejuvenating the curriculum and bringing newer teaching and learning practices into the classroom. They felt that the introduction of integrated pedagogy and contemplative practices in the New Student Seminar would generate change throughout the curriculum. Professors who had spent their careers at West Shores College or other colleges with similar traditional curricula were against any change that decreased the professor- and teacher-focus to one that was more learner-centred. Other professors, both long-standing members of the college community and some new to the institution, objected to the inclusion of contemplative practices in their classroom teaching. Initiative members argued that the approach advanced in the proposal was congruent with the spiritual traditions of Historically Black Institutions.

Despite her involvement on the Initiative, during the faculty senate meeting Dr. Charest launched a particularly vigorous opposition to the proposal. She cited cases where the incorporation of religion into secular institutions resulted in a drift away from academic rigor. The curriculum in these cases became more focused on student personal growth at the expense of rigorous academic study. She, and other professors who supported her perspective, felt that these practices were too personal to be included in the professional and impartial space of the classroom. For them, spirituality, like religion, belonged in students' personal space, not the classroom.

Questions to Consider
- What are some of the differences between religion and spirituality?
- What is the role of spirituality in secular institutions?
- How can the ideas of holism, authenticity, and meaning making be incorporated into academic curricula?

After rigorous and rancorous debate in the faculty senate, the proposal for the New Student Seminar failed to be approved by a narrow two-vote margin. One of the points raised by the senators speaking against the curricular change was the power shift they feared would result if integrative pedagogy and contemplative practices were brought into the curriculum. Students, they argued, would take less responsibility for their learning with such an approach. Proponents of the integrative pedagogy approach argued that students in colleges and universities with such a curriculum worked harder than when learning was teacher-centered. Students are empowered, they argue, to take responsibility for their learning. This was the overall goal of integrative pedagogy and contemplative practices; to encourage students to be active participants in the process of making meaning in their lives.

Questions to Consider
- How do you interpret "meaning making" in the context of higher education?
- What dynamics are at play when power in the classroom shifts from being teacher-centered to being learner-centered? What traditional roles are challenged?
- What is gained when students are more spiritually and holistically engaged? What is lost?

The Provost Takes Action

Despite the lack of approval by the faculty senate, the proposal was instituted by Dr. Laureano who believed that this was one of several ways necessary to update the curriculum. He argued that both the provost and faculty senate had the authority to institute curricular changes. He knew he was taking a chance by going against the faculty senate vote but believed the political risk was worth it given the narrow vote in the senate. He further believed that this innovative curricular effort could be used during admissions recruitment to portray West Shores College as a place that valued students in holistic and complete ways. To show his support for the effort to incorporate integrated pedagogy and contemplative practices into the curriculum, Dr. Laureano placed his name in consideration as one of the professors to teach the New Student Seminar.

Questions to Consider

- What is the provost's role in changing the curriculum?
- If you were an admissions professional, how would you explain the integrated learning and contemplative practices approaches to prospective students? Do you see this as a positive or negative aspect of the college's academic program?
- What is the place of spiritual practices such as meditation and mindfulness in the classroom and higher education generally?
- What is your comfort level with contemplative practices? As an instructor? As a student?

10

CONCLUSIONS

INTRODUCTION

Higher education faculty, staff, and administrators perform their life's work in extremely ambiguous, multifaceted, and politically charged settings. By understanding the theories and models offered in this book, effective programs can be built, stimulating curriculum shaped, and meaningful policy and planning created.

THE MODELS FROM DIFFERENT INSTITUTIONAL PERSPECTIVES

A unique aspect of higher education institutions is the presence of various groups who are involved in their operation. Internally, students, faculty, administrators, and staff navigate the organizational milieu from their unique perspective. Externally, parents, the public, and government officials, among others, are concerned with the success of higher education institutions. Internal participants and external stakeholders can best influence higher education by acquiring a firm understanding of how these organizations work. This final chapter offers suggestions for ways that different groups can use the information about the organizational models summarized in this book to understand higher education institutions.

The suggestions in this chapter are made in the context of understanding organizational theory from a multi-model perspective in which one model cannot explain all the intricacies of higher education institutions. An inclusive approach to organizational functioning warrants the fullest understanding of how higher education institutions work. Each model provides strengths and weaknesses and a unique perspective on colleges or universities. As one embraces the diversity of these organizational models, a fuller understanding of the institution in which one works is possible.

Faculty

Given the time-consuming nature of academic life, faculty may not have the luxury of time to fully understand the many organizational perspectives at play within the college or university. A faculty member's focus must be on the activities and priorities of the colle-gium, a focus that means that other important perspectives may be ignored or downplayed. This sometimes myopic view of a college or university may be frustrating to those who see a different perspective from that offered by the collegium. But, it is wise to remember that each group within higher education brings strengths and weaknesses to the enterprise.

Faculty are urged to understand that other organizational perspectives exist to enable the operation of these complex institutions. Faculty can look beyond the narrow disci-plinary approach of their program or department to gain an institutional view. Although their discipline has served a faculty member well and is one to which they have dedicated their life's work, insights from other points of view can be enriching.

Faculty, contingent, tenured, and tenure track, cannot play their important institu-tional roles without effective administrative practices that enable their work to proceed. Likewise, administrators and staff are urged to understand the crucial importance of the collegium. Education cannot proceed and higher education institutions cannot be effect-ively managed and administered without an understanding of the different institutional roles, cultures, and ways of being.

An essential role of faculty in higher education organizations is that of institutional historian and holders of academic values. Birnbaum's (1991) caution about the role of faculty to hamper overly-ambitious administrators is an important one. With a pen-chant for discussion and deliberation, faculty can urge complete vetting of issues, careful attention to institutional purpose and goals, and thoughtful consideration of the long- and short-range implications of a change in direction.

The dynamics of modern higher education often drive faculty and administrators into an "us versus them" position. Both sides may lose sight of the fact that the overall mission of the institution is education. The information contained in this book can assist faculty and administrators to understand the perspectives from which the other comes. Faculty can better understand the operating values and constraints of administrators. Not every-thing is possible, even if it is a great idea. Administrators can understand the time-consuming and all-encompassing role that faculty play in teaching, research, and service. Both "sides" have much to offer the institution but only if respect for the varied roles in the college or university is achieved.

Undergraduate Students

Students, the raison d'être for higher education, are frequent participants on institu-tional committees and decision-making bodies. Students are board of trustee members, participants in institutional governance bodies, and search committee members, among other roles. Obviously, students have a dissimilar perspective on the college or univer-sity than would be held by a faculty member, administrator, or staff member.

As people who will be associated with the institution for life as alumni/ae, students often have the fiercest investment in the institution's survival and success. And, as new-comers to institutional functioning, they are not burdened with past impressions and understandings of the "ways things are done." As such, students have valuable perspec-tives on the most up-to-date means to achieve goals, whether through technology or other innovations. Their most unusual ideas have the potential to become the most effective way to achieve a result.

Important members of the community, students primary although not singular role is academic. Their main role is not on the committee on which they may be serving.

Students cannot be expected to be familiar with the intricacies of organizational functioning as detailed in this book. As one works with students on committees and boards,
it is important to remember that they do not have access to the same information as
administrators or faculty members on the committee. Although this lack of knowledge
is often viewed as naïve, their unconstrained approach to organizational functioning can
reveal solutions and ways of operating not considered by those more seasoned about
college and university procedures.

Can you imagine the institution from their perspective? What information do they
need to most effectively represent students on the committee? What do you know about
the organization that provides insights not available to students? What are the most
important ways to share those perspectives? Students cannot be expected to read a book
such as *Organizational Theory in Higher Education* but how can information from this
book be shared with them to assist them most effectively to share their perspective, a
perspective that may significantly affect institutional functioning.

Staff

The ideas about organizational functioning are as relevant to staff members as they are
to students, faculty, and administrators. The models advanced in this book can be an
inspiration for staff who want to exercise their voice concerning issues within the college
or university. The feminist and gendered model can be used to advocate for equity
regarding salaries, benefits, and resources. The collegial approach can be a model upon
which to base staff relations. The political model can be used to better understand the
ways staff power can be exercised within the institution.

Staff are a frequently overlooked resource of a college or university. Long-term staff
members often serve as the backbone of an office or program. Institutional knowledge is
stored in the minds of staff members who have worked at the college or university for
years. Effective ways to change a program, manage an administrative task, or introduce
an innovation can be discovered by asking a staff member.

Staff members can be viewed as full members of the college or university whose
ongoing education is essential for the effective functioning of the institution. Familiarity
with the organizational models contained in this book can provide valuable information
for their professional development and continued success.

Administrators

With past experiences and successes as their model, all administrators are susceptible to
fossilization. Ideas become tried and true and expediency dictates that solutions that
worked in the past could be an answer to a current problem. But, higher education today
is different from even a few months ago. The higher education institution of the future
requires forward-thinking action to discover valuable innovations and advances.

The challenges facing U.S. higher education are greater today than perhaps at any
point in its history. The roles and responsibilities of administrators have expanded
and compounded in ways unimaginable 20 years ago. As recommended in the multi-
model approach, no one organizational model will succeed in all situations and
administrators must be nimble in their ability to understand and apply a range of
models. The traditional models of bureaucracy, collegium, cultural, organized
anarchy, and political described in this book are necessary to fully understand today's
higher education institutions. The newer perspectives of feminist and gendered

approaches, organizational spirituality, and institutionalization inspire new means of working on old problems.

In addition to fossilization, a danger faced by administrators is the privilege their positions provide. Upper administration roles in colleges and universities afford privileges that may not seem obvious: to hire others with whom you are comfortable, speak without interruption, accept the deference afforded by others, and obtain a salary significantly above other institutional members. The current climate of higher education institutions implies that many privileges be eschewed in the name of egalitarianism and fairness. Administrators can keep perspective on their privilege—perspective often lost when one interacts primarily with those immediately in one's closest circle, by getting into the classroom to teach and experience the collegial perspective, attending SGA meetings and viewing student politics first hand, and insisting on the inclusion of LGBT people, women, people of color, and other disenfranchised institutional communities to obtain a broader perspective on issues of importance within the college or university.

For All Within the Higher Education Community

Because higher education institutions are intellectual communities, there is an obligation to read contemporary concepts such as queer, critical race, and feminist theory. The newer ideas espoused in these theories can engender informed perspectives about privilege, leadership, collaboration, and inclusion. To remain contemporary, all within higher education communities can consider jumping on the bandwagon of a trend. These trends become means to transform higher education.

MULTI-MODEL APPROACH

Complex organizations demand multifaceted analytical tools. Comprehensive understanding of the ever-changing world of higher education necessitates that faculty, administrators, students, and staff use multiple models and theories in their work. The organizational theories and models in this book provide a potent means to analyze problems, craft initiatives, build relationships, and determine a vision for higher education. When one model becomes the explanation for all situations and contexts, that understanding fails to provide a broad or deep perspective concerning higher education functioning. No matter how explanatory any one model may seem, analysis of an organization must proceed using multiple models. Different models allow diverse insights and assessments.

The use of multiple models with which to view the organization can lead to creative solutions, more informed decision making, and increased organizational effectiveness. Technology, complex budget approaches, social media, and the presence of a wide variety of students means that the use of multiple perspectives with which to view higher education is more important now than ever before.

A multi-model approach is additionally valuable because different parts of the organization reflect different theories. While one person may have a preference for one particular model, a diverse perspective can help them understand how others view the organization. In other words, walking in others' shoes and seeing the organization from a different perspective can assist in understanding how people make the choices they do.

PARTING THOUGHTS

In addition to the organizational models and cases presented in this book, the following thoughts are offered as we reconceive higher education for the future.

- Global climate change raises questions about whether higher education can continue using its current model of on-campus attendance that requires fossil-fuel driven transportation. Steps toward sustainability and net zero campuses are a necessity.
- Student demands and the changing nature of and accessibility to knowledge due to the internet is driving the need for more innovative curricula and pedagogy.
- Internationalization and globalization have expanded the reach of individual institutions and the systems in which they exist.
- Integrative pedagogy and learner-centered approaches could be embraced in lieu of the traditional approaches of lecture and instructor-centered teaching.
- The teaching, research, and service model of faculty work is no longer sustainable. Rather than pursuing these three aspects of faculty work simultaneously, models that acknowledge the ebb and flow across these three areas could better fit the generative nature of faculty work.
- Administrative increases built up over the last 20 years could be reassessed and reduced to achieve flatter organizations and decreased expenditure. This goal could be accompanied with refocused attention on the fundamental priorities of higher education institutions.
- Distance and online learning combined with consortia and interinstitutional partnerships could save valuable resources and provide more options for students.
- The competition established between and among higher education institutions has built an arms race where all lose. The race to build the best amenities and facilities has distracted the attention of students, faculty, staff, and administrators alike from the fundamental purposes of higher education: the achievement of a high quality education.
- The four-year model of progress to graduation is a myth worth abandoning. Reimagined academic calendars, less rigid course delivery approaches, and improved ways to organize class times can help faculty consider how students learn over time in ways unencumbered by the restrictions of a four-year graduation expectation.
- The push toward interdisciplinary learning requires that faculty look beyond their home disciplines to discover the ways that academic areas inform and enrich one another.
- All involved in higher education can shape an expectation that the wisdom of higher education comes from all who are involved in the enterprise: faculty, students, administrators, staff, and stakeholders.

These recommendations require shifts in thinking from competition to collaboration, teaching to learning, passivity to engagement, elitism to inclusion, bureaucracy to inclusion, and scarcity to abundance.

The purpose of this book was to expand the number of models used to consider higher education organizational structures. The traditional models of collegial, political, cultural, and anarchic (Birnbaum, 1991) were expanded to include contemporary models as well as those infrequently discussed in the higher education literature. Traditional and contemporary perspectives have much to offer higher education. As institutions increase in complexity, particularly in complexity by function, all involved in higher education require wide-ranging knowledge to meet the challenges before us.

REFERENCES

Acker, J. (1990). Hierarchies, jobs, bodies: A theory of gendered organizations. *Gender & Society, 4*(2), 139–158.

Acker, J. (2006). Inequality regimes: Gender, class, and race in organizations. *Gender & Society, 20*(4), 441–464.

Acker, J. (2009). From glass ceiling to inequality regimes. *Sociologie du Travail, 51*(2), 199–217.

Afshar, V. (2014). Ten hottest disruptive technologies in higher education. Retrieved from www.slideshare.net/ValaAfshar/8699-educauseslideshare-v3.

Allen, K. E., & Cherrey, C. (2000). *Systemic leadership: Enriching the meaning of our work.* Lanham, MD: University Press of America.

Alpert, D. (1985). Performance and paralysis: The organizational context of the American research university. *Journal of Higher Education, 56*(3), 241–281.

Altbach, P. G. (2011). Patterns of higher education development. In P. G. Altbach, P. J. Gumport, & R. O. Berdahl (Eds.), *American higher education in the twenty-first century: Social, political, and economic challenges* (pp. 15–36). Baltimore: Johns Hopkins University Press.

Altbach, P. G., Gumport, P. J., & Berdahl, R. O. (Eds.). (2011). *American higher education in the twenty-first century* (3rd ed.). Baltimore: Johns Hopkins University Press.

American Association of Colleges and Universities. (2002). *Greater expectations: A new vision for learning as a nation goes to college.* Washington, DC: Author.

American Association of University Professors. (1968). *Statement on faculty workload with interpretive comments.* Washington, DC: Author.

American Association of University Professors. (1970). *Statement of principles on academic freedom and tenure with 1970 interpretive comments.* Washington, DC: Author.

American Association of University Professors. (1990). *Statement of principles on academic freedom and tenure with 1970 interpretive comments.* Washington, DC: Author. (Original work published 1940).

American Association of University Professors. (1999a). *Post-tenure review: An AAUP response.* Washington, DC: Author.

American Association of University Professors. (1999b). *Recommended institutional regulations on academic freedom and tenure.* Washington, DC: Author. (Original work published 1957).

American Association of University Professors. (2007). Trends in faculty status, 1975–2007 all degree-granting institutions; national totals. Retrieved from www.aaup.org/AAUP/pubsres/research/.

American Association of University Professors. (2008). *Policy documents and reports* (11th ed.). Baltimore: Johns Hopkins University Press.

American Council on Education. (2012). *The American college president.* Washington, DC: Author.

Amey, M. J., Jessup-Anger, E., & Tingson-Gatuz, C. R. (2009). Unwritten rules: Organizational and political realities of the job. In M. J. Amey & R. M. Reesor (Eds.), *Beginning your journey: A guide for new professionals in student affairs* (pp. 15–38). Washington, DC: NASPA.

Andrews, J. G. (May–June 2006). How can we resist corporatization? *Academe, 92*(3), 16–19.

Annamma, S. A., Connor, D., & Ferri, B. (2013). Dis/ability critical race studies (DisCrit): Theorizing at the intersections of race and dis/ability. *Race Ethnicity and Education, 16*(1), 1–31.

Armacher, R. C., & Meiners, R. E. (2004). *Faculty towers: Tenure and the structure of higher education.* Oakland, CA: The Independent Institute.

Aronowitz, S. (2000). *The knowledge factory: Dismantling the corporate university and creating true higher learning.* New York: Beacon Press.

Astin, A. (2004). Why spirituality deserves a central place in higher education. *Spirituality in Higher Education Newsletter, 1*(1), 1–12.

Astin, A. W. (2016). "Spirituality" and "religiousness" among American college students. *About Campus, 6*(20), 16–22.

Astin, A. W., Astin, H. S., & Lindholm, J. A. (2010). *Cultivating the spirit: How college can enhance students' inner lives.* San Francisco: Jossey-Bass.

Austin, I., & Jones, G. A. (2015). *Governance of higher education: Global perspectives, theories, and practices.* New York: Routledge.

Baden-Fuller, C., & Stopford, J. M. (1994). *Rejuvenating the mature business: The competitive challenge.* Boston: Harvard Business School Press.

Baldridge, J. V. (1971a). *Academic governance: Research on institutional politics and decision making.* Berkeley, CA: McCutchan.

Baldridge, J. V. (1971b). Introduction: Models of university governance—Bureaucratic, collegial, and political. In J. V. Baldridge (Ed.), *Academic governance: Research on institutional politics and decision making* (pp. 1–19). Berkeley, CA: McCutchan.

Baldridge, J. V. (1971c). *Power and conflict in the university.* New York: Wiley.

Baldridge, J. V., Curtis, D. V., Ecker, G., & Riley, G. L. (1974). *Alternative models of governance in higher education* (Research and Development Memorandum, No. 129). Stanford, CA: School of Education, Stanford University.

Baldridge, J. V., Curtis, D. V., Ecker, G., & Riley, G. L. (1978). *Policy making and effective leadership.* San Francisco: Jossey-Bass.

Barbera, K. M. (2014). *The Oxford handbook of organizational climate and culture.* Oxford: Oxford University Press.

Barbezat, D. P., & Bush, M. (2014). *Contemplative practices in higher education: Powerful methods to transform teaching and learning.* San Francisco: John Wiley & Sons.

Bastedo, M. N. (2004). Strategic decoupling: Building legitimacy in educational policy environments. Presented at the Annual Meeting of the American Sociological Association, San Francisco, August 14–17.

Bastedo, M. N. (2006a). Activist trustees in the university: Reconceptualizing the public interest. In P. D. Eckel (Ed.), *The shifting frontier of academic decision making* (pp. 127–141). Santa Barbara, CA: Greenwood Publishing Group.

Bastedo, M. N. (2006b). Tuition cuts: The political dynamics of higher education finance. *NASFAA Journal of Student Financial Aid, 36*(2), 33–48.

Bastedo, M. N. (2007). Bringing the state back in: Promoting and sustaining innovation in public higher education. *Higher Education Quarterly, 61*(2), 155–170.

Bastedo, M. N. (2009a). Conflicts, commitments, and cliques in the university: Moral seduction as a threat to trustee independence. *American Educational Research Journal, 46*(2), 354–386.

Bastedo, M. N. (2009b). Convergent institutional logics in public higher education: State policymaking and governing board activism. *The Review of Higher Education, 32*(2), 209–234.

Bastedo, M. N. (2011). Curriculum in higher education: The historical roots of contemporary issues. In P. G. Altbach, R. O. Berdahl, & P. J. Gumport (Eds.), *American higher education in the twenty-first century: Social, political, and economic challenges* (2nd ed., pp. 462–485). Baltimore: Johns Hopkins University Press.

Bastedo, M. N. (Ed.). (2012). *The organization of higher education: Managing colleges for a new era.* Baltimore: Johns Hopkins University Press.

Beatty, R. W., & Ulrich, D. O. (1991). Re-energizing the mature organization. *Organizational Dynamics, 20*(1), 16–30.

Bell, D. A. (1980). Brown v. Board of Education and the interest-convergence dilemma. *Harvard Law Review, 93*(3), 518–533.

Bell, D. A. (1992). *Faces at the bottom of the well: The permanence of racism.* New York: Basic Books.

Bendl, R., Fleischmann, A., & Walenta, C. (2008). Diversity management discourse meets queer theory. *Gender in Management: An International Journal, 23*(6), 382–394.

Bendl, R., Fleischmann, A., & Hofmann, R. (2009). Queer theory and diversity management: Reading codes of conduct from a queer perspective. *Journal of Management & Organization, 15*(5), 625–638.

Benschop, Y., & Verloo, M. (2015). Feminist organization theories: Islands of treasure. In R. Mir, H. Willmott, & M. Greenwood (Eds.), *The Routledge companion to philosophy in organization studies* (pp. 100–112). New York: Routledge.

Bergquist, W. H., & Pawlak, K. (2008). *Engaging the six cultures of the academy* (2nd ed.). San Francisco: Jossey-Bass.

Berrett, D. (2014, November 13). Professors' place in the classroom is shifting to the side. *The Chronicle of Higher Education*.

Bess, J. L., & Dee, J. R. (2008). *Understanding college and university organization: Theories for effective policy and practice* (Volume 1). Sterling, VA: Stylus.

Bills, D. B. (2016). Living, learning, and the new higher education. *Contemporary Sociology: A Journal of Reviews* 45(6), 690–695.

Birnbaum, R. (1991). *How colleges work: The cybernetics of academic organization and leadership*. San Francisco: Jossey-Bass.

Birnbaum, R. (1992). *How academic leadership works: Understanding success and failure in the college presidency*. San Francisco: Jossey-Bass.

Blake-Beard, S. D., Finley-Hervey, J. A., & Harquail, C. V. (2008). Journey to a different place: Reflections on Taylor Cox, Jr.'s career and research as a catalyst for diversity education and training. *Academy of Management Learning & Education, 7*(3), 394–405.

Bleiklie, I., & Powell, W. W. (2005). Universities and the production of knowledge—Introduction. *Higher Education, 49*, 1–8.

Block, P. (1993). *Stewardship: Choosing service over self-interest*. San Francisco: Jossey-Bass.

Bok, D. (2003). *Universities in the marketplace: The commercialization of higher education*. Princeton, NJ: Princeton University Press.

Bok, D. (2015). *Higher education in America*. Princeton, NJ: Princeton University Press.

Bollinger, S. J. (2016). Between a tomahawk and a hard place: Indian mascots and the NCAA. *Brigham Young University Education & Law Journal, 1*, 73–115.

Bordas, J. (2012). *Salsa, soul, and spirit: Leadership for a multicultural age* (2nd ed.). San Francisco: Berrett-Koehler.

Bott, S. E., Banning, J. H., Wells, M., Hass, G. & Lakey, J. (2006). A sense of place: A framework and its application to campus ecology. *College Services, 6*(5), 42–47.

Bowen, W. G., & Tobin, E. M. (2015). *Locus of authority: The evolution of faculty roles in the governance of higher education*. Princeton, NJ: Princeton University Press.

Briskin, A. (1996). *The stirring of soul in the workplace*. San Francisco: Jossey-Bass.

Briskin, A., Erickson, S., Ott, J., & Callanan, T. (2009). *The power of collective wisdom: And the trap of collective folly*. San Francisco: Berrett-Koehler.

Broadbridge, A., & Simpson, R. (2011). 25 years on: Reflecting on the past and looking to the future in gender and management research. *British Journal of Management, 22*, 470–483.

Brown, M. C., Lane, J. E., & Zamani-Gallaher, E. M. (2010). *Organization and governance in higher education* (6th ed.). Boston: Pearson Custom.

Brubacher, J. S. (1990). *On the philosophy of higher education*. San Francisco: Jossey-Bass.

Bruns, J. W., & Bruns, D. L. (2007). Effecting change in colleges and universities. *Journal of Leadership Studies, 1*(2), 53–63.

Burnes, B. (1996). Organizational change: What we know, what we need to know. *Journal of Management Inquiry, 4*(2), 158–171.

Butler, J. (1990). *Gender trouble: Feminism and the subversion of identity*. New York: Routledge.

Cabrera, N. L., Watson, J. S., & Franklin, J. D. (2016). Racial arrested development: A critical Whiteness analysis of the campus ecology. *Journal of College Student Development, 57*(2), 119–134.

Cai, Y., & Mehari, Y. (2015). The use of institutional theory in higher education research. In M. Tight & J. Huisman (Eds.), *Theory and method in higher education research* (pp. 1–25). Bingley, UK: Emerald Group Publishing Limited.

Calás, M. B., & Smircich, L. (1999). Past postmodernism? Reflections and tentative discussions. *Academy of Management Review, 24*(4), 649–671.

Calás, M. B., & Smircich, L. (2006). From the "Woman's Point of View" ten years later: Towards a feminist organization studies. In S. R. Clegg, C. Hardy, T. B. Lawrence, & W. R. Nord (Eds.), *The Sage handbook of organization studies* (pp. 284–346). Thousand Oaks, CA: Sage.

Cantwell, B., & Kauppinen, I. (Eds.). (2014). *Academic capitalism in the age of globalization*. Baltimore: Johns Hopkins University Press.

Carnegie Foundation. (2015). Classification description. Retrieved from http://carnegieclassifications.iu.edu/.

Chait, R. P. (Ed.). (2002). *The questions of tenure.* Cambridge, MA: Harvard University Press.

Chait, R. P., Holland, T. P., & Taylor, B. E. (1996). *Improving the performance of governing boards.* Phoenix, AZ: Oryx Press.

Chambers, A. C., and Burkhardt, J. C. (Eds.). (2015). *Higher education for the public good: Emerging voices from a national movement.* San Francisco: John Wiley & Sons.

Cheslock, J. J., Ortagus, J. C., Umbricht, M. R., & Wymore, J. (2016). The cost of producing higher education: An exploration of theory, evidence, and institutional policy. In M. B. Paulsen (Ed.), *Higher education: Handbook of theory and research* (pp. 349–392). New York: Springer International Publishing.

Chickering, A. W. (2006). Authenticity and spirituality in higher education: My orientation. *Journal of College & Character, 7*(1), 1–5.

Chickering, A. W., Dalton, J. C., & Stamm, L. (2005). *Encouraging authenticity and spirituality in higher education.* San Francisco: Jossey-Bass.

Childers, M. E. (1981). What is political about bureaucratic-collegial decision making? *The Review of Higher Education, 5*(1), 25–45.

Ching, D., & Agbayani, A. (2012). *Asian Americans and Pacific Islanders in higher education: Research and perspectives on identity, leadership, and success.* Washington, DC: NASPA.

Clark, B. R. (1963). Faculty culture. In T. Lunsford (Ed.), *The study of campus cultures* (pp. 39–54). Boulder, CO: Western Interstate Commission for Higher Education.

Clark, B. R. (1972). The organizational saga in higher education. *Administrative Science Quarterly, 17*(2), 178–184.

Clark, B. R. (1980). *Academic culture.* New Haven, CT: Institute for Social and Policy Studies.

Clark, B. R. (1986). *The higher education system: Academic organization in cross-national perspective.* Berkeley, CA: University of California Press.

Clark, B. R. (2007). Development of the sociology of higher education. In P. Gumport (Ed.), *Sociology of higher education: Contributions and their contexts* (pp. 3–16). Baltimore: Johns Hopkins University Press.

Clark, B. R. (2008). *On higher education: Selected writings, 1956–2006.* Baltimore: Johns Hopkins University Press.

Clark, B. R., & Trow, M. (1966). The organizational context. In T. M. Newcomb & E. K. Wilson (Eds.), *College peer groups: Problems and prospects for research* (pp. 17–70). Chicago: Aldine.

Clark, D. L. (1985). Emerging paradigms in organizational theory and research. In Y. Lincoln (Ed.), *Organizational theory and inquiry: The paradigm revolution* (pp. 43–78). Beverly Hills, CA: Sage.

Clemons, S. A., McKelfresh, D., & Banning, J. (2005). Importance of sense of place and sense of self in residence hall room design: A qualitative study of first-year students. *Journal of the First-Year Experience, 17*(2), 73–86.

Coburn, C. (2015). Negotiation conflict styles. Retrieved from https://hms.harvard.edu/sites/default/files/assets/Sites/Ombuds/files/NegotiationConflictStyles.pdf.

Cohen, A. M., & Brawer, F. B. (2003). *The American community college.* San Francisco: John Wiley & Sons.

Cohen, M. D., & March, J. G. (1986). *Leadership and ambiguity* (2nd ed.). Boston: Harvard Business School Press.

Cohen, M. D., March, J. G., & Olsen, J. P. (1972). A garbage can model of organizational choice. *Administrative Science Quarterly, 17*(1), 1–25.

Conley, T. (2016, January 19). 4 trends shaping higher education in 2016. *Ed Surge News.* Retrieved from www.edsurge.com/news/2016-01-19-4-trends-shaping-higher-education-in-2016.

Cox, T., Jr. (1993). *Cultural diversity in organizations: Theory, research and practice.* San Francisco: Berrett-Koehler.

Cox, T., Jr. (2001). *Creating the multicultural organization: A strategy for capturing the power of diversity.* San Francisco: Jossey-Bass.

Cox, T., & Beale, R. L. (1997). *Developing competency to manage diversity.* San Francisco: Berrett-Koehler.

Cox, T. H., & Blake, S. (1991). Managing cultural diversity: Implications for organizational competitiveness. *The Executive, 5*(3), 45–56.

Crichlow, W. (2015). Critical race theory: A strategy for framing discussions around social justice and democratic education. Paper presented at the Higher Education in Transformation Conference, Dublin, May 31–April 1 (pp. 187–201). Dublin: Dublin Institute of Technology. Retrieved from http://arrow.dit.ie/cgi/viewcontent.cgi?article=1004&context=st2.

Curry, J. R., Laws, A. L., & Strauss, J. (2013). *The buck stops elsewhere.* Washington, DC: NACUBO.

Cyert, R. M., & March, J. G. (2011). A behavioral theory of organizational objectives. In J. M. Shafritz, J. S. Ott, & Y. S. Jang (Eds.), *Classics of organization theory* (7th ed., pp. 139–148). Boston: Wadsworth. (Original work published 1959).

Dacin, M. T., Goodstein, J., & Scott, W. R. (2002). Institutional theory and institutional change: Introduction to the special research forum. *Academy of Management Journal, 45*(1), 45–56.

Daft, R. L. (2007). *Organization theory and design* (10th ed.). Mason, OH: Cengage Learning.

Daloz, L. A. P., Keen, C. H., Keen, J. P., & Parks, S. D. (1996). *Common fire: Lives of commitment in a complex world.* Boston: Beacon Press.

Deal, T. E., & Kennedy, A. A. (1982). *Corporate cultures: The rites and rituals of corporate life.* Reading, MA: Addison-Wesley.

DeCuir, J. T., & Dixson, A. D. (2004). "So when it comes out, they aren't that surprised that it is there": Using critical race theory as a tool of analysis of race and racism in education. *Educational Researcher, 33*(5), 26–31.

DeGeorge, R. T. (2003). Ethics, academic freedom and academic tenure. *Journal of Academic Ethics, 1*(1), 11–25.

Delgado, R., & Stefancic, J. (2012). *Critical race theory: An introduction* (2nd ed.). New York: New York University Press.

DiMaggio, P. J., & Powell, W. W. (1983). The iron cage revisited: Institutional isomorphism and collective rationality in organizational fields. *American Sociological Review, 48*, 147–160.

DiMaggio, P. J., & Powell, W. W. (1991). Introduction. In W. W. Powell & P. J. DiMaggio (Eds.), *The new institutionalism in organizational analysis* (pp. 1–38). Chicago: University of Chicago Press.

Dobbin, F., Schrage, D., & Kalev, A. (2015). Rage against the iron cage: The varied effects of bureaucratic personnel reforms on diversity. *American Sociological Review, 80*(5), 1014–1044.

Doeringer, P. B. (1987). Make way for mature industries. *Labor Law Journal, 38*(8), 453–457.

Dowd, A. C., Sawatzky, M., & Korn, R. (2011). Theoretical foundations and a research agenda to validate measures of intercultural effort. *The Review of Higher Education, 35*(1), 17–44.

du Gay, P. (2005). *The values of bureaucracy.* Oxford: Oxford University Press.

Duncan, J. C. (1999). The indentured servants of academia: The adjunct faculty dilemma and their limited legal remedies. *Indiana Law Journal, 74*(2), 514–526.

Eckel, P. D. (2000). The role of shared governance in institutional hard decisions: Enabler or antagonist? *The Review of Higher Education, 24*(1), 15–39.

Eckel, P., Green, M., & Barblan, A. (2015). The new (and smaller) world of higher education. *International Higher Education, 29*, 2–3.

Eddy, P. L., & Cox, E. (2008). Gendered leadership: An organizational perspective. In J. Lester (Ed.), *Gendered perspectives on community colleges* (New Directions for Community Colleges, No. 142, pp. 69–80). San Francisco: Jossey-Bass.

Eddy, P. L., & Van Der Linden, K. E. (2006). Emerging definitions of leadership in higher education: New visions of leadership or the same old "hero" leader. *Community College Review, 34*(5), 5–26.

Ehrenberg, R. G. (2012). American higher education in transition. *The Journal of Economic Perspectives, 26*(1), 193–216.

Ellis, S. (2016). The political dimensions of decision making. In G. S. McClellan & J. Stringer (Eds.), *The handbook of student affairs administration* (pp. 457–477). Washington, DC: NASPA.

Endres, D. (2015). American Indian permission for mascots: Resistance or complicity within rhetorical colonialism? *Rhetoric & Public Affairs, 18*(4), 649–689.

Evans, C. & Holmes, L. (Eds.). (2016). *Re-Tayloring management: Scientific management a century on.* New York: Routledge.

Fayol, H. (1916/2016). General principles of management. In J. M. Shafritz, J. S. Ott, & Y. S. Jang (Eds.), *Classics of organizational theory* (8th ed., pp. 53–65). Boston: Wadsworth. (Original work published 1916)

Ferguson, K. (1985). *The feminist case against bureaucracy.* Philadelphia: Temple University Press.

Ferguson, K. E. (1994). On bringing more theory, more voices and more politics to the study of organization. *Organization, 1*(1), 81–99.

Ferren, A. S., & Anderson, C. B. (2016). Integrative learning: Making liberal education purposeful, personal, and practical. In M. M. Watts (Ed.), *Finding the why: Personalizing learning in higher education* (New Directions for Teaching and Learning, No. 145, pp. 33–40). San Francisco: Jossey-Bass.

Finkin, M. W., Post, R. C., Nelson, C., & Benjamin, E. (2007). Freedom in the classroom. *Academe, 93*(5), 54–61.

Fleischmann, A. (2009). Queering the principles: A queer/intersectional reading of Frederick W. Taylor's *The Principles of Scientific Management.* In M. Èzbilgin (Ed.), *Equality, diversity and inclusion at work: A research companion* (pp. 159–170). Northampton, MA: Edward Elgar Publishing.

Frost, P. J., Moore, L. F., Louis, M. R., Lundberg, C. C., & Martin, J. (Eds.). (1985). *Organizational culture.* Thousand Oaks, CA: Sage.

Fry, L. W. (2003). Toward a theory of spiritual leadership. *The Leadership Quarterly, 14*(6), 693–727.

Fumasoli, T., & Huisman, J. (2013). Strategic agency and system diversity: Conceptualizing institutional positioning in higher education. *Minerva, 51*(2), 155–169.

Fumasoli, T. & Stensaker, B. (2013). Organizational studies in higher education: A reflection on historical themes and prospective trends. *Higher Education Policy, 26*(4), 479–496.

Gardner, H. (1993). *Multiple intelligences: The theory in practice.* New York: Basic Books.

Gardner, H. (1995). *Leading minds: An anatomy of leadership.* New York: Basic Books.

Gardner, H. (2003). Multiple intelligences after twenty years. Paper presented at the American Educational Research Association, Chicago, April 21.

Gardner, H. (2006). *Multiple intelligences: New horizons.* New York: Basic Books.

Geertz, C. (1973). *The interpretation of cultures.* New York: Basic Books.

Gibson-Graham, J. K. (2003). Poststructural interventions. In E. Sheppard & T. J. Barnes (Eds.), *A companion to economic geography* (pp. 95–110). Oxford: Blackwell Publishing.

Giddens, A. (1979). *Central problems in social theory: Action, structure, and contradictions in social analysis.* Berkeley, CA: University of California Press.

Giddens, A. (1984). *The constitution of society: Outline of the theory of structuration.* Berkeley, CA: University of California Press.

Giddens, A. (1993). *New rules of sociological method* (2nd ed.). Stanford, CA: Stanford University Press.

Gillett-Karam, R. (2013). The future-shaping function of the governing board. In G. Myran, C. L. Ivery, M. H. Parsons, & C. Kinsley (Eds.), *The future of the urban community college: Shaping the pathways to a multiracial democracy* (New Directions for Community Colleges, No. 162, pp. 37–44). San Francisco: Jossey-Bass.

Gilligan, C. (1982). *In a different voice: Psychological theory and women's development.* Cambridge, MA: Harvard University Press.

Giroux, H. (2002). Neoliberalism, corporate culture, and the promise of higher education: The university as a democratic public sphere. *Harvard Educational Review, 72*(4), 425–463.

Giroux, H. (2014). *Neoliberalism's war on higher education.* Chicago: Haymarket Books.

Goldman, E. (1910). *Anarchism and other essays.* New York: Mother Earth.

Goleman, D. (1998). *Working with emotional intelligence.* New York: Bantam.

Goodman, P. (1962). *The community of scholars.* New York: Random House.

Gouldner, A. (1957). Cosmopolitans and locals: Toward an analysis of latent social roles. I. *Administrative Science Quarterly, 2*(3), 281–306.

Gouldner, A. (1958). Cosmopolitans and locals: Toward an analysis of latent social roles. II. *Administrative Science Quarterly, 2*(4), 444–480.

Govindarajan, V., & Trimble, C. (2010). *The other side of innovation: Solving the execution challenge.* Cambridge, MA: Harvard Business Press.

Green, M. F., Eckel, P. D., & Barblan, A. (2002). *The brave new (and smaller) world of higher education: A transatlantic view* (Vol. 1). Washington, DC: American Council on Education.

Greenfield, T. B. (1986). Leaders and schools: Willfulness and nonnatural order in organizations. In T. J. Sergiovanni & J. E. Corbally (Eds.), *Leadership and organizational culture: New perspectives on administrative theory and practice* (pp. 142–169). Chicago: University of Illinois Press.

Greenleaf, R. (2008). *The servant as leader.* Newton Center, MA: Greenleaf Center.

Greenwood, R., Oliver, C., Sahlin, K., & Suddaby, R. (2008). Introduction. In R. Greenwood, C. Oliver, R. Suddaby, & K. Sahlin (Eds.), *The SAGE handbook of organizational institutionalism* (pp. 3–45). Los Angeles: Sage.

Gruenewald, D. A. (2003). Foundations of place: A multidisciplinary framework for place-conscious education. *American Educational Research Journal, 40*(3), 619–654.

Guetzkow, H. (1965). Communications and organizations. In J. G. March (Ed.), *Handbook of organizations* (pp. 534–573). Chicago: Rand McNally.

Guiliano, J. (2015). *Indian spectacle: College mascots and the anxiety of modern America.* New Brunswick, NJ: Rutgers University Press.

Guinier, L. (2015). *The tyranny of meritocracy: Democratizing higher education in America.* Boston: Beacon Press.

Gulick, L. (2016). Notes on the theory of organization. In J. M. Shafritz, J. S. Ott, & Y. S. Jang (Eds.), *Classics of Organizational Theory* (8th ed., pp. 84–92). Boston: Wadsworth. (Original work published 1937).

Gumport, P. J. (Ed.). (2007). *Sociology of higher education: Contributions and their contexts.* Baltimore: Johns Hopkins University Press.

Gumport, P. (2012). Strategic thinking in higher education research. In M. N. Bastedo (Ed.), *The organization of higher education* (pp. 18–41). Baltimore: Johns Hopkins University Press.

Gunnlaugson, O., & Vokey, D. (2014). Evolving a public language of spirituality for transforming academic and campus life. *Innovations in Education and Teaching International, 51*(4), 436–445.

Hacker, S. (2016). Is the workplace a zombie breeding ground? *The Journal for Quality and Participation, 39*(1), 4.

Hagberg, J. (1994). *Real power.* Salem, WI: Sheffield.

Hamada, T. (1989). Perspective on organizational culture. *Anthropology of Work Review, 10*(3), 5–7.

Han, C. W. (2016). No fats, femmes, or Asians: The utility of critical race theory in examining the role of gay stock stories in the marginalization of gay Asian men. In M. Zhou & A. C. Ocampo (Eds.), *Contemporary Asian America: A multidisciplinary reader* (3rd ed., pp. 312–330). New York: New York University Press.

Harper, S. R. (2009). Race, interest convergence, and transfer outcomes for Black male student athletes. In L. S. Hagedorn & D. Horton Jr. (Eds.), *Student athletes and athletics* (New Directions for Community Colleges, No. 147, pp. 29–37). San Francisco: Jossey-Bass.

Haskins, C. H. (1984). *The rise of universities.* New York: Cornell University Press.

Hatch, M. J., & Cunliffe, A. L. (2006). *Organization theory: Modern, symbolic, and postmodern perspectives.* Oxford: Oxford University Press.

Haviland, D., Alleman, N. F., & Allen, C. C. (2015, November). "Separate but not quite equal": Collegiality experiences of full time, non-tenure-track faculty members. Paper presented at the Annual Meeting of the Association for the Study of Higher Education. Denver, CO.

Hazelkorn, E. (2015). *Rankings and the reshaping of higher education: The battle for world-class excellence.* New York: Springer.

Hedlund, G. (1986). The hypermodern MNC—A heterarchy? *Human Resource Management, 25*(1), 9–35.

Helgesen, S. (1990). *The female advantage: Women's ways of leadership.* New York: Doubleday Currency.

Helgesen, S. (1995). *The web of inclusion: A new architecture for building great organizations.* Frederick, MD: Beard Books.

Helgesen, S. (2006). Challenges for leaders in the years ahead. In F. Hesselbein & M. Goldsmith (Eds.), *The leader of the future 2: Visions, strategies, and practices for the new era* (pp. 183–190). San Francisco: Jossey-Bass.

Hendrickson, R. M., Lane, J. E., Harris, J. T., & Dorman, R. H. (2013). *Academic leadership and governance of higher education: A guide for trustees, leaders, and aspiring leaders of two-and four-year institutions.* Sterling, VA: Stylus Publishing.

Hofmann, S. (2005). The elimination of indigenous mascots, logos, and nicknames: Organizing on college campuses. *The American Indian Quarterly, 29*(1), 156–177.

Huber, M. T., & Hutchings, P. (2004). *Integrative learning: Mapping the terrain. The academy in transition.* Washington, DC: Association of American Colleges and Universities.

Hurtado, S., Milem, J., Clayton-Pedersen, A., & Allen, W. (1999). *Enacting diverse learning environments* (ASHE-ERIC Monograph, *26*, No. 8). Washington, DC: The George Washington University.

Immergut, E. M. (1998). The theoretical core of the new institutionalism. *Politics and society, 26,* 5–34.

Iverson, S. (2011). Glass ceilings and sticky floors: Women and advancement in higher education. In J. L. Martin (Ed.), *Women as leaders in education: Succeeding despite inequity, discrimination, and other challenges* (pp. 79–105). Santa Barbara, CA: Praeger.

Jablonski, M. A. (Ed.). (2001). *The implications of student spirituality for student affairs practice* (New Directions for Student Services, No. 95). San Francisco: Jossey-Bass.

Jamieson, D., & Vogel, J. (2010). In our own voices: The contributions and challenges of OD practitioners of color. *OD Practitioner, 42*(2).

Jaschik, S. (2017, January 5). When colleges rely on adjuncts, where does the money go? *Inside Higher Education.* Retrieved from www.insidehighered.com/news/2017/01/05/study-looks-impact-adjunct-hiring-college-spending-patterns.

Johnson, A. B. (2008). Privilege as paradox. In P. Rothenberg (Ed.), *White privilege: Essential readings on the other side of racism* (pp. 117–121). New York: Worth.

Kanter, R. M. (1977). *Men and women of the corporation.* New York: Basic Books.

Kark, R. (2004). The transformational leader: Who is (s)he? A feminist perspective. *Journal of Organizational Change Management, 17*(2), 160–176.

Kaur, M., & Kaur, D. (2014). The power of organizational spirituality: Its effect on job satisfaction, quality of work life and occupational stress. *International Journal of Research in Organizational Behavior and Human Resource Management, 2*(2), 356–369.

Keeling, R., & Hersh, R. (2016). *We're losing our minds: Rethinking American higher education.* New York: Springer.

Kerr, C. (2001). *The uses of the university.* Cambridge, MA: Harvard University Press.

Kessler, R. (2000). *The soul of education: Helping students find connection, compassion, and character at school.* Alexandria, VA: Association for Supervision and Curriculum Development.

Kezar A. (2001). *Understanding and facilitating organizational change in the 21st century: Recent research and conceptualizations* (ASHE-ERIC Higher Education Report, *28*, No. 4). San Francisco: Jossey-Bass.

Kezar, A. (2006). Rethinking public higher education governing boards performance: Results of a national study of governing boards in the United States. *The Journal of Higher Education, 77*(6), 968–1008.

Kezar, A. (2010). Organizational theory. In J. H. Schuh, S. R. Jones, & S. R. Harper (Eds.), *Student services: A handbook for the profession* (pp. 226–241). San Francisco: Jossey-Bass.

Kezar, A. (2011). Organizational culture and its impact on partnering between community agencies and postsecondary institutions to help low-income students attend college. *Education and Urban Society, 43*(2), 205–243.

Kezar, A. (2012). Organizational change. In M. N. Bastedo (Ed.), *The organization of higher education: Managing colleges for a new era* (pp. 181–222). Baltimore: Johns Hopkins University Press.

Kezar, A. (2013). Understanding sensemaking/sensegiving in transformational change processes from the bottom up. *Higher Education, 65*(6), 761–780.

Kezar, A. (2014a). Higher education change and social networks: A review of research. *The Journal of Higher Education, 85*(1), 91–125.

Kezar, A. (2014b). *How colleges change: Understanding, leading, and enacting change.* New York: Routledge.

Kezar, A., Chambers, A. C., & Burkhardt, J. C. (Eds.). (2005). *Higher education for the public good: Emerging voices from a national movement.* New York: John Wiley & Sons.

Kezar, A., Lester, J., & Anderson, G. (2006). Challenging stereotypes that interfere with effective governance. *Thought and Action, 22*(2), 121–134.

Kimberly, J. R. (1980). Initiation, innovation, and institutionalization in the creation process. In J. R. Kimberly, R. H. Miles, & Associates (Eds.), *The organizational life cycle: Issues in the creation, transformation, and decline of organizations* (pp. 18–43). San Francisco: Jossey-Bass.

Kleiner, A. (2002). Karen Stephenson's quantum theory of trust. *Strategy + Business, 29,* 1–14.

Ko, C. M. (2012). Transformative leadership: The influence of AAPI college student organizations on the development of leadership for social change. In D. Ching & A. Agbayani (Eds.), *Asian American and Pacific Islanders in higher education: Research and perspectives on identity, leadership, and success* (pp. 121–142). Washington, DC: NASPA.

Kolodny, A. (2008, September–October). Tenure, academic freedom, and the career I once loved: We're being underfunded out of existence. *Academe, 94*(5). Retrieved from www.aaup.org/AAUP/pubsres/academe/2008/SO/.

Kraatz, M. S., & Block, E. S. (2008). Organizational implications of institutional pluralism. In R. Greenwood, C. Oliver, K. Sahlin-Andersson, & R. Suddaby (Eds.), *The Sage handbook of organizational institutionalism* (pp. 243–275). Los Angeles: Sage.

Kroeger, N. (2014). "Micropolitics" and communication: An exploratory study on student representatives' communication repertoires in university governance. (MSc dissertation). Retrieved from www.lse.ac.uk/media@lse/research/mediaWorkingPapers/MScDissertationSeries/2013/msc/110-Kroeger.pdf.

Kuh, G. D. (Ed.). (1993). *Cultural perspectives in student affairs work.* Lanham, MD: University Press of America.

Kuh, G. D. (2008). *High impact educational practices: What they are, who has access to them, and why they matter.* Washington, DC: Association of American Colleges and Universities.

Kuh, G. D., Kinzie, J., Schuh, J. H., Whitt, E. J., & Associates. (2010). *Student success in college: Creating conditions that matter.* San Francisco: Jossey-Bass. (Original work published 2005)

Kuh, G. D., Schuh, J., Whitt, E., & Associates. (1991). *Involving colleges: Successful approaches to fostering student learning and development outside the classroom.* San Francisco: Jossey-Bass.

Kuh, G. D., & Whitt, E. J. (1988). *The invisible tapestry: Culture in American colleges and universities* (ASHE/ERIC Higher Education Report, No. 1). Washington, DC: ERIC Clearinghouse on Higher Education.

Laden, B. V., Millem, J. F., & Crowson, R. L. (2000). New institutional theory and student departure. In J. Braxton (Ed.), *Reworking the student departure puzzle* (pp. 235–255). Nashville, TN: Vanderbilt University Press.

Ladson-Billings, G. J. (1998). Just what is critical race theory and what's it doing in a nice field like education? *International Journal of Qualitative Studies in Education, 11*(1), 7–24.

Ladson-Billings, G. (2013). *Critical race theory—What it is not!* In M. Lynn & A. D. Dixson (Eds.), *Handbook of critical race theory in education* (pp. 34–47). New York: Routledge.

Lamont, M., & Lareau, A. (1988). Cultural capital: Allusions, gaps and glissandos in recent theoretical developments. *Sociological Theory, 6*(2), 153–168.

Lawrence, J., & Ott, M. (2013). Faculty perceptions of organizational politics. *The Review of Higher Education, 36*(2),145–178.

Lechuga, V. M. (2016). *The changing landscape of the academic profession: Faculty culture at for-profit colleges and universities.* New York: Routledge.

Leider, R. J. (2015). *The power of purpose: Find meaning, live longer, better* (3rd ed.). San Francisco: Berrett-Koehler.

Leiser, B. M. (1994). Threats to academic freedom and tenure. *Pace Law Review, 15*(1), 15–53.

Levin, J. S., Haberler, Z., Walker, L., & Jackson-Boothby, A. (2014). Community college culture and faculty of color. *Community College Review, 42*(1), 55–74.

Levine, A. (2000, March 13). The soul of a new university. *New York Times*. Retrieved from www.nytimes.com/2000/03/13/opinion/the-soul-of-a-new-university.html?pagewanted=all&src=pm.

Levine, A. (2001). Higher education as a mature industry. In P. G. Altbach, P. J. Gumport, & D. B. Johnstone (Eds.), *In defense of American higher education* (pp. 38–58). Baltimore: Johns Hopkins University Press.

Lewis, P., & Simpson, R. (2012). Kanter revisited: Gender, power and (in)visibility. *International Journal of Management Reviews, 14*(2), 141–158.

Lincoln, Y. S. (Ed.). (1985). *Organizational theory and inquiry: The paradigm revolution*. Thousand Oaks, CA: Sage.

Lincoln, Y. S., Lynham, S. A., & Guba, E. G. (2011). Paradigmatic controversies, contradictions, and emerging confluences, revisited. In N. K. Denzin & Y. S. Lincoln (Eds.), *The SAGE handbook of qualitative research* (4th ed., pp. 97–128). Thousand Oaks, CA: Sage.

Lipman-Blumen, J. (1992). Connective leadership: Female leadership styles in the 21st century workplace. *Sociological Perspectives, 35*(1), 183–203.

Lipman-Blumen, J. (1998). Connective leadership: What business needs to learn from academe. *Change, 30*(1), 49–53.

Lipman-Blumen, J. (2002). The age of connective leadership. In F. Hesselbein & R. Johnson (Eds.), *On leading change: A leader to leader guide* (pp. 89–101). San Francisco: Jossey-Bass.

Lipman-Blumen, J. (2014). The essentials of leadership: A historical perspective. In G. R. Goethals, S. T. Scott, & M. Roderick (Eds.), *Conceptions of leadership: Enduring ideas and emerging insights* (pp. 15–37). London: Palgrave Macmillan.

Lucas, H. (2014). Surviving disruptive technologies (Coursera), University of Maryland, College Park [online course]. Retrieved from www.mooc-list.com/course/surviving-disruptive-technologies-coursera.

Macfarlane, B. (2013). *Intellectual leadership in higher education: Renewing the role of the university professor*. New York: Routledge.

Mahoney, A. I. (2002, October). Recalibrating for the customer. *Association Management Magazine*. Retrieved from www.asaecenter.org/PublicationsResources.

Manning, K. (1997, April). Student affairs in the mature industry of higher education. Speech given at the National Association of Student Personnel Administrators Region V, Washington State University, Pullman, WA.

Manning, K. (2000). *Rituals, ceremonies, and cultural meaning in higher education*. Westport, CT: Bergin & Garvey.

Manning, K. (2001). Infusing soul into student affairs. In M. A. Jablonski (Ed.), *The implications of student spirituality for student affairs practice* (New Directions for Student Services, No. 95, pp. 27–35). San Francisco: Jossey-Bass.

Manning, K., Kinzie, J., & Schuh, J. (2014). *One size does not fit all: Traditional and innovative models of student affairs practice* (2nd ed.). New York: Routledge.

March, J. G. (1981). Footnotes to organizational change. *Administrative Science Quarterly, 26*(4), 563–577.

March, J. G. (1994). *A primer on decision making: How decisions happen*. New York: Free Press.

March, J. G., & Shapira, Z. (2007). Behavioral decision theory and organizational decision theory. In G. R. Ungson & D. N. Braunstein (Eds.), *Decision making: An interdisciplinary inquiry* (pp. 293–345). Boston: Kent.

Martin, J. (2000). Hidden gendered assumptions in mainstream organizational theory and research. *Journal of Management and Inquiry, 9*(2), 207–216.

Martin, J. (2002). *Organizational culture: Mapping the terrain*. Thousand Oaks, CA: Sage.

Martin, R., Manning, K., & Ramaley, J. (2001). The self-study as a chariot for strategic change. In J. Ratcliffe, E. S. Lubinescu, & M. A. Gaffney (Eds.), *How accreditation influences assessment* (New Directions for Higher Education, No. 113, pp. 95–115). San Francisco: Jossey-Bass.

Martinez-Saenz, M., & Schoonover, S. (2015). The new era of "hire" education. *Liberal Education, 101*(1/2), 68–71.

Mather, P. C. (2010). Positive psychology and student affairs practice: A framework of possibility. *Journal of Student Affairs Research and Practice, 47*(2), 157–173.

Matsuda, M. J., Lawrence, C. R., Delgado, R., & Crenshaw, K. W. (1993). *Words that wound: Critical race theory, assaultive speech, and the First Amendment*. Boulder, CO: Westview Press.

Mayo, E. (1946). *The human problems of an industrial civilization* (2nd ed.). Boston: Graduate School of Business Administration, Harvard University.

Mendez, J. P., Bonner II, F. A., Méndez-Negrete, J., & Palmer, R. T. (Eds.). (2015). *Hispanic serving institutions in American higher education: Their origin, and present and future challenges*. Sterling, VA: Stylus Publishing.

Merton, R. K. (2011). Bureaucratic structure and personality. In J. M. Shafritz, J. S. Ott, & Y. S. Jang (Eds.), *Classics of organizational theory* (7th ed., pp. 107–115). Boston: Wadsworth. (Original work published 1957)

Meyer, J. W., Ramirez, F. O., Frank, D. J., & Schofer, E. (2007). Higher education as an institution. In P. Gumport (Ed.), *Sociology of higher education: Contributions and their contexts* (pp. 187–221). Baltimore: Johns Hopkins University Press.

Meyer, K. (2010). The role of disruptive technology in the future of higher education. Retrieved from http://er.educause.edu/articles/2010/3/the-role-of-disruptive-technology-in-the-future-of-higher-education.

Meyerson, D. E., & Kolb, D. M. (2000). Moving out of the "armchair": Developing a framework to bridge the gap between feminist theory and practice. *Organization, 7*(4), 553–570.

Michigan State University. (2010). Faculty handbook. Retrieved from www.hr.msu.edu/documents/facacadhandbooks/facultyhandbook/incompetence.htm.

Miller, S. D. (2014, February 4). Welcome to the campus of 2019. *Huffington Post*. Retrieved from www.huffingtonpost.com/dr-scott-d-miller/welcome-to-the-campus-of-_b_4694887.html.

Mintzberg, H., & Westly, F. (2010). Decision making: It's not what you think. In P. C. Nutt & D. C. Wilson (Eds.), *Handbook of decision making* (pp. 73–82). Hoboken, NJ: Wiley.

Morgan, A. (2001). Danah Zohar and Ian Marshall: SQ—Spiritual intelligence, the ultimate intelligence. Unpublished paper.

Morgan, G. (2006). *Images of organization* (3rd ed.). Thousand Oaks, CA: Sage.

Mullins, L. B. (2014). Pink tape: A feminist theory of red tape. *Public Voices, 13*(2), 33–42.

Museus, S. D. (2007). Using qualitative methods to assess diverse institutional cultures. In S. R. Harper & S. D. Museus (Eds.), *Using qualitative methods in institutional assessment* (New Directions for Institutional Research, No. 136, pp. 29–40). San Francisco: Jossey-Bass.

National Center for Educational Statistics. (2015). *Digest of education statistics*. Washington, DC: U.S. Department of Education.

National Education Association. (n.d.). The truth about tenure in higher education. Retrieved from www.nea.org/home/33067.htm.

Nevarez, C., Wood, J. L., & Penrose, R. (2013). *Leadership theory and the community college: Applying theory to practice*. Sterling, VA: Stylus Publishing.

Newman, F., Couturier, L., & Scurry, J. (2004). *The future of higher education: Rhetoric, reality, and the risks of the market*. San Francisco: Jossey-Bass.

Obear, K., & Martinez, B. (2013). Race caucuses: An intensive, high-impact strategy to create social change. In S. K. Watt & J. L. Linley (Eds.), *Creating successful multicultural initiatives in higher education and student affairs* (New Directions for Student Services, No. 144, pp. 79–86). San Francisco: Jossey-Bass.

Oliva, M., Rodríguez, M. A., Alanís, I., & Cerecer, P. D. Q. (2013). At home in the academy: Latina faculty counterstories and resistances. *The Journal of Educational Foundations, 27*(1/2), 91.

Oliveira, A. (2004). The place of spirituality in organizational theory. *Electronic Journal of Business Ethics and Organization Studies, 9*(2), 17–21.

Olsen, J. P. (2001). Garbage cans, new institutionalism, and the study of politics. *American Political Science Review, 95*(1), 191–198.

Olsen, J. P. (2005). Maybe it is time to rediscover bureaucracy. *Journal of Public Administration Research and Theory, 16*, 1–24.

Orton, J. D., & Weick, K. E. (1990). Loosely coupled systems: A reconceptualization. *The Academy of Management Review, 15*(2), 203–223.

Ospina, S., & Foldy, E. (2015). Enacting collective leadership in a shared-power world. In J. L. Perry & R. K. Christensen (Eds.), *Handbook of public administration* (3rd ed., pp. 489–507). San Francisco: Jossey-Bass.

Ouchi, W. G. (1982). *Theory Z: How American business can meet the Japanese challenge*. Reading, MA: Addison-Wesley.

Palfreyman, D., & Tapper, T. (2013). *Oxford and the decline of the collegiate tradition*. New York: Routledge.

Parker, M. (2000). *Organizational culture and identity: Unity and division at work*. Thousand Oaks, CA: Sage.

Pasque, P. A. (2007). Seeing more of the educational inequalities around us: Visions strengthening relationships between higher education and society. In E. P. St. John (Ed.), *Confronting educational inequality: Reframing, building understanding, and making change* (Vol. 22, pp. 37–84). New York: AMS Press.

Patton, L. D., McEwen, M., Rendón, L., & Howard-Hamilton, M. (2007). Critical race perspectives on theory in student affairs. In S. R. Harper & L. D. Patton (Eds.), *Responding to the realities of race on campus* (New Directions for Student Services, No. 120, pp. 39–54). San Francisco: Jossey-Bass.

Peppers, C., & Briskin, A. (2000). *Bringing your soul to work: An everyday practice*. San Francisco: Berrett-Koehler.

Peters, M. A. (2013). Managerialism and the neoliberal university: Prospects for new forms of "open management" in higher education. *Contemporary Readings in Law and Social Justice, 5*(1), 11–26.

Peters, T. J., Waterman, R. H., & Jones, I. (1982). *In search of excellence: Lessons from America's best-run companies*. New York: Harper and Row.

Peterson, M. W. (2007). The study of colleges and universities as organizations. In P. J. Gumport (Ed.), *Sociology of higher education: Contributions and their contexts* (pp. 147–184). Baltimore: Johns Hopkins University Press.

Pettigrew, A. M. (2014). *The politics of organizational decision-making*. New York: Routledge.

Pfeffer, J. (2005). Understanding the role of power in decision making. In J. M. Shafritz, J. S. Ott, & Y. S. Jang (Eds.), *Classics of organizational theory* (6th ed., pp. 289–303). Boston: Wadsworth. (Original work published 1991).

Pope, R. L., Reynolds, A. L., & Mueller, J. A. (2014). *Creating multicultural change on campus*. San Francisco: John Wiley & Sons.

Powell, W. W. (1990). Neither market nor hierarchy: Network forms of organization. *Research in Organizational Behavior, 12*, 295–336.

Powell, W.W. (2007). The new institutionalism. In S. R. Clegg & J. R. Bailey (Eds.), *The international encyclopedia of organizational studies* (pp. 975–979). Thousand Oaks, CA: Sage.

Pryor, J. H., Hurtado, S., DeAngelo, L., Palucki Blake, L., & Tran, S. (2010). *The American freshman: National norms fall 2010*. Los Angeles: Higher Education Research Institute, UCLA.

Pullen, A., Thanem, T., Tyler, M., & Wallenberg, L. (2013). Sexual politics, organizational practices: Interrogating queer theory, work and organization. *Gender, Work and Organization, 23*(1), 1–6.

Pusser, B. (2003). Beyond Baldridge: Extending the political model of higher education organization and governance. *Educational Policy, 17*(1), 121–140.

Pusser, B. (2015). A critical approach to power in higher education. In A. Martínez-Aleman, B. Pusser, & E. M. Bensimon (Eds.), *Critical approaches to the study of higher education: A practical introduction* (pp. 59–79). Baltimore: Johns Hopkins University Press.

Quatro, S. A. (2004). New age or age old: Classical management theory and traditional organized religion as underpinnings of the contemporary organizational spirituality movement. *Human Resource Development Review, 3*(3), 228–249.

Reay, T., & Hinings, C. R. (2009). Managing the rivalry of competing institutional logics. *Organization Studies, 30*(6), 629–652.

Rendón, L. I. (2009). *Sentipensante (sensing/thinking) pedagogy: Educating for wholeness, social justice and liberation*. Sterling, VA: Stylus Publishing.

Rhoades, G. (2007). The study of the academic profession. In P. J. Gumport (Ed.), *Sociology of higher education: Contributions and their contexts* (pp. 113–146). Baltimore: Johns Hopkins University Press.

Rhoades, G., & Slaughter, S. (2004). Academic capitalism in the new economy: Challenges and choices. *American Academic, 1*(1), 37–60.

Rhoades, G., Kiyama, J. M., McCormick, R., & Quiroz, M. (2008). Local cosmopolitans and cosmopolitan locals: New models of professionals in the academy. *The Review of Higher Education, 31*(2), 209–235.

Rhoads, R. A., & Liu, A. (2009). Globalization, social movements, and the American university: Implications for research and practice. In J. C. Smart (Ed.), *Higher education: Handbook of theory and research* (Vol. 24, pp. 273–315). Netherlands: Springer Science + Business Media.

Roethlisberger, F. J. (1941). *The Hawthorne Experiments: Classics of organizational behaviour*. Danville, IL: Interstate Printers.

Rogers, E. M. (1962). *Diffusion of innovations*. New York: Free Press.

Rogers, E. M. (1976). New product adoption and diffusion. *Journal of Consumer Research, 2*(4), 290–301.

Rogers, E. M. (2003). *Diffusion of innovations* (5th ed.). New York: Free Press. (Original edition published 1962).

Rogers, J. (2003). Preparing spiritual leaders. *About Campus, 8*(5), 19–26.

Rogers, J., & Dantley, M. (2001). Invoking the spiritual in campus life and leadership. *Journal of College Student Development, 42*(6), 589–603.

Rosser, V. J. (2003). Historical overview of faculty governance in higher education. In M. Miller & J. Caplow (Eds.), *Policy and university faculty governance* (pp. 3–18). Charlotte, NC: Information Age.

Rost, J. (1993). *Leadership for the twenty-first century*. Westport, CT: Praeger.

Rudolph, F. (1990). *The American college and university: A history*. Athens, GA: The University of Georgia Press.

Ryan, S. (2016, May 3). Illinois to select new mascot; Chief Illiniwek backers "not going to stop." *Chicago Tribune*. Retrieved from www.chicagotribune.com/sports/college/ct-university-of-illinois-mascot-chief-illiniwek-20160502-story.html.

Saltzman, G. M. (2008). Dismissals, layoffs, and tenure denials in colleges and universities. *The NEA 2008 almanac of higher education* (pp. 51–65). Retrieved from www.nea.org/home/32972.htm.

Sandberg, S. (2013). *Lean in: Women, work, and the will to lead*. New York: Random House.

Santiago, C. R. V. (2004). Countering Kulturkampf politics through critique and justice pedagogy, race, Kulturkampf, and immigration. *Seton Hall Law Review, 35*, 1155.

Schein, E. H. (2010). *Organizational culture and leadership* (4th ed.). San Francisco: Jossey-Bass.

Schrecker, E. (2010). *The lost soul of higher education: Corporatization, the assault on academic freedom, and the end of the American university*. New York: The New Press.

Selznick, P. (1996). Institutionalism "old" and "new." *Administrative Science Quarterly, 41*(2), 270–277.

Selznick, P. (2016). Foundations of the theory of organization. In J. M. Shafritz, J. S. Ott, & Y.-S. Jang (Eds.), *Classics of organizational theory* (8th ed., pp. 116–125). Boston: Wadsworth. (Original work published 1948).

Shaw, K. M., Valadez, J. R., & Rhoads, R. A. (Eds.). (1999). *Community colleges as cultural texts: Qualitative explorations of organizational and student culture.* Albany, NY: SUNY Press.

Simon, H. A. (1955). A behavioral model of rational choice. *The Quarterly Journal of Economics, 69*(1), 99–118.

Simon, H. A. (1956). Rational choice and the structure of the environment. *Psychological Review, 63*(2), 129–138.

Simon, H. A. (1957). *Models of man: Social and rational.* Oxford: Wiley.

Simon, H. A. (1979). Rational decision making in business organizations. *American Economic Review, 69*(4), 493–513.

Slaughter, S., & Leslie, L. L. (1997). *Academic capitalism: Politics, policies, and the entrepreneurial university.* Baltimore: Johns Hopkins University Press.

Slaughter, S., & Rhoades, G. (2004). *Academic capitalism and the new economy: Markets, state, and higher education.* Baltimore: Johns Hopkins University Press.

Small, J. L. (Ed.). (2015). *Making meaning: Embracing spirituality, faith, religion, and life purpose in student affairs.* Sterling, VA: Stylus.

Smircich, L. (1983). Concepts of culture and organizational analysis. *Administrative Science Quarterly, 28*(3), 339–358.

Solórzano, D., Ceja, M., & Yosso, T. (2000). Critical race theory, racial microaggressions, and campus racial climate: The experiences of African American college students. *Journal of Negro Education, 69*(1), 60–73.

Stegman, E., & Phillips, V. F. (2014). *Missing the point: The real impact of native mascots and team names on American Indian and Alaska Native Youth.* Washington, DC: Center for American Progress.

Stephenson, K. (2001). What knowledge tears apart, networks make whole. *Internal Communication Focus, 36*, 1–6.

Stephenson, K. (2004, Winter). Space: A dialectic frontier. *Reveal*, 20–21.

Stephenson, K. (2005). Trafficking in trust: The art and science of human knowledge networks. In L. Coughlin, E. Wingard, & K. Hollihan (Eds.), *Enlightened power: How women are transforming the practice of leadership* (pp. 242–265). San Francisco: Jossey-Bass.

Stephenson, K. (2006). Trusted connections. *World Business, 6*, 56–59.

Stephenson, K. (2007). The community network solution. *Strategy + Business, 49*, 32–37.

Stephenson, K. (2009). Neither hierarchy nor network: An argument for heterarchy. *People and Strategy, 32*(1), 4–7.

Stephenson, K. (2010). Neither hierarchy nor network: An argument for heterarchy. *Perspectives.* Retrieved from www.rossdawsonblog.com/HRPS_Heterarchy.pdf.

Stephenson, K. (2011). From Tiananmen to Tahrir: Knowing one's place in the 21st century. *Organizational Dynamics, 40*, 281–291.

Strange, C. C. (2001). Spiritual dimensions of graduate preparation in student affairs. In M. A. Jablonski (Ed.), *Implications of student spirituality for student affairs* (New Directions for Student Services, No. 95, pp. 57–67). San Francisco: Jossey-Bass.

Sue, D. W. (2010). *Microaggressions in everyday life: Race, gender, and sexual orientation.* New York: John Wiley & Sons.

Svokos, A. (2015, September 8). Why are college buildings still named after White supremacists? *Huffington Post.* Retrieved from www.huffingtonpost.com/2015/06/11/college-buildings-white-supremacists_n_7554958.html.

Taylor, F. W. (1947). *Scientific management.* New York: Harper and Row.

Teasdale, W. (1999). *The mystic heart: Discovering a universal spirituality in the world's religions.* Novato, CA: New World Library.

Temple, J. B., & Jari Ylitalo, J. (2009). Promoting inclusive (and dialogic) leadership in higher education institutions. *Tertiary Education and Management, 15*(3), 277–289.

The Chronicle of Higher Education. (2011). President, University of Utah [job advertisement].

Thomas, D. A., & Ely, R. J. (1996). Making differences matter: A new paradigm for managing diversity. *Harvard Business Review, 74*(5), 79–90.

Thomas, K. W. (1976). Conflict and conflict management. In M. D. Dunnette (Ed.), *Handbook of industrial and organizational psychology* (pp. 889–935). Chicago: Rand McNally.

Thomas, K. W. (1977). Toward multidimensional values in teaching: The example of conflict behavior. *Academy of Management Review, 2*, 484–490.

Thornton, P. H., & Ocasio, W. (2008). Institutional logics. In R. Greenwood, C. Oliver, & K. Sahlin-Andersson (Eds.), *The SAGE handbook of organizational institutionalism* (pp. 99–129). Los Angeles: Sage.

Tierney, W. (1998). Tenure is dead. Long live tenure. In W. Tierney (Ed.), *The responsive university: Restructuring for high performance* (pp. 38–61). Baltimore: Johns Hopkins University Press.

Tierney, W. (2004). *Competing conceptions of academic governance: Negotiating the perfect storm.* Baltimore: Johns Hopkins University Press.

Tierney, W. (2006). *Trust and the public good: Examining the cultural conditions of academic work.* New York: Peter Lang.

Tierney, W. G. (2008). *The impact of culture on organizational decision-making: Theory and practice in higher education.* Sterling, VA: Stylus.

Tierney, W. (2012). Creativity and organizational culture. In M. N. Bastedo (Ed.), *The organization of higher education: Managing colleges for a new era* (pp. 160–180). Baltimore: Johns Hopkins University Press.

Tierney, W. G., & Lanford, M. (2015). An investigation of the impact of international branch campuses on organizational culture. *Higher Education, 70*(2), 283–298.

Tierney, W. G. & Lanford, M. (2016). Conceptualizing innovation in higher education. In M. Paulsen (Ed.), *Higher education: Handbook of theory and research* (pp. 1–40). New York: Springer.

Tight, M. (2014). Collegiality and managerialism: A false dichotomy? Evidence from the higher education literature. *Tertiary Education and Management, 20*(4), 294–306.

Tight, M. (2015). Theory development and application in higher education research: The case of academic drift. *Journal of Educational Administration and History, 47*(1), 84–99.

Tirri, K., & Nokelainen, P. (2008). Identification of multiple intelligences with the Multiple Intelligence Profiling Questionnaire III. *Psychology Science Quarterly, 50*(2), 206–221.

Tirri, K., Nokelainen, P., & Ubani, M. (2006). Conceptual definition and empirical validation of the spiritual sensitivity scale. *Journal of Empirical Theology, 19*(1), 37–62.

Tisley, A. (2010, July 2). New policies accommodate transgender students. *The Chronicle of Higher Education,* pp. A19–A20.

Toma, J. D. (2012). Institutional strategy, positioning for prestige. In M. N. Bastedo (Ed.), *The organization of higher education: Managing colleges for a new era* (pp. 118–159). Baltimore: Johns Hopkins University Press.

Trondal, J. (2015). Ambiguities in organizations and the routines of behavior and change. *International Journal of Organizational Analysis, 23*(1), 123–141.

Turner, V. W., & Bruner, E. M. (Eds.). (1986). *The anthropology of experience.* Chicago: University of Illinois Press.

Urrieta Jr, L., & Villenas, S. A. (2013). The legacy of Derrick Bell and Latino/a education: A critical race testimonio. *Race Ethnicity and Education, 16*(4), 514–535.

U.S. Department of Education. (2006). *A test of leadership: Charting the future of U.S. Higher education.* Washington, DC: The Secretary of Education's Commission on the Future of Higher Education.

Valdez, P. L. (2015). Anatomy of the Hispanic-Serving Institution (HSI) designation: An overview of HSI policy formation. Paper presented at the conference, Hispanic-Serving Institutions in the 21st century: A convening. University of Texas at El Paso, TX.

Van Note Chism, N., Baldwin, R. G., & Chang, D. A. (Eds.). (2010). *Faculty and faculty issues in universities and colleges* (3rd ed.). Boston: Pearson Custom.

Villalpando, O. (2004). Practical considerations of critical race theory and Latino critical theory for Latino college students. In A. Ortiz (Ed.), *Addressing the unique needs of Latino American students* (New Directions for Student Services, No. 105, pp. 41–50). San Francisco: Jossey-Bass.

Walsh, M. (1992). Authentic anarchy and the transformation of the residence hall [unpublished manuscript]. Higher Education and Student Affairs, University of Vermont, Burlington, VT.

Weber, M. (1947). *The theory of social and economic organization* (A. M. Henderson & T. Parsons, Trans.). London: W. Hodge.

Weber, M. (2016). Bureaucracy. In J. M. Shafritz, J. S. Ott, & Y. S. Jang (Eds.), *Classics of organizational theory* (8th ed., pp. 78–83). Boston: Wadsworth. (Original work published 1946)

Weick, K. E. (1976). Educational organizations as loosely coupled systems. *Administrative Science Quarterly, 21*(1), 1–19.

Weick, K. E. (1989). Loose coupling: Beyond the metaphor. *Current Contents, 20*(12), 14.

Whitt, E. J. (1993). "Making the familiar strange": Discovering culture. In G. D. Kuh (Ed.), *Cultural perspectives in student affairs work* (pp. 81–94). Lanham, MD: American College Personnel Association.

Whittington, R. (1992). Putting Giddens into action: Social systems and managerial agency. *Journal of Management Studies, 29*(6), 693–712.

Wolfe, B. L., & Dilworth, P. P. (2015). Transitioning normalcy: Organizational culture, African American administrators, and diversity leadership in higher education. *Review of Educational Research, 85*(4), 667–697.

Yakoboski, P. J. (2016). Adjunct views of adjunct positions. *Change: The Magazine of Higher Learning, 48*(3), 54–59.

Zajonc, A. (2013). Contemplative pedagogy: A quiet revolution in higher education. In L.A. Sanders (Ed.), *Contemplative studies in higher education* (New Directions for Teaching and Learning, No. 134, pp. 83–94). San Francisco: Jossey-Bass.

Zemsky, R. (2008). Tenure Wild Cards. *Academe, 94*(5), 19.

Zohar, D. (1997). *ReWiring the corporate brain: Using the new science to rethink how we structure and lead organizations.* San Francisco: Berrett-Koehler.

Zohar, D. (2010). Exploring spiritual capital: An interview with Danah Zohar. *Spirituality in Higher Education Newsletter, 5*(5), 1–8.

Zohar, D., & Marshall, I. (2000). *SQ: Connecting with your spiritual intelligence.* New York: Bloomsbury.

Zohar, D., & Marshall, I. (2004). *Spiritual capital: Wealth we can live by.* San Francisco: Berrett-Koehler.

INDEX

Page numbers in *italics* denote tables.